SUFISM : EVOLUTION AND PRACTICE

ENCYCLOPAEDIC SURVEY OF ISLAMIC CULTURE SERIES—7

Sufism Evolution and Practice

Edited by

MOHAMED TAHER

ANMOL PUBLICATIONS PVT. LTD.

New Delhi-110 002

ANMOL PUBLICATIONS PVT. LTD.
4374/4B, Ansari Road, Daryaganj
New Delhi-110 002

Sufism· Evolution and Practice

First Edition 1997
Reprint, 2003
ISBN 81-7488-541-2

PRINTED IN INDIA

Published by J.L. Kumar for Anmol Publications Pvt. Ltd., New Delhi-110 002 and Printed at Mehra Offset Press, Delhi.

Preface

The Encyclopaedic Survey of Islamic Culture is a unique reference source. This series seeks to anthologise the most important primary and secondary materials on a wide variety of topics and writers of Islamic culture and civilisation. The scholar, the student and the layman will find in various volumes not only a generous selection of reprinted articles, but original essays, bibliographies, and other materials brought for the first time in a comprehensive and exhaustive fashion.

The need for this collation grew out of our awareness that there is no comprehensive source of information for the study and research of the field. Other published works are too specialised in the topics discussed or neglect the institutional as well the individual role which the Islamic system plays. Few encyclopaedic works do exist, and few anthologies also have appeared. Fewer books, again, have systematically covered such topics as Islam in Africa, Islamic sociology, Islamic polity, Islamic thought, etc. Although these topics have been addressed separately, no attempt has been made to discuss them as part of a united treatment of the literature of the field.

Islam brought a total change in all spheres of life. It revolutionised many societies, both in the east and the west. But this is not always accepted and acknowledged. To quote Major Arthur Leonard from his work: Islam; her moral and spiritual value:

"Never to this day has Europe acknowledged in an honest and whole hearted manner the great and everlasting debt she owes to Islamic culture and civilisation. Only in a lukewarm and perfunctory way has she recognised that when, during the dark ages, her people were sunk in feudalism and ignorance, Muslim civilisation under the Arabs reached a high standard of social and scientific splendour that kept the flickering members of European society from utter decadence."

"Do not we, who now consider ourselves on the top most pinnacle ever reached by culture and civilisation, recognise that, had it not been for the high culture, the civilisation and intellectual, as well as the social splendours of the Arabs and soundness of their school system, Europe would to this day have remained sunk in the darkness of ignorance. Have we forgotten that the Muslim maxim was that, the real learning of a man is of more public importance than any particular religious opinions he may entertain, that Muslim liberality was in striking contrast with the then intolerant state of Europe? Does the magnificent valour of the Arabs, inspired as it was by a theism as lofty as it was pure, not appeal to us? Does not the moderation and comparative toleration shown by them to the conquered, notwithstanding the fierce and burning ardour to regenerate mankind that impelled them onward to conquest, also appeal to us? Does it not all the more appeal to us when we contrast this with the bitterness of the attitude of the Christian sects towards one another? Especially when we consider that in Christendom, as it was then constituted, extortion, tyranny and imperial centralisation, combining with ecclesiastical despotism and persecution, had practically extinguished patriotism, by substitution in its place schismatic and degenerate Church?"

Further the same writer continues to say:

"Is it possible that Europe is unmindful of, and has the ingratitude to ignore the splendid services of the scientists and philosophers of Arabic? Are the names of Assamh, Abu Othman, Alberuni, Albeithar, Abu Ali Ibn Sina (Avicenna) the great physician and philosopher, Ibn Rushd (Anempace) besides a host of others but dead letters? Is the great work that they have done and the fame they have left behind them in their books to be consigned to the limbo of oblivion, by an ungrateful but antipathetic Europe?

"It cannot be that already we have lost sight of the amazing intellectual activity of the Muslim world during the earlier part of the `Abbaside' period more especially. It cannot be that we have quite forgotten the irrecoverable loss that was inflicted on Arabian literature, and on the world at large, by the wanton destruction of thousands of books that was promoted by Christian bigotry and fanaticism? It cannot be surely said of Christian Europe that for centuries now she has done her best to hide obligations to the Arabs; yet most assuredly, obligations such as these, are far too sacred to lie much linger hidden."

This is one side of the story. The other side is that the West has definitely absorbed much of the Islamic contributions and is "unaware." To quote Marcus Marby and William Underhill "Bold new visions from ancient landscapes" (Newsweek May 29, 1995): Christian and Islamic civilizations have been in conflict for most of their history. But as often as they have clashed, they have enriched each other. In this ninth century, Moors brought advanced architecture, astronomy and medicine to occupied Spain. While Europe lingered in the Dark Ages, courtly poetry from Persia inspired the troubadours, whose verse evolved into the literature of the early French Renaissance. Even whiling away hours over coffee and conversation—the basis for the cafe—came from Arab culture... France's most popular dish today is not escargots but couscous. French slang is peppered with Arab words like kif-kif (50-50) and Insha Allah (God willing). The hottest new music is Arab-inspired rai" (p. 28). The list of Arabic borrowed words in English and Western usages are many more, not mere algebra, alchemy, azimuth, albatross, timbal, zenith, etc.

There is, in short, a lot of misinformation and incorrect representation about Islam. And more so there is a need today to describe and interpret the issues and express in clear terms what this thought actually deals with. Due to social and cultural changes, the salient aspects of the field require examination. The post cold war era has left the world with a unipolar political system. Islam is a system which promises the world that if applied in toto it would solve the multi-dimensional problems of the modern era. But is there any one who wishes to test this module and try it in a space and time to see the truth of the statement?

The primary purpose of this encyclopaedic survey is to serve as a basic handbook on significant topics of Islamic culture. To facilitate an understanding of the field, the series presents a survey and an analysis of the various socio-cultural forces that shape both the structure and functions of the field as well as by the way this society has changed. We also analyse the larger forces outside the community, such as assimilation and acculturation, and forces inside the community, like, role of the leadership, role of the social and cultural groups and the so much alleged 'imbalance' in the theory and practice of the faith.

We are confident that this work will make a permanent and significant contribution to the study of Islam. Its style is simple, and it is presented in a style accessible to a wide audience. Its target audience is faculty, students, and all concerned with the understanding of the faith of the second largest following in the world. While it has scholarly materials, it is nevertheless also of use to those who have no knowledge of the field, as well as to those who are working in related and allied fields. Most important, we hope that this series will be useful in teaching and learning as an educational resource in the academic world.

The series is planned to be both, multi-volume and multi-facted set, which will run into hundreds of numbers. The compilation of such a huge set is a gigantic task and requires the support and encouragement of all concerned. It requires feed-back and also support from the literary market place and literary circles all over.

A collection of articles, or an anthology, has many benefits, like, it renews our acquaintance with literature which we have neglected, it reveals to us material of which we were ignorant, and it exposes relationships where we did not suppose them to exist. This is the ultimate purpose of our efforts and we wish and pray that this is fulfilled.

A word of acknowledgement is due to the inspiration of the idea of a comprehensive, commulative and compact set of literary works on the Islamic culture. These inspirers are from all walks of life and their efforts must be acknowledged which includes, contributors, authors and editors, as well as the publishers who have graciously contributed to this project and we duly acknowledge their cooperation. The well wishers are many more and listing all the concerned by names is impossible here. Each must be duly rewarded for this gesture, and this is our sincere prayer.

Editor

Contents

1

Sufism: Its Evolution and Practice

MOJIBUR RAHMAN

Describes the origin of Sufism; its borrowings from other schools; and the evolution of sufi orders. It focuses on the level of influence of other schools on Sufism.

There is no task more delicate than to assess the factors which go to determine the nature and degree of influence exerted by one thought upon another. Commercial and historical contact may tend to ease mental fusion, yet even without this, thought travels unbridled on wings of imagination whether the political relations of the people concerned are friendly or hostile. Thoughts expressed in literature wait for literary analysis to prove their worth. Thus ideas of inherent value spread far and wide and do not stop at political frontiers.

If one side is to give and the other side is willing to take, this implies recognition of superiority of the side whose thought is being taken. The Greeks' exquisite poetry and prose have inspired countless writers all the world over; there are profound and rich ponderings on the meaning of life and exploration of delicate personal situations in Arabic and Persian literatures that appeal to and satisfy our senses and imagination. Love palpitates with fantastic imagery and literary refinement among the elite finding expression in the simple and passionate songs of the people.

While new ideas of chivalry inspired the upper classes in almost all European countries, we find Arabic poetry striding in the desert with measured steps (like their camels) in rhyme and mater to prepare the norms for polished ode and short lyric to enable the "love laden heart to assuage its grief at parting from some beloved" in a dignified manner. The Persians could write "timeless truths" in a way that makes the reader feel that he is taking a walk in a quiet wood or bathing in a cool stream—it soothes the spirit. This lyrical poetry paved the way for the emergence of a distinctive type of Platonic love that embraced ethical elements.

The name of Ibn-i Dawud of Baghdad is dear to many who regard *The Book of Venus* almost as a book of devotion. It depicts in soul-stirring verse, all the aspects of love its nature, laws, forms of expression and effects." It dealt with the ideal love of which the holy Prophet said: "One who loves and conceals his love and remains chaste, dies a martyr."

Ibn-i Hazm (d. 1064 A.D.) of Spain, a proverbial name in Islam for purity in religious thought, came out with his own treatise in verse on love, namely *Tawq al-Hamama*.[1] The majesty and beauty of the language in which he clothed his ideas caught the imagination of the western scholars who honoured him, declaring him as the founder of the science of Comparative Religion. He believes the Platonic theory of love being the means to attain union between earthly and heavenly beings.

With the exception of Spaniards, the Europeans of those days were of opinion that Arabic and Persian were nothing more than fables narrated from the mouth of birds and animals, as they were acquainted with only *Kalila wa Dimma* of Sanskrit origin, (panchatantra), translated by Ibn al-Muqaffa' into Arabic in the 8th century, which was rended into Spanish for Alfanso, the Wise (1252-1284). Its Latin version *Directorium Humanae Vitae* by John of Capua evaluated its worth and opened the floodgates for translation into almost all other languages of the West.

The infiltration of eastern thought into medieval Europe led to an intellectual movement of vast dimensions. Latin suffered due to the lack of originality and Greek due to the passage of time. Hence and learned were compelled to look elsewhere in their literary quest and lyrical thirst. Greece that once supplied food to the intellect was languishing; and Arabia, that looks a desert, produced intellectual giants. The military superiority of the Arabs was well established; now Europe had to recognise their intellectual pre-eminence as well.

History records that Arabic studies were pursued in Dante's time in Italy with much vigour and interest. Books like *Legends of Tundal, St., Patrick Purgatory* and *Divine Commedia* were profoundly influenced by elements of Muslim Cosmogony and the ascent of the holy Prophet to heaven. Dante marvellously succeeded in fusing into one magnificent synthesis the Christian and classical mysticism.

The richest and highly developed doctrines of the early sufis taught the western scholars to realise that our daily life in our religion; faith cannot be separated from actions or one's belief from one's occupation. Worship is not a window to open and shut: The spirit of worship should infuse in that—it must be translated into action. In worshipping Go we cannot rise higher than the angels who praise Him day and night. Then why have we been created?

It was the effect of such writings that made Sir William Jones once observe: "No appreciation of Asiatic poetry was possible without a scholarly knowledge of the peoples and natural history of Asia."[2] And without making a proper assessment of Asiatic poetry, to assess the spiritual heritage of the orient will be an effort, undoubtedly, at second hand.

It was at one time held that the word "sufi" was synonymous with the word "mystic." But the word "sufi", as used in Arabic, Persian, Turkish and Urdu, has a religious connotation. According to the sufis themselves, the word is derived from an Arabic root "safa" (purity). This view is also held by Bashr al-hafi, the barefooted (d. 841-42 A.D.) and Junaid Baghdadi (d. 909-10). According to them the sufi is he who keeps his heart pure with God.[3]

Noldeke has conclusively established that the word was derived from an Arabic word "suf" meaning coarse wool and was originally applied to those Muslim mystics who wore coarse woollen garments as a sign of self renunciation and penitence.

Ibn Khaldun says that coarse woollen garments were put on so that those who wore them might be distinguished from those who indulged in luxury. According to Qushayri, the term "sufi" got currency before the close of 200 A.H (815-816 A.D.). According to Jami, Abu Hashim of Kufa (d. 778 A.D.) was the first sufi of Islam. According to Gibb, the West can still learn, in respect of mystical psychology and speculation, something from the East, though it had learned much during the Middle Ages when Muslim philosophy and science radiated from Spain through Christian Europe. Thomas Aquinas Eckhart and Dante heavily drank from it, as mysticism was the common ground where Islam and Christianity touched each other in those days. They seem to bear the stamp of one and the same spiritual genius. Towards the second decade of the 7th century (719-816 A.D.) history records the name of sufi, in Mesopotamia probably derived from `suf', coarse woollen garb donned by Muslim and Christian ascetics. This goes to show their affinity in the matter of choosing dress.

The sufis claim to have inherited their doctrines direct from the teachings of the holy Prophet, who, strictly speaking, has given no dogmatic or mystical theology. The Qur'an of course supplies raw material for both when it say: Allah is the highest of the heaven and the earth (XXIV-35); He is the First and the Last, the Outward and the Inward (LVII-3); there is no God but He; everything is to perish except He (XXVIII-88); I breathed into Man, My spirit (XV-29); I have created man and I know what his soul suggests to him, for I am near to him than his jugular vein (I-15); wheresoever you turn, there is the face of Allah (II-109); To whom Allah gives no light, he has no light at all (XXIV-40).

Compare the above verses with those of Bhagvad Gita (the Yoga of ths vision of Universal form—the dialoge betwen Shri

Krishna and Arjuna) which reads thus: I am the generator of all (Gita—8).[4] "Thou art the Supreme Eternal," Arjuna says to Krishna, "the Supreme abode, the Supreme purity, eternal divine man, primeval Deity, unborn, the Lord (V-12); whatsoever is glorious, good, beautiful and mighty,· and thou emanates from a fragment of my splendour (V-41); If thou thinkest that by me, it can be seen, O Lord! Lord of Yoga, then show me thine imperishable self (11 discourse, V-4). "My Lord! show me thyself so that I may look upon thee." But God said: "You cannot bear to see Me, look at the Mount Senai, have a flash of Me if it can bear to stand, (Qur'an vii-143).

The English poet while giving vent to his feeling about the unity in diversity had the same conception of divine being as held by the sufis and the Bhaktas:

> Thou art, O God! The life and light
> Of all the wondrous world we see
> Its glow by day, its smile by night
> Are but reflection caught from Thee.

And read with it the verses of Bhagvad Gita:-

> Father of worlds, of all that moves and stands
> Worthier of reverence than the Guru Self
> There is none like to Thee, who passeth Thee?
> Pre-eminent Thy power in all the worlds.

Rites and creeds count for little with God. He dwells neither in mosque nor church nor temple, but in the pure heart. A voice cannot carry the tongue and the lips that give it wings. One must seek the Ether Alone; alone and without his nest the eagle flies across the sea.

Reverting to the Qur'anic verses referred to before, there is o doubt that they contain mystical nuclei, but the passages in regard to the Prophet's ascension to heaven,[5] gave a spur to the sufis to attain mystical experience. Along with this, the political upheaval in Europe made the sufis face new problems. With the opening of a new horizon of time and place new ideas began to infiltrate in Muslim society. They came into contact with the ideas of older civilization both in the West and the East.

Before Islam *Hellenism* ruled supreme in European countries. Theologeans of Islam were extremely busy in controversies with Christian and Greek mystics on one side, and with the Manichaeans and the Zoroastrians on the other. The result was that after 1000 A.D. sufism began absorbing Christian asceticism and Hellenic gnosticism. The Christian monks or hermits were known as "Raheb" who renounced the world to attain divine knowledge. They took refuge in some solitary cave, mountain or forest as the holy Prophet, in his early days, did in the cave of Hira. As there was a fear that his pious and overzealous followers should make it a model for their life the well-known verse appeared: "there is no nunnery in Islam". This in fact meant disapproval of the Christian ideal of asceticism.

The purpose of all religions is to discipline the human behaviour and create an atmosphere in which men could live in peace and harmony. But man is a queer combination of contradictions. The devil in man keeps him always tempted and lured by fascinating objects. Penal codes by temporal powers may discipline his mind and regulate his conduct for a while, but sooner or later it turns like a curly tail. The religious codes and the sufi's preachings about "Hell and Heaven" are a powerful deterrent to keep mankind within bounds, organised and disciplined. Philosophers, scientists and educationists, in their own ways, do the same by conquering new fields of production that go a long way to contribute to the advancement of civilization, so that the world may enjoy peace and progress.

When Islam spread to Persia and India, the sufis had an amazing experience of going through the Manichaeans and the Zoroastrians' esoteric expositions of their holy scriptures. The sufis felt that the precious corn from the rich granary of the East may be fruitfully gathered. "Birds alight where they pick up grains, and the inn of generosity remains ever crowded" is an old maxim, The sufis began taking interest in the Vedas that contained much of the sublime verses of the Vedas, as they testified to the veracity of the Qur'an wherein Allah says: "I sent my apostles and messengers to all people in all countries."

According to Vedantic philosophy we find that in the whole course of a soul's journey from eternity to the days of resurrection, few events are so epoch-making as those of the strong and genuine love for God which is called "bhakti." This transforms the whole human nature. A Bhakta rests content only when he comes to realise that there is one thing alone existing in the Universe called, "Ekamevadwitiyam Brahma" (the only God without a Second). Charles Darwin through his theory of "Naturalism" asserted that the species of all things in nature spring from the same fountain-head, namely, minerals, vegetables, animals or mankind. Jalaluddin Rumi, even though not believing in the theory of "Transmigration of Souls", could not resist his Zoroastrian influence.

This is nothing but the theory of "Evolution of Soul" which is in contrast to the Darwin's theory of evolution of the human body. Rumi's rejoinder to Darwin would be: If by assimilation "matter can turn into man," there can be no obstacle in the way of evolution of a man acquiring the qualities of God and thereby uniting with the infinite from where he has come.

Every religion has evolved its own method for the realisation of God. The actual names of rituals may vary as also the details but they lead to the same consequence. According to Vedanta, which is the fountain-head of Bhakti, there are three such paths to God: (a) Janamarga (path of knowledge), (b) Bhaktimarga (path of devotion), (c) Karmamarga (path of service), and these relate to the "head, he heart and the hands of man, respectively."

Zoroaster (Zarathushtra of the Avesta) emphasised the path of service (the fifth cardinal truth contained in the Avesta) to be the royal road leading to God. Knowledge is indispensable to realisation of the supremacy of God and understanding of the wondrous creations fashioned by Him. Consequently love and devotion should be enshrined in one's heart to realise the aforesaid objective. The love of God can be displayed either through complete surrender to His will and utter devotion to Him, or through love of serving humanity, as it has been said: "To serve man is to serve God." And this is the dawn of wisdom on the part of mankind. Hence the Avesta enjoins "Service to Humanity" on all the adherents of this faith. Humanitarian projects of pious benevolence have been stressed and eulogised through ages in Christianity as well.

The Quintessence of Sufism

The fundamental of sufism is God, Man and the relation between them, which is Love. The whole sufi theosophy revolves on these three pivots. From God sprang the theory of "tawhid" (divine unity), of "nur" (divine light), of "zat wa sifat" (divine essence and attributes) and the theory of "hama ust" (all is He).

From "man" emerged the theories of "ruh" (soul), "qurbat" (divine proximity), "hulul" (infusion of divine spirit). From "the relation between God and Man" the idea of *`Ishq* (divine love), *Fana* (self-annihilation), *Baqa* (abiding in God), etc. came into being. Hence the sufis believe in the real one God who is all merciful and loving and whom a man can approach with a loving heart. He is a friend, a comrade and a beloved; He longs to unite with His creatures and they, in their turn, pine for union with Him, to which Rumi refers.

Metaphysically, God is the embodiment of light, life of all the universe. The universe is the only place where His manifestation (*Mazhar*) can be seen by men of divine vision, radiant with eternal glory. This conception leads us to believing that His essence and attributed and nothing but light. Hence His "zat" and "safat" are one and absolutely one.

Man's outward shape in temporary and perishable (*fani*); man has come from God and he will be one with Him. The present existence of man, according to oriental mystics, is the cause of his separation from God. That is why the sufis like the bhaktas neglect the body and take every possible care for the development of the soul. They practise severe mortification, austerity and physical hardships for seeking deliverance by overcoming the lust of flesh (*nafs*) that keeps him in a prison-body.

> 'Ishq or love is the only criterion of their creed and the guiding principle of their mundane life that sustains the relation between God and man. The union of his desideratum and life-long longing, which is metaphorically expressed by the sufis by words like *khamr, mai, bada* and *sharab* (wine and liquor, etc.), all attributing to the esoteric love for the real being. Hafiz, while composing the following, had the same ecstatic effulgence in mind:-
>
> O cup-bearer! illuminate the cup with lustrous wine,
> Lyrist! Touch the chord of mirth and joy,
> My World in tune in dancing fine!

Saqi (cup-bearer) in sufi terminology means God.

Nicholson observes: "Sufism was not an outcome of a single definite cause. Some say it was a reaction of the Aryan mind against the Semitic conqueror, and as such the product of Indian or Persian thought. If we take this to be true, how can we explain the historical fact that some of the leading pioneers among them were the natives of Egypt and Syria and Arabs by race. Similarly to those who hold that it was of a Buddhistic or Vedantic origin, one may ask: why did Islamic theology, philosophy and science shoot their luxuriant stems in countries which were under Hellenistic culture, whereas Islamic civilization admitted Indian influence at a later epoch? Whether it was influenced by Christianity, Neoplatonism, Gnosticism or Buddhism or the Vedas, sufism in the Islamic world has a specific religious connotation."[6]

The sufis prescribe four stages for the aspirants to attain communion with God:-

(1) The first stage is called Shari'at wherein a devotee has to follow strictly the rules of religion. At this stage of learns how to annihilate himself. This is also called 'Fana fi al-Dhat'. This happens in the natural state of every human being living in the world, technically called "'Alam-i-Nasut. But the sufi 'Fana' means self-mortification before actual death.

(2) The second stage is called "Tariqat" wherein a devotee has to follow blindly the commands of his mentor which is termed as "Fana fi al-Shaikh". Herein the aspirant starts traversing the path of spiritual journey leading to the world of angels, technically called "'Alam-e Malakut".

(3) The third stage is called "Ma'rifat" wherein a devotee follows rigidly the teaching of the holy Prophet. In the language of the sufis it is called "Fana fi al-Rasul". Here the devotee attains some power; divine knowledge dawns on him; his soul is strengthened enabling him to take strides further toward the "world of pre-destination," called "Alam-i Jabarut".

(4) The fourth and the final state is called "Haqiqat," wherein the difference between the devotee and God is little. He becomes part and parcel of God by self-annihilation. In sufi terminology it is called "Fana fi Allah". The goal of the journey is reached and the aspirant unites with Truth. This state of the world is called "`Alam-e Lahut". It may also be noted that `Haqiqat' is also named as wasl.

'Arsh:-According to the sufis, there are nine heavenly spheres, each higher than the preceding one. The highest is called the "Heaven of Heavens" or the throne of God. Each of these spheres possesses of soul and an intelligence higher in order of merit. The `Arsh contains the "Primal intelligence."

'Allama Iqbal refers to this "'Alam-i Lahut" in his "Bang-i Dara," reprimanding those who seemed contented with the bond of slavery under the British rule in India:-

O Bird of heaven! Death is far better than the livelihood, which fetters the flight into blue heaven.

Sufi movement in India, we know, commenced in the 11th century A.D. Information about the orders to which the sufis belonged is scanty. It must be remembered that eastern people are highly impressionable to systematic devotion of any sort. The institution of pilgrimage which gathers together millions of Muslims with their religious emotions facilitated the propagation of sufi doctrines to an extraordinary degree by different orders of the sufis in different periods. Though the various forms of devotion, prevalent in Islam, are remarkably systematic and unitary, yet there is some variance in views among the different Orders of the sufis.[9]

The absorption of Aryan civilization of Iran and of Greece by Islam stimulated mystic speculation resulting in the spread of various sufi orders in

A'in-e Akbari furnishes us with a list of sufi orders that existed in India during the time of Akbar the Great (1556-1605). The names of their founders with dates of their deaths in chronological order are as follows:

(1) Habibiya Order founded by Khwaja Habib 'Ajami, contemporary of Hasan Basari (d. 728 A.D.).
(2) Zaidiya Order founded by Shaikh `Abdu'l Wahid b. Zaid (d. 743 A.D.)
(3) Adhamiya Order founded by Khwaja Ibrahim b. Adham Balkhi (d. 777 A.D.)
(4) 'Iyaziya Order established by Khwaja Fudail b. Ayaz (d. 803 A.D.)
(5) Karkhiya Order established by Ma'ruf Karachi (d. 815 A.D.)
(6) Saqatiya Order established by Abu'l Hasan Sari Saqati (d. 867 A.D.)
(7) Taifuriya Order established by Bayazid Bastame Taifuri Shami (d. 874 A.D.)

(8) Hubairiya Order established Khwaja Hubairatu'l Basri (d. 900 A.D.)

(9) Junaidiya Order established Junaid Baghdadi (d. 910 A.D.)

(10) Chishtiya Order established Abu Ishaq Chisti (d. 967 A.D.)

(11) Kaziruniya established by Abu Ishaq Kaziruni (d. 1034 A.D.)

(12) Suhrawardiya established by Shaikh Shahabuddin Abu Nasib Suhrawardi (d. 1167 A.D)

(13) Firdausiya established by Shaikh Najmuddin Kubra Firdausi, (d. 1221 A.D.)

(14) Tusiya established by Alau'dding Tusi (contemporary of Najmuddin Kubra)

Abul Fadl admits that the above list contains only the prominent orders existing upto the 16th century in India.[8] There were others who rose to prominence afterwards:-

(15) Shattariya Order established by Shattar (probable date 1200-1300 A.D.)

(16) Qadirya Order established by Abdu'l Qadir Jilani (1078-1166).

(17) Qalandariya established by Qalandar Yusuf al-Andlusi (Not known).

(18) Naqshbandiya established by Bahau'ddin Naqsh Band (d. 1389 A.D.)

(19) Uwasiyia Order established by Uwais Qarani, contemporary of Prophet

Names of the sufis who introduced the orders in India with probable dates of introduction are as under:-

(1) Chishtiya Order—Khwaja Mo'inu'ddin Chishti (d. 1236 A.D.) introduced

(2) Suhrawardiya Order (a) Jalalu'ddin Tabrizi (d. 1225 A.D.) introduced before 1200 A.D.

		(b)	Qazi Hamiduddin Naguri (d. 1246 A.D.) introduced in 1200 A.D.
		(c)	Bahau'ddin Zakariya Multani (d. 1266 A.D) introduced in (1193 1200 A.D.)
(3)	Junaidiya Order	(a)	Data Gunj Bakhsh Lahore (d. 1072 A.D.) introduced before 1072 A.D.
		(b)	Baba Ishaq Maghribi (d. before 1400 A.D.) introduced in (1324-51 A.D.)
(4)	Shattariya Order		'Abdu'llah Shattari (d. 1406 A.D.) introduced before 1400 A.D.
		(b)	Syed Ni'matullah (d. 1430 A.D.) introduced before 1400 A.D.
		(c)	Syed Md. Ghawth al-Jili (d. 1517 A.D.). introduced in 1482 A.D.
(6)	Uwaisiya Order	—	Badrudding Shah Madar (d. 1436 A.D.) introduced in about 1400 A.D.
(7)	Naqshbandiya Order	—	Khwaja Baqibillah (d. 1603 A.D.) introduced before 1600 A.D.

Out of these seven only three orders enjoy high popularity, viz. the Chishtiya, the suhrawardiya, and the Qadiriya. Next come the names of Naqshbandiya and Firdausiya, which of late have risen to prominence. The Qadiriya order had a favourable time for its diffusion among the Indians who regard it as the most puritanic of all sufi orders. Maulana 'Abdu'l Haq Muhaddith Dehlavi (d. 1641 A.D.) has echoed the general reverence of the people of India in the following lines composed in honour of Hadrat 'Abdu'l Qadir al-Jilani, the founder of this order:-

> Ghauth-i-'Azam, the guide and light of the Path (the God),
> Is undoubtedly the leader of religious divines,
> Like the royal falcon among saints and savants;
> He stands exalted as the Prophet stood amongst the apostles.
> The saints reverentially his Chariot draw,
> And to mount his shackle on their neck, they bow.

The *Kitabu'l Luma'* by Abu Nasr al-Sarraj and *Qutui Qulub* by Abu Talib al-Makki are the first systematic and general works on sufi doctrines written during the century following the death of Hallaj (922 D.A) at Baghdad. The books contain valuable material from sources which are not extinct. Sufism in this period was drifting from its monistic anchorage towards Pantheism due to the influence of "Emanation" theory of Greek philosophy, the traces of which we find in the life and sayings of the Persian mystic. Abu Sa'id Abu'l Khair (967-1049 A.D.).

According to him, a true saint goes in and out amongst people and eats and sleeps with them, buys and sells in the market and enjoys matrimonial life but never forgets God for a single moment. All creatures should be seen through the eyes of the creator, he said. Charity and loving kindness he practised to win over the hearts of people and that was the best way of attaining to God.

Qushairi's famous epistle written in (1045) presents a contrast with the piety of the early sufis strictly following the "sunna", and the hypocrisy prevailing amongst the sufis of his own time. This was further endorsed by `Ali Hujwiri, thirty years later in his famous work *Kashfu'l Mahjub* wherein he asserts: They name `Law' to their lusts; and `senseless fancies' are called `divine knowledge'; affections of the animals soul and heart's desire are termed as `divine love'; purity had degenerated into scepticims, and poverty appeared in the garb of heresy.[9]

This was the worst period of Islamic theology and tradition. Scholars were busy in scholastic duel, each trying to prove his superiority. It seemed that no means of preserving the vitals of the Faith was left. But God chose a man who in his younger days had been a sceptic, Imam Abu Hamid al-Ghazali (1058-1111 A.D.), who after having been cured of his malady by a mystical experience, dedicated his whole life to search of absolute truth. Scholastic theology and study of philosophy that he pursued as a professor in Madrasah Nizamia of Baghdad, led him nowhere.

Ultimately he turned to the writings of Harith al-Muhasibi (an old teacher of 3rd century A.H.) to attain mystical knowledge. He realised that sufism cannot be learned from books; it can be had by experience, ecstasy and inward transformation, being with the true sufis. By his personal experience, he gathered the truth that law with mystics and which he put in his immortal work the *Ihyau'l 'Ulum* which led to the revival of Islamic learning on a permanent basis.

Al-Ghazali insists on the saints' believing in the supreme authority of the holy Prophet whose laws must be obeyed in letter and spirit. In his *Mish-katu'l-Anwar*, he emphasised that "Allah is the Sun and besides that there is only its rays." This makes him a Pantheist. But the language used does not exhibit his real mind, as he says forcefully: "God is the creator of this world by His absolute will."

But as the unifying force of Islam grew feebler, foreign elements (Greek and Egyptian) penetrated the life and teachings of the sufis, especially after the collapse of the caliphate at Baghdad. The result was that the pantheistic theory gained ground in far-flung areas of Muslim world. It culminated in Muhiyu'ddin Ibnu'l 'Arabi's (1165-1240) *Fususul Hikam* (Bezels of Wisdom) and 'Abdu'l Karim Jili's (d. 1410 A.D.) *Al-Insan-i Kamil* (Perfect man). The mysticism interpreted by Jalalu'ddin Rumi (1207-73 A.D.), Hafiz (726-79 A.H.) and Sa'di (1184-1291 A.D.) etc. swayed the intelligentsia and the sufis alike.

Another characteristic feature of this period was that the saints with their disciples started living in a convent (khanqah) like the monastic orders in medieval Christian countries. Thus free association and personal contact with the shaikh (mentor) gave birth to a sense of brotherhood (fellow disciples), each tracing its descent through its founder saint to the line of the holy Prophet. Religious norms and rituals may vary in different orders (silsila), but they all faithfully observe the tenets of Islam.

REFERENCES

1. Edited with an intro. by Peterof, Leiden, 1914.
2. H A R Gibb, - quoted in the Legacy of Islam, ed by Thomas Arnold and Alfred Guillaume, Oxford, 1931.
3. H R Nicholson, Literary history of the Arabs, p. 228.
4. Bhagvad Gita, 5th ed., June 1226, Madras, G A Nateson & Co., 10th discourse.
5. Quran, (xvii-1; liii, 1-18)
6. R A Nicholson, The mystics of Islam, p. 12.
7. Dr. Margolioth, Muhamm. p. 213.
8. Mirza Md. Akhtar, Tadhkirah-i-Awliya-i Hind, pt. III, p. 5.
9. R A Nicholson, articles in The Legacy of Islam, Oxford, 1943, p. 220.

(Revised and edited; originally appeared in Islamic Culture April 1978).

2

The Nature and Meaning of Tawakkul in Sufism

DARSHAN SINGH

Tawakkul, or Trust in God, is discussed in the contextual framework of Islam and Sufism.

We may begin by relating a story from the Sufi literature:

> "I have read that when Ibrahim Khawwas was asked concerning the reality of faith he replied: `I have no answer to this question just now, because whatever I say is a mere expression, and behoves me to answer by my actions; but I am setting out for Mecca: do thou accompany me that thou mayest be answered.' The narrator continues: I consented. As we journeyed through the desert, every day two cups of water appeared. He gave one to me and took the other for himself. One day an old man rode up to us and dismounted and conversed with Ibrahim for a while; then he left us. I asked Ibrahim to tell me who he was. He replied: `This was Khidr, who begged me to let him accompany me, but I refused, for I feared that in his company I might put confidence in him instead of in God, and then my trust in God (*tawakkul*) would have been vitiated. Real faith is trust in God."[1]

Although the story primarily is told in the context of *Iman*, it is as much relevant in the context of *tawakkul*. It points out a very crucial problem characteristic of the realm of mystical experience.

The meaning of specifically mystical 'terms' cannot be expressed at the level 'mere expression' because the meaning that they enshrine always eludes expression at the literal or conceptual level. This perhaps is the reason that the role of language in this realm of experience is more symbolic and metaphorical than literal and conceptual. Myths and symbols, metaphors and ideograms[2] are more frequently used in this realm than ideas and concepts.

The term *tawakkul* belongs to the same category of terms which are more symbolic and metaphorical than conceptual or rational. In the words of Rudolf Otto we can say that it is an 'ideogram,' an analogy borrowed from ordinary human experience in order to express something 'wholly other.' It is employed to designate a vast and rich realm of meanings which are not only mystical and experiential but also ethical and practical, not only rational but also paradoxical. The meaning of such terms can more easily be suggested than taught. I am tempted to find recourse to another small story to make the above point clear:

> "I heard an old man relate that one day he went to the place where al-Daqqaq held his meetings, with the intention of asking him about the state of those who trust in God (*mutawakkilan*). Al-Daqqaq was wearing a fine turban manufactured in Tabaristan, which the old man coveted. He said to al-Daqqaq: 'What is trust in God?' The Shaykh replied: 'To refrain from coveting people's turbans."[3]

Any attempt to abstract and analyse the meanings of these 'terms' or categories such as *tawakkul* is bound to be inadequate, for their reality is revealed not only in thoughts but also in action based on emotional responses. It is better to know of these limitations at the beginning so that one does not get upset at the end.

The doctrine of *tawakkul* is firmly grounded in the revelation and the tradition of Islam. In following this doctrine the Sufis were not following, as was maintained by Margaret Smith, "in the steps of the Christian ascetics and mystics who had preceded them."[4] *Tawakkul* in fact is one of the basic doctrines of Islam and it is from this doctrine that the faith derives its name. The attitude of submission (Islam) is the logical outcome of the doctrine of.trust in God (*tawakkul*).[5] Without putting trust in God submission cannot be practised. Many verses in the Qur'an explicitly enjoin upon the believers to have full trust in God:

> So put your trust (in Allah) if ye are indeed believers.(V:23)
> In Allah let believers put their trust.(XIV: 11)
>
> And trust thou in the Living One who death not, and hymn His praise. He sufficeth as the knower of His bondmen's sins.(XXV: 58)
>
> And will provide for him from (a quarter) whence he hath no expectation, and whosoever putteth his trust in Allah, He will suffice him.(LXV: 3)

And there is a tradition of the Prophet which says: "If ye trusted in God as ye should, He would sustain you even as He sustains the birds, which in the morning go forth hungry and return in the evening filled."[6]

Another important source of the doctrine of *tawakkul* in Sufism is the doctrine of *Tauhid*. Islam in its insistence on the doctrine of Oneness of God is almost uncompromising. Ibrahim b. Adham's pupil Shaqiq of Balkh (d. 194/810) is said to be the first man to define *tawakkul* as a mystical state (*hal*).[7] He has defined the interrelationship between the doctrine of *Tauhid* and the doctrine of *tawakkul* as follows:

> "There are three things which a man in bound to practice. Whosoever neglects any one of them must needs neglect them all, and whosoever cleaves to any one of them must needs cleave to them all. Strive, therefore, to understand, and consider heedfully.
>
> "The *first* in this, that with your mind and your tongue and

your actions you declare God to the One; and that, having declared Him to be One, and having declared that non benefits you or harms you except Him, you devote all your actions to Him alone. If you act a single jot of your actions for the sake of another, your thought and speech are corrupt, since your motive in acting for another's sake must be hope or fear; and when you act from hope or fear of other than God, who is the lord and sustainer of all things, you have taken to your self another god to honour and venerate.

"*Secondly*, that while you speak and act in the sincere belief that there is no God except Him, you should trust Him more than the world or money or uncle or father or mother or any of the face of the earth.

"*Thirdly*, when you have established these two things, namely sincere belief in the unity of God and trust in Him, it behoves you to be satisfied with Him and not to be angry on account of anything that vexes you. Beware of anger! Let your heart be with Him always, let it not be withdrawn from Him for a single moment."[8]

Following the above interpretation of Shaqiq we may say that *tawakkul* is the only mode of expression of one's genuine faith in the unity of God. Among the other possible secondary sources of the doctrine may be enumerated the Islamic emphasis on predestination and man's weakness and sinfulness against the overpowering might and fear of God. These doctrines also inevitably lead man to put trust in God—the only way to escape the wrath of God. But the positive commandments in the Qur'an, the doctrine of *Tauhid* and tradition of the Prophet are the only primary sources of the doctrine of *Tawakkul.*

The doctrine of *tawakkul* is the central doctrine in the Sufi path of purification. It is a basic category or a key concept for the only who is interested in understanding the nature of the Sufi path. "The definition of *tawakkul*, says Annemarie Schimmel, "is of central importance for an understanding of classical Sufi thought."[9] Schimmel continues, "The importance of the problem of *tawakkul* for early Sufi thought and practice can be understood from the fact that the earliest standard work on mysticism, Abu Talib al-Makki's *Qut al-qulub*, contains sixty pages (big folio with every small print) about the topic, more than about any other aspect of Sufism."[10] In the systematized Sufi path *tawakkul* is just one step in the forward journey, but in actual practice its importance if far greater.

It is only in theoretical discussion that the Sufi path is divided into certain 'states' and 'stages,' but in the actual practice these 'states' and 'stages' may not be distinguishable. "Should he venture to make a map of this interior ascent it will not correspond exactly with any of those made by previous explorers."[11] The division and distinction of the 'stations' and 'states' are later rational formulations. In its actual practice the Sufi path may be described in two categories, i.e. 'asceticism' and 'love'. The *nafs* in the Islamic faith represents the lower self, base instincts and the material nature of man. It is the cause of all the blameworthy actions, sins, and base qualities, and the holy war in the Sufi sense of the term is struggle against the perverse nature of the *nafs*.[12] The *nafs* cannot be destroyed,[13] but as a restive horse, it can be tamed and trained. Other ascetic practices which help to keep the *nafs* under control are repentance, abstinence, renunciation, poverty, patience, etc.

At the other end of the journey is God—the 'Lord of the Worlds,' Beneficent,' 'Merciful', 'Owner of the Day of Judgement'.[14] The only appropriate response to God can be of loving adoration. Rabi'a (d. 185/801) perhaps is the first woman mystic who introduced the element of love in the formative period of the path. The ideal form of love can be found expressed in her sayings:

> "O God: If I worship Thee is fear of Hell, burn me in Hell; and if I worship Thee in hope of Paradise, exclude me from Paradise; but if I worship Thee for Thine own sake, withhold not thine everlasting beauty!"[15]

The goal of the Sufi is to subdue God by the bonds of love,[16] and the discipline of the Sufis is to tame the *nafs* by mortifications in order to put it into service to reach the goal. Now, *tawakkul* as the central doctrine of the Sufi path refers both to the discipline and the goal. It incorporates both asceticism and divine love. Viewed in relation to *nafs, tawakkul* is asceticism, and viewed in relation to God *tawakkul* is love of God.

Trust as an attitude is a mixed response of the two basic opposing feelings of fear and love. We trust God because He is All Powerful and Overwhelming; also because He is Gracious and the Bestower of sustenance. It is surrender and faith at the same time—surrender because of His all-Compassing Lordliness, faith because of His graciousness and benevolence. As one grows stronger and stronger in *tawakkul*, the feeling of fear withers away and only the feeling of love remains.[17] As we have seen in Rabi'a, this is an attitude of loving God for the sake of love alone. It is the type of mixed and ever-changing attitude that the Sufis have described either in its inception, or in its perfection or in the intermediate stage. Here we would like to quote a few definitions of *tawakkul* by the prominent Sufis. We have tried to classify these definitions into three groups so that they may be read as supporting the above view of beginning, middle and perfection.

Group One:

> Sari al-Saqati said: "Trust is stripping of power and strength."[18]
>
> Ibn Masruq said: "Trust is resignation to the course of the decrees of fate."[19]
>
> Dhu'l-Nun said: "*Tawakkul* is abandonment of the changeableness of the *nafs* and ridding of oneself of might and power."[20]

Group Two:

> Sahl said: "Trust is being at ease before God."[21]

Abu Sa'id al-Kharraz said: "The Lord granted sufficiency to the people of His Kingdom, and they dispensed with the stations of trusting in God is order that He might suffice: for how unseemly a thing it is for the people of purity to make stipulations."[22]

'Ibn 'Ata' was asked of the reality of *tawakkul*, and he said: "That no distress occurs to you on account of material means in spite of your dire need for them, and that you continue in real reliance on God in spite of your having stopped short of it."[23]

Group Three:

Abu 'Abdillah al-Qurashi said: "Trust is abandoning every refuge except God."[24]

Sahl said: "All the stations have a face and a back with the exception of trust: trust is a face without a back." He refers to the trust that is of care (for God), not the trust that is for sufficiency (from God).[25]

Shibli said: "It means that you are with respect to God as if you were not, and God is with respect to you as He is eternally."[26]

Al-Junayd said that "it is for heart to find its support in God under all conditions."[27]

In Sufism a mere attitude of trust does not mean anything unless it is practised in active life. Rather the basic meaning of trust consists in its practice. Junayd b. Muhammad has said: "*Tawhid* (i.e. the pure monotheistic belief in God) is a `saying of the heart' (*qawl al-qalb*), while *tawakkul* (i.e. the complete reliance on God) is a `doing of the heart' (*`amal al-qalb*)."[28] The Sufis were fully aware of the real nature and meaning of *tawakkul*. It is not surprising that in the classical Sufi literature there are more stories about the actual practice of *tawakkul* than its theoretical definitions. Al-Sarraj related the story of Abu `Abdillah

b. al-Jalla who refused to speak on the subject of trust in God (*tawakkul*) until he had given away four small coins which he possessed[29]. We have already seen in the stories of Ibrahim Khawwas and al-Daqqaq that the real meaning of *tawakkul* lies in its practice rather than its theory. In Sufi literature most of the stories that tell of the practice of *tawakkul* primarily are those which are related to its extreme from such as the following:

> "A dervish fell into the Tigris. Seeing that he could not swim, a man on a bank cried out, `Shall I tell someone to bring you ashore?' `No,' said the dervish. `Then do you wish to be drowned? `No.' `What, then, do you wish?' The dervish replied, God's Will be done! What have I to do with wishing?"[30]

Other stories relating to the practice of *tawakkul* tell of similar incidents in the lives of Sufis, such as having absolutely no trust in individual initiative or exertion, remaining indifferent in the face of anger, not storing food and clothes, travelling without provisions, not asking for anything even at the time of dire need, abstaining from medicine during serious illness, etc. *Tawakkul* understood in the light of the above discussion is complete resignation to the Will of God and full confidence in His grace and benevolence.

The function of *tawakkul* in the life of the seeker can easily be understood in terms of the station (*maqam*) following immediately after the station of *tawakkul*— in the systematized Sufi path. This is the station of acquiescence (*rida'*). Schimmel perhaps has the same perspective in mind when he says, "*tawakkul* results in perfect inner peace.'[31] Mansur b. `Ammar is reported to have said, "the hearts of those who trust (*mutawakkilin*) are vessels of acquiescence (*rida'*).."[32] Abu Ya'qub al-Susi says of the people of *tawakkul* that they find rest from the troubles of the this world and the next.[33] The reward of the *mutawakkilin* in the next world is mentioned in the Qur'an (Sura V: 119).

The fire is not only in hell but it is in this world also. In this world it is in the form of passions represented in Islamic theology by *nafs*. Sometimes the *nafs* is personified as a dog (representing greed). The perfection of *tawakkul* redeems the seeker from the worldly fire of *nafs*, because at this stage the *nafs* is under check. The perfection of *tawakkul* thus results in a balanced personality. In adversity and in prosperity the remains in the state of equipoise. Dwelling on the question of what type of personality it shaped by *tawakkul*, Nicholson says, "at best, a harmless dervish who remains unmoved in the midst of sorrow, meets praise and blame with equal indifference and accepts insults, blows, torture and death as mere incidents in the eternal drama of destiny."[34] *Tawakkul* thus relieves the seeker of many unnecessary worries and cares of the world and gives inner calm and equipoise. Such an ideal state is the goal of many faiths. The man of steady wisdom (*sthitaprajna*) in the *Bhagavadgita* is very close to the above ideal of *mutawakkilin*.

But the practice of *tawakkul* in Sufism has not always been a source of blessings. Sometimes its practice was carried to the extreme, at the cost of the other aspect of the Sufi path, and led to suspicion about the practice of *tawakkul* even in Sufi circles. We have already seen an example of this extreme form of practice of *tawakkul* in the story of the dervish in the Tigris. There are many other stories in Sufi literature in which only the extreme form of *tawakkul* has come to be identified with the Sufi path. For example, the trust that God will provide *rizq* to everybody under all circumstances had led many Sufis to abstain from undertaking any type of exertion. Schimmel says: "The faith in the rizq that will reach man was certainly carried too far by an early mystic who forbade his disciple to stretch out his hand to grasp a dried-up melon skin."[35] This type of practice is more a form of testing God, instead of putting trust in Him. But this type of misplaced emphasis in the practice of *tawakkul* seems to have its root in the tradition itself. It derives its strength from the doctrine of predestination which has repeatedly been maintained in Islam. It is the result of the imbalance of emphasis between the doctrine of predestination and practice of *Sunnah*. Such a notion of *tawakkul* may shape strange characters, such as the dervish in the Tigris, or, as Nicholson says, "a useless drone and hypocrite preying upon his fellow-creatures."[36] The ethical implications of such a doctrine may not be very healthy. These are some of the possible risks of the doctrine of *tawakkul*. But the extreme from of *tawakkul* was never the essential doctrine of the Sufi path. The earlier Sufi Shaykhs were fully aware of the possible misinterpretation of the doctrine, therefore they always preached a healthy balance between the doctrine of predestination and the commands of the Qur'an and the rules of the *Sunnah*. Al-Junayd said: "The proper method of earning is to engage in works which bring one nearer to God, and to occupy oneself with them in the same spirit as with works of supererogation commended to one, not with the idea that they are the means of sustenance or advantage."[37] Shal said: "It is not proper for those who put all their trust in God to acquire, except for the purpose of following the *Sunnah*; but for others it is not proper, except for the purpose of mutual assistance."[38] Al-Khawwas said: "Do not trouble yourself with anything that is done for you, and do not neglect anything that you are bound to do for yourself," i.e. `do not trouble yourself with destiny, for what is destined from eternity will not be changed by your efforts, and do not neglect His commandments, for you will be punished if you neglect them.'[39] Rumi has related a very long and interesting story about the same controversy of destiny and exertion in relation to trust.[40] A very fine balance between destiny and exertion has been maintained since early times. Some examples of the extreme form of trust are the result of just a misplaced emphasis; they do not form the core of the doctrine.

In conclusion we can say that the importance of *tawakkul* in the Sufi path is far greater than just a small 'station' among others. Rather, it is a central doctrine in the Sufi path. It is one of the basic principles of Islam and Sufism, and its real nature and meaning can only be understood in the total perspective of Islamic theology and practice. Historically, *tawakkul* has come to be misunderstood as blind faith is destiny; but its proper understanding and practice may lead to a balanced moral life and perfect inner peace. In this sense, its practice leads to the realization of the highest goal in the Sufi path.

REFERENCES

1. Ali b. Uthman al-Jullibi al-Hujwari, The Kashf al-Mahjub, trans. R A Nicholson (London, Luzac, 1911), pp. 289-90.
2. An `ideogram like myth' is an illustrative and symbolic substitute for concepts especially coined by Rudolf Otto, The idea of the Holy (London, Oxford Univ. Press, 1980), first printed 1923, Eng. trans. by John W Harvey.
3. Al-Hujwiri, p. 163.
4. Margaret Smith, The way of the mystics: The early Christian mystics and the rise of the Sufis (New York, Oxford Univ., Press, 1978, first in 1931), p. 172.
5. H A R Gibb, Mohammedanism: An historical survey (New York, Oxford Univ. Press, 1979, first 1949), p. 1.
6. Ahmad b. Hanbal, Musnad, I, pp. 30-52. A J Arberry, Sufism: An account of the mystics of Islam (New York, Harper, 1970), p. 27.
7. L Massignon, "Tasawwuf" in Encyclopaedia. of Islam, p. 683a.
8. R A Nicholson, The mystics of Islam (London, Routledge, 1970), pp. 42-43.
9. A. Schimmel, Mystical dimensions of Islam (Chapel Hill, University of North Carolina Press, 1978, first, 1975), p. 117
10. Ibid., p. 120
11. Nicholson, op. cit., p. 28
12. Schimmel, p. 112.
13. Nicholson, op. cit., p. 40.
14. The meaning of the Glorious Koran, p. 31.
15. Nicholson, op. cit., p. 115.
16. A Hadith Qudsi States: "My earth and my Heaven contain me not, but the heart of my faithful servant containeth me." A J Arberry, Sufism: An account of the mystics of Islam, p. 28.
17. Al-Sarraj also in his chapter XXVI on the `station' of trust, describes three types of twakkul: trust of the faithful, trust of the elect (ahl al-khusus) and the trust of the elect of the elect (Khusus al-khusus). Al-Sarraj, The kitab al-Luma, ed with critical notes, and abstract of contents by R A Nicholson (London, Luzac, 1963).

18. Abu Bakr al-Kalabadhi, The doctrine of the sufis(trans. by A J Arberyy, Lahore, Sh. Muhammad Ashraf, 1966), p. 101.
19. Ibid.
20. Al-Sarraj (trans. by Carl W Ernst), Chapter XXVI.
21. Al-Kalabadhi, p. 101.
22. Ibid. 102
23. Al-Qushayri, Al-Risala al-Qushayriya, ed by Abd al-Halim Mahmud and Mahmud ibn al-Sharif, 2 vols. (Cairo, Dar al-Kutub al-Hadiths, 1974, trans. by Carl W Ernst).
24. Al-Kalabadhi, p. 101.
25. Ibid., p. 102.
26. Al-Sarraj, Chapter XXVI.
27. Ibid.
28. Toshihiko Izutsu, The concept of belief in Islamic theology (Yokohama, Yurlndo Pub. co., 1965), p. 173.
29. Al-Sarraj, Chapter LXXI.
30. Nicholson, The mystics of Islam, p. 41.
31. Schimmel, p. 119.
32. Hujwiri, p. 126.
33. Margaret Smith, p. 172.
34. Nicholson, op. cit., pp. 44-45.
35. Schimmel, p. 118
36. Nicholson, op. cit., p. 44.
37. Al-Kalabadhi, p. 81.
38. ibid.
39. Hujwiri, p. 146.
40. Jalaluddin Rumi, The mathnawi, Book I, trans by R.A Nicholson (London, Luzac, 1977, first 1926), pp. 50-56, verses 900-990.

(Revised and edited, originally appeared in Islamic Culture, October 1982).

3

Foreign Terms in Sufism: A Survey of Chinese Influences

AHMAD ANANI

Sufism has imported much from other philosophies of the world. In this process it has borrowed terms, concepts, and practices. Chinese influences in this direction are the scope of this paper. It deals with terms like, suf, pir-i Mughan, Malang, etc.

It is worth to start from a broader plain in understanding the speicific terms and concepts in the Chinese socio-cultural context. Let's first see what is the relationship between matter and spirit in the Chinese literature. Chinese alchemy, for instance, is at once both exoteric, or alchemy proper, and esoteric, or mysticism because in each it aims at immortality. In fact alchemy started by making gold-preparations as drugs of rejuvenation, which later promised longevity and finally everlasting youth. The adepts in the art played an important role by promising elixirs of life and by finally making themselves "elixirs personified." They thus became the bestowers of immorality. Accordingly it explains the veneration bestowed upon the Masters of the cult of immorality by their disciples. There were, however, different degrees of adepts, the foremost being addressed as Shih-Fu, from which the Arabic world Sufi is derived. Shih, originally refers to "military commander," and was transferred to denote Master, such as of a prisoner, now a slave, who naturally had to obey and venerate the Master as a military commander. Fu would be Father; the absolute authority in an ancient family system. Hence Shih-Fu, Master-cum-Father, would be a benevolent despot, etymologically a more powerful term than Guru, in Sanskrit, but can be properly identified with it. Shih-Fu, in the Ningpo dialect, is Sz-Fu. This was Arabicized as Sa-Fu and with the interchange of vowels, it mutated into Su-Fa. This term existed in pre-Islamic Arabic though usually ignored. To it was added the Arabic suffix, "i", meaning "my" resulting in Su-Fa-I, My Master and Father, abbreviated as Sufi-My Guru.

Shih, in the term Shih-Fu, connotes Master, and coming overland from Szechwan, was Persianized as Shah. This is different from the real Persian word Shah, for King. In Hindustani, the honorific word, Saheb or Mister, was added as suffix to Shah, the Master, thereby giving the term, Shah-Saheb, for addressing Sufis. Etymologically speaking, here is a duplication, for each of these two words means Master. In a title, like Shah Waliullah, the word Shah is the same Chinese word Shih, as in Shih-Fu, meaning Master, and no King. Thus Shah (Saheb) and Sufi both originate from the same Chinese source and signify a Master of the cult of immortality, which Sufism is. Likewise, Dervish comes from the Szechwan term, Dao-Erh Yin-Shi, meaning, Recluse Scholar of Taoism or of divinity. Here the word Shi-Teacher, whereas in Shih-Fu, Shih-Master, as that of a slave. Then the full term, Dao-Erh-Yin-Shi was Persianized as Dar-Vi-Shi, abbreviated to Dervish, a Recluse Scholar. Qalander is another Szechwan term adapted into Persian, the original being Khun-Lun-Dao-Erh, which signifies one proficient in Taoism but wandering all over. Khun-Lun is the fabulous mountain, corresponding to Meru in Aryan mythology. In Chinese mythology an immortal, who did not ascend to heaven, not being spiritually high enough for it, remained at the next best station, which was the highest mountain on earth and as such the nearest to heaven. Then the ascetic wandering about in search of the Khun-Lun range became the type of a wanderer always hoping to reach the "mountain of immortals."[1]. Whereas Sufi comes highest in spiritual rank and next, Dervish, by contrast, Qalander would be much lower than either. It is to be noted that in Dervish the prefix, "Dar" and in Qalandar the suffix, "Dar" are the same. The original Chinese term is Dao-Erh. Dao-Taoism or mysticism and Erh-Master, the one proficient in it.

Then Dao-Erh-Master of Mysticism, or simply Master.

As a new word we have Malang. It is not found in the large Turkish Dictionary of Redhouse,[2] but is given in the Persian Dictionary of Babibullah Amozkar[3]. There it is rendered as an eccentric 'self-neglecting (individual, even) a naked fakir," like some ascetics, and majzubs. J. Shakespear's Dictionary[4], published in 1849, describes Malang as, "a Mohammadan dervish...with hair growing to full length," as is the case with some hippies today. Plats[5] reproduces all that Shakespear had said, further adding that, Malang is " a careless and inconsiderate fellow." *Nurul Loghath*[6] mentions that, "Malang is the disciple of Shah Madar." According to this information these two words should be etymologically connected. The Chinese word, Mang, is given by Fenn[7], as signifying People, but is also translated as Gypsies. These being nomads, the word, Mang, can be better appreciated as wanderers, like the sannyasis. Giles[8] transliterates the same word as Meng, character 7790, rendering it also as People. He gives the term Lieu-Meng, for Gypsies, whereas Fenn renders the same sense by the single word, Mang. The word Lieu, character 7248 in Giles, means "to circulate," whence Lieu-Meng would signify, "circulating people," like ascetics, always on the move. Thus Meng, as people, would not refer to a nation but to people of low social status, like nomads, or better, as ascetics. This explains how Fenn equates, Mang-Gypsies. Incidentally it may be noted that Fenn transliterates the same word as Mang, while Giles has it as Meng. Lang, character 6777 in Giles, is the "term for respect, a gentleman." Accordingly Mang-Lang would mean, Mr. Wanderer, or Mr. Ascetic, or Majzub Saheb in Hindustani. The terminal "ng" sound of Lang can be reduced to "n" and further omitted, as is the case with the French word Monsieur, which is pronounced with the "n" sound totally absent. Thus Mang has been simplified to ma, when Mang-Lang became Ma-Lang or Malang. This would now designate a wandering ascetic, a Majzub type of Sufi, always on the move. As *Nurul Loghath* indicates, Malang should be the disciple of Madar. In Madar we have two syllables, Ma-Dar. Ma is the same Mang, or the ascetic, as in Ma-Lang above. "Dar" is the abbreviated from of the Chinese term, Dao-Erh, explained above. There are two allied terms in Chinese Dau-Shi and Dau-Erh. Shi means a Teacher and Dao connotes Taoism, when Dao-Shi would be Teacher-of-Taoism, a Taoist-Priest. Al-most as synonym, would be Dao-Erh. Here, literally, Erh-Boy, but never-theless Erh is an honorific term for a Devotee, and as such Dao-Erh, literally, Taoist-Boy, signifies Taoist-Master. Madar can be taken to Mang-Dao-Erh which would deliver Ma-Dar. When we compare the two Chinese terms, Mang-Lang, venerable ascetic and Mang-Dao-Erh, the Master ascetic, the two terms mutate as Malang and Madar, respectively. They mutually reveal their relationship as junior and senior, the former as Reverend ascetic, the latter as the Master or Guru. This explains how *Nurul Loghath* states that Malang is the disciple and Madar, the Master. To understand the dual significance of Erh, as Boy and as Master, we have, in Hindustani, the word Miyan which also signifies both a Son as also Master. A boy can be called Miyan, as also a Sufi. Briefly, Erh-Miyan-Boy-Master. Even in English Master can be the word of address for a junior, legally underage, as one Master Paul, in contrast to his father, who would be Mister Paul. Here again Master can signify a Boy, nevertheless one worthy or regard. Depending upon circumstances, the word Master can signify a boy, worthy of regard, or a gentleman definitely deserving of respect. Now near Karachi there is a shrine named after a Sufi, as Mango-Pir. Mango can be split up into Mang and Go. Mang is the Wanderer or sannyasi, already established. Go, according to Fenn, means Elder Brother. A disciple or Murid of a Pir, or of a Spiritual Guide, would preferably address his Master as Bhai, meaning Senior Brother in Hindustani. Likewise an employees of some status would address his chief also as Bhai. Thus Bhai becomes a term of respect and endearment for the immediate Chief or Master. The Chinese word Go, is identical with the word Bhai, hence also a term for the Chief. Then the words Mang-Go, together, would mean Ascetic-Chief, signifying. My Chief, the Ascetic. Such a term becomes meaningful when we can conceive another like "Sannyasi hai" in Hindustani, signifying Ascetic

Master. Mang-Go could be effectively paraphrased as Majzub-Bhai, Majzub Master, My Guru. The word Pir, found in the term Mango-Pir, would clearly denote a saint or at least a sage Literally Pir-Old man, but it signifies Chief. Even in Germany an assistant would speak of his chief as "der Alte," the "Old one," meaning the senior or Veteran, and thus the Chief. Then in the term, Mango-Pir, there is a duplication, Pir, a Persian word signifying Master or Chief, and Mango, the Chinese term, as the Chief-ascetic. The site, Mango-Pir, there is a duplication, Pir, a Persian word signifying Master or Chief, and Mango, the Chinese term, as the Chief-ascetic. The site, Mango-pir, must have a long history for it has preserved signs of ancient paganism. Its special feature is the presence, in an adjoining pool, of crocodiles. These used to be numerous before but the survivors are still being fed by the pilgrims visiting the shrine. Further, there are springs of hot and cold water which have the reputation of curing such diseases as leprosy and others. Altogether the site has been a sacred place. The crocodiles enjoy a sanctified position, similar to that in ancient Egypt, where a village was called Crocodilopolis and the animals used to be pampered by being decorated with jewellery. Crocodile is an emblem of fertility and paganism institutes its worship. At Mango-Pir the presence of crocodiles is therefore a relic of past paganism. Peter Mayne [9]on visiting the site, found one crocodile specially large which "was considered most sacred and called, More-Saheb, Mr. Peacock." Peacock is an emblem of the Sun and as such as equally vital emblem or fertility, for sun is the power that makes everything grow. Now this large crocodile. "Mr. Peacock," is made to "wear a vermilion mark on the head" and in paganism, to smear redness on an object is to deify or to vivify it, sometimes both.

However, the crocodile, as emblem of fertility, is a potential donor of longevity-cum-immortality. As such a Master of the cult of immorality is bound to protect the crocodile. It then becomes a fellow-protege, a comrade of others, who are the regular disciples of the Master. This explains how the term, Malang, for the ascetic disciple, as protege, was transferred to the crocodile, as another protege. My friend, Hakim Jami Saheb Akbarabadi, kindly tells me that, in the Kanpur District, in India, the country-folks call a crocodile Malang, Mang, Mag and even simply as Ma. And we have also seen how Mang, the Chinese word, can mutate to Ma, while the word Madar was discussed. Likewise Mang gives, as another form of transmutation, Mag, recognized by the word Magi. Another friend, Dr. G.M. Mehkri, who hails from Mysore, also confirms that Malang is a complementary word there for crocodile. This from Karachi to Mysore crocodile would also be called Malang. Briefly we have as synonyms, Malang-Mang-Mag-Ma.

We have now to deal with the term, Pir-i Mughan, in which Mughan is the plural of Mugh. Mugh, in Redhouse (1918) is translated as 'a Magian." It is explained by its synonym as 'a fire-worshipper, a Zorastrian." However the Encyclopedia Britannica[10] (482) points out that, "it is disputed whether the Magi were, from the beginning, the followers of Zoraster and his first propagandists." They are mentioned first in an inscription of Darius dated 522 B.C. and would "rather appear constituting a priesthood *serving several religions*." This is perhaps the most essential feature of the Magi. The same Encyclopedia states that "its Greek form was Magoi, as given in Horodotus, and it was Latinized as Magus, with its plural as Magi." Then the real word, without the Greek and Latin suffixes, would be Marg, and this can be traced to the Chinese word Mang, as wandering ascetic or sannyasi. A word, on entering a foreign tongue, can mutate in different ways. We have considered Mang becoming Ma, but Mang can also drop its nasal "n", when it becomes Mag, the basic word, of which the Latin plural is Magi. Thus Magi in Latin would be the Chinese word Mang. Realizing that the Magi were "free worshippers," corresponding to "free thinkers," they must have radically differed from the orthodox religion of fire worship and explains their rising, as heretics which was easily curbed by Darius. We also know Sufis, radically differing from orthodox islam, having been individually maltreated. This could also apply to Magi as "the Sufis" of the times of Darius. Further, to understand their faith, we have, as precedence, the sannyasis among the Hindus. Once an individual becomes a sannyasi he is no longer a Hindu, and is free to worship as he likes. We have then to realize that the *Magi were ascetics*, whatever else they may have been and Zorastrism shuns asceticism. As such I felt safe in interpreting Magi as the loan word from Chinese for an ascetic and a Wanderer. With the attributes, like those of the Hindu ascetic, the Magi would be above any codified religion. Moreover in India sannyasis are known to dabble in different kinds of magical practices, even indulging in human sacrifice to acquire magical powers. Their Chinese prototypes, the Mang or Magi, could have easily been magicians as well. This enables us to identify, Mang-Wandering ascetics-Magicians. I[11] have shown before that the word, Magnates, in Arabic, can be ultimately traced to the Chinese term, Mang-Nan-Thie-Shi, Pointing-South-iron-Stone, or Loadstone. Here another word, Mang, has also entered Persian as Mugh. Then Mang, signifying Sannyasi, has likewise become Mugh, and given the plural form, Mughan. Pir, the Persian word, as discussed before, means Chief, whence Pir-i Mughan-Chief ascetic. Sometimes the sannyasis move in a group which then has a Chief of the group of wanderers. Pir-i Mughan would therefore denote such a Guru. To briefly recall the stages in the history of the word Mughan we have the series Mang (Chinese)—Mang (the basic word of the Greek Magoi)—Magi (Latin plural) Mugh (Persian singular)—Mughan (plural)—Wandering ascetics or Majzubs, with Pir-i Mughan, the Guru-ascetic, the Arch-ascetic.

Sufism, like other form of mysticism, represents "the spirit" of religion, as opposed to its "letter". One can however find enough material to present a caricature of Sufism. But according to a proper vocabulary of Sufism, as compiled by Mohammad Zauqi [12](110), "Murshid-i Kamil (one higher than Insan u'l Kamil), the perfect spiritual guide, is also called Pir-i Mughan." Then by now Mughan is a group of ascetics, and Pir-i Mughan the Chief ascetic, the Guru sannyasi. Since Pir-i Mughan signifies "perfect spiritual guide", no title can supersede it. It has therefore become the model term for a veteran in the filed, deserving of general respect and worthy of a following. Thus Pir-i Mughan-Venerable Veteran-Master of his field—Guru-Dev. The Hindu term Guru-Dev, literally Guru-God, would be Super-Guru, Archguru. Zauqi (306) also gives the term, Mugh-Bachcha. Redhouse' (1918) translates it as "Magian Boy". Mugh is rendered by him as Magian, and Baccha as Boy, hence he offers the term Magian Boy. It is however too literal a translation to signify anything. Let us consider the Chinese term, Mang-Erh. Mang is best rendered by now, as sannyasi or Majzub. Erh, literally Boy, but like the Hindustani word Muyan, also signifies Master. We then have the synonyms, Erh-Boy-Master-Miyan. To remind again, Master in English can be the word of address for a junior, or a Boy, while it clearly means Chief. Miyan in Hindustani has the same dual significance, of Boy and of Master. And Erh in Chinese is identical with the English word Master, and with the Hindustani word Miyan. It is obvious that Miyan is the word of address for a boy which implies endearment. As such Bachcha, the Persian word, literally meaning a child, would be used for a junior, or a Boy, as a term of endearment. Then Bachcha would signify "a dear junior." Accordingly, Mugh-Bachcha would connote "the beloved junior ascetic." There are two synonyms in Chinese, Erh-Child-Boy and Tzu-Son-Boy. Erh would denote one lower in rank, but would be a term of greater endearment, as for a child who is dear as the protege of his parents. Then as effective paraphrase, Mugh-bachcha-Khalifa, the future successor, the one beloved of the Chief ascetic, as his Child or Bachcha. Here full justice is being done to the significance of the word by the series, Erh-Child-Master-Khalifa. We have to admit that Pir-i Mughan would be, what the HIndu call, Guru-Dev, Super-Master, who then has, as his dear Khalifa, or successor-designate, Mugh-bachcha. Briefly, Pir-i Mughan is the Ascetic Chief, Mugh-Bachcha, his Khalifa, and Malang, the ordinary ascetic disciples. Zauqi (306), on the contrary, speaks of Mugh-Bachcha in very vague terms as "One upon whom the secret knowledge (of mysticism) has become apparent." Redhouse alone attempts a translation, as Magian-Boy, though itself imperfect.

For the sake of completion three terms given by Zauqi (239), may be briefly discussed. He described the term, "Shaikh-i kamil, as an adept, himself perfect but cannot make others likewise." But Insan-i Kamil is described as the perfect devotee, with no stage left unattainable so much so that, Insan-i Kamil-the Prophet Mohammad. Here the adjective Kamil, perfect, reveals its full significance. But the same does not qualify the "Shaikh" or Master, There is obvious discrepancy in Zauqi, as revealed by the terms Insan-i Kamil and Shaikh-i Kamil. Now I[13] have shown that the term, Insan-i Kamil, is an effective translation of the Chinese term, Chen-Jen, literally True-Man, which is a synonym in Chinese of the term, Chin-Jen, literally, Golden-Man, in Persian Adam-e Zarrin. Both these terms signify Immortal Man, and immortality marks the climax of spiritual attainment. Insan-i Kamil, or Perfect-Man, was translated into Greek as Anthropos teleios, and Golden Man as Chrusanthropos. The term, Perfect Man, would be shared by Sufism and alchemy, whereas Golden Man, though its synonym, would particularly belong to alchemy. Higher in rank to Shaikh-i Kamil, according to Zauqi, would be "Shaikh-i Akmal, who is a perfect devotee himself, and can make others likewise, but does not do so, due to over-concentration on perfecting himself." The highest position of a devotee would be occupies by Shaikh-i Mukammal, "perfect himself and making others perfect." These three terms belong to the class of Insan-i Kamil, the Perfect Man of which the Chinese original is Chen-Jen, in Greek Anthropos telios.

Zauqi (117) also records two other terms, Tarsa and Tarsa-bachcha. According to him, Tarsa would be, one who has made himself "other-worldly," devoting himself to the acquisition of spiritual attributes. As one word, Tarsa-Devotee, Tarsa-bachcha is placed higher in rank, as Perfect master or, "Shaikh-i Mukammal perfect himself, and capable of making others likewise." He leaves us in no doubt as to the seniority of Tarsa-bachcha over Tarsa. This would be reverse of Mugh-bachcha, who is the Khalifa of Pir-i Mughan, the Chief ascetic. But as opposed to Zauqi, Redhouse (532) renders TArsa, as "a mystic, a heathen, a fire worshipper," making Tarsa a synonym of Mugh or Magi. And then Redhouse translates Tarsa-Bachcha as "Pagan Boy," which harmonizes with his translation of Mugh-Bachcha, as "Magian Boy." Accepting the rendering of Redhouse once there is a Pagan-Boy or TArsa-bachcha, this would be the junior of another, who would automatically be Tarsa, as the senior. The significance of Tarsa has then to be established etymologically. The original Chinese term to Tao-Erh-Tzu, Persianized as Ta-R-Sa, Tarsa. Tao-Taoism, mysticism, Erh-Child or Boy and Tzu-Son, or Boy. But Erh-Tzu is a regular term in Chinese, literally meaning Boy, but signifying Master. In Hindustani Erh-Miyan-Child-Master, and Tzu-Baba-Son-Master. A sufi, as Master, can be addressed as Miyan, or, as Baba, again each literally meaning Son or Boy, but signifying Master. Then Tao-Erh-Tzu, as Ta-R-Sa, or Tarsa would denote a Master of Taoism of mysticism. In Pir-i Mughan the word, Pir, had to be added for a Chief mystic, but Tarsa, incorporates the Chinese term Erh-Tzu, which connotes Master. Thus Pir-i Mughan has for its synonym the term Tarsa, both denoting Chief. Every such chief has next in rank, as successor, or Khalifa, one who is dear as a child to him, and the word for child in Bachcha in Persian. Thus the term Tarsa-Bachcha would signify the Khalifa, dear as child to Tarsa, the Chief ascetic. We can then equate Pir-i Mughan-Tarsa and correspondingly Mugh-Bachcha-Tarsa-bachcha To recall again, according to Redhouse, Mugh-Bachcha-Magian Boy and Tarsa-Bachcha-Pagan Boy. However, each would specify the Khalifa of his Chief.

Now Zauqi is inconsistent in assigning seniority to Tarsa-bachcha over Tarsa. It is however possible to explain even this. In the Persian term Pir-i Mughan, for the Chief devotee, the word Pir, for chief, was added. In Chinese the word Tzu, in preference to Erh, is the word of chose for Master, and Tzu is incorporated in TArsa (Tao-Erh-Tzu). Confucius in Chinese in Khung-Tzu, literally the Boy-Khung, but the name signifies Master-Khung. In Hindustani he could have been designated Khung-Miyan the (Boy) Khung, Master Khung. A great Sufi of Khairabad, near

Lucknow, whose demise occurred now very long ago, was known as Maqbool-Miyan.

Then since Tzu-Boy-Master, Tarsa-Tzu, Tarsa-Boy, would be Master-Tarsa. Tarsa-Tzu partially translated into Persian would be Tarsa-Bachcha. I have been facing two problems here, one to show that Zauqi has not rightly interpreted the term, Tarsa-bachcha, and if he is correct, what does Bachcha mean here, which it does not in Mugh-Bachcha. Common sense requires two terms being intimately associated, as disciple and master, as Malang and Madar, or as Khalifa (Successor) and Pir (Chief), as Mugh-Bachcha and Pir-i Mughan in one case and as Tarsa-Bachcha and Tarsa in the other. But TArsa is left as an unknown word, connoting either Chief or his Khalifa. Pir-Tarsa then would specify the Chief, and tarsa-Tzu would be Master-Tarsa, the Chief ascetic.

Many a beginner in Sufism recites the words Allah-Hu like a spiritual formula, which the more it is repeated the sooner would it lead to its realization. Redhouse (2172), as a lexicographist, gives some grammatical forms of the word Hu, translated as: "1. He,; 2. God; 3. Any individual called to." It is obvious that mystic can only call out to God, so that the implied addressee is God. God then becomes another meaning of the word Hu. But when the word God is replaced by a pronoun this would be "He," which gives the third meaning of Hu, above. Redhouse also translates the terms, "Allah-Hu-O! God, and Ya-Hu -O! thou, to whom I speak." Then the term O! God, clearly signifies that the being "calling out to" is God, properly connoting the word, Hu. Now Giles gives, as character 4912, the word Hu, translating it as "to call out to". Thus the word, Hu, was taken over from the Chinese, without any change, either in form or in sense. Gruner[14] (125) briefly discusses the word, "Breath" as signifying spirit. He gives Hu as the Sufi term for Ruh, spirit. He nevertheless correctly reproduces the Chinese word Hu, the same as character 4912 in Giles. It is difficult to explain how he missed the sense of the Chinese word, Hu, as in the term Allah-Hu. According to its implied sense, Hu can only mean God, while to equate Hu-Ruh, as he does, would be a free translation.

A Sufi can also be addressed as Mivan. Formerly the terms of respect discussed have been Erh and. Tzu, with the dual significance of son or Child, as also Chief or Master. But Meng, character 7795 in Giles has been translated as "Chief, Eldest". But the inscribed character of the word, Meng, centains as component, the pictograph of child so that here "eldest" implicitly signifies "eldest child", thereby allied to Tzu. Then, according to its sense. Meng, character 7785, would be identical with Miyan in Hindustani. It has been generalized, as have also been the words, Erh, and Tzu, in Chinese. In Hindustani Bhai and Miyan each would connote a respectable gentleman. Among my lamented friends have been Husaain Bhai (Bandukwala) as also (Prof) Miyan Mohammad Sharif, where Bahi-Miyan, each is a term of respect, apart from other meaning. We have considered how Bhai can signify Chief, now Miyan would be another. Then Miyan-Meng as ideal equivalents. Now what is required is to show that Meng was formerly pronounced Miyan in some Chinese dialect. Karlgren[15] (198) gives several words now pronounced, Min, as having been pronounced as Miyan before. But Meng, the word for Chief, was pronounced Mang. Here three considerations appear before me, Miyan in Hindustani does not reveal its origin while Miyan is identical in sense with the Chinese word Meng Words sounding Miyan did exist in pre-Tang Chinese but are now obsolete. Possibly in some dialect of that period Meng was pronounced Miyan. It tracing the Chinese word Hsien, the immortal to Jin, neither Karlgren nor Giles proved helpful. Nevertheless Rev. Edkins incidentally offers such a transliteration making Hsien-Jin which then became the Arabic word for Geni. Likewise I feel Meng-Miyan, even though there is no authority available in its favour at present. Those who emphasize the precise meaning of words would be inclined to agree that Meng-Miyan. This would explain Miyan becoming a general term for a gentleman and as such worthy of addressing a Sufi.

Summary

Malang: The Chinese term is Mang-Lang, revered sannyasi. It became Ma-Lang, in Persian, for a Wandering Majzub. Madar: The origin is Mang-Dao-Erh, which became Ma-Da-R, Chief Sannyasi, with Malangs as disciples and proteges. The syllable Ma, in Malang and in Madar, is Mang, meaning Wanderer. Mango-Pir: Pir is the Persian for Chief, like Shaikh in Arabic. Mango-Mang+Go. Mang Mang is sannyasi, or Majzub, and Go-Brother-Chief.

Mango-Chief Sannyasi-Majzub Bhai in Hindustani. Mango-PIr-the Majzub Chief. Malang; Crocodile, as emblem of fertility, became a protege of Mango-Pir, like any disciple as protege, and was also called Malang. Pir-i Mughan: Singular is Mugh, in Latin Mug. As plural Mughan—Magi. The Chinese word, Mang, of the term Mang-Lang became Mugh, with its plural Mughan, meaning Majzubs. Pir-i Mughan would be Chief Majzub, as synonym of Mang-Go (Pir). Mugh-Bachcha: The hypothetical Chinese term is Mang-Erh. Mang is ascetic, and Erh, literally Boy, but the term, Mang-Erh, signifies a Devotee. Mang was Persianized as Mugh, and Erh translated as Bachcha, when Mugh-Bachcha, otherwise literally translated as Magian-Boy, conveys no sense, for Boy here signifies Khalifa, dear to his chief like a child. Tarsa; The Chinese term, Tao-Erh-Tzu, was Persianized as Ta-R-Sa, Tarsa Tao-Taoism, mysticism Erh-Child-Boy-Master and Tzu-Son, Boy-Master. In Chinese the two words, Erh-Tzu, constitute a regular term, literally Boy, but signifying Master. In Hindustani we have as parallel Miyan-Son-Boy-Master (like Erh) and Bab-Child-Boy-Master (like Tzu) Sufi, as Master, can be addressed as Miyan or as Baba, when each word, literally as Boy, signifies Master. Then Tarsa, incorporating the word Tzu, would be Master. Tzu here is the same as in the Chinese name, Khung-Tzu, literally Boy-Khung, but designating Master, Khung Confucius. Then Tarsa, as Master, would have, as his immediate junior, the future successor or Khalifa, as Tarsa-Bachcha, literally Majzub-Boy. It is to be noted that Mughan meant ascetics and Pir had to be prefixed to give the term, Pir-i Mughan, the Chief ascetic.

In Mango, Go-Brother-Chief, but its significance remaining unknown. Pir was prefixed to specify the Chief ascetic. Pir-i Mughan and Mango Pir are synonyms. Tarsa itself incorporates Tzu, the word for Chief, but the concept is not obvious. But as Tarsa-Tzu, it is Master Tarsa, where Tzu-Master-Bachcha, and Tarsa-Tzu was rendered as Tarsa-Bachcha. Redhouse explains Mugh-Bachcha as Magian-Boy, whereas it means the Khalifa of Pir-i Mughan, and Tarsa-Bachcha as Pagan-Boy, which really signifies Khalifa of Tarsa, the Chief ascetic; Mugh-bachcha and Tarsa-bachcha are synonyms.

Hu: This Chinese word means "to call out to." As word and as sense it has entered Arabic quite unchanged. A devotee would only call out to God. Allah Hu, O! God, signifies, (I) call out to (God). Miyan, a form of address for a Sufi, is a synonym of Baba. Pre-Tang China or possibly some dialect pronounced the word Meng as Miyan, and Meng means Chief, Master.

REFERENCES

1. See my article: "The Chinese Origin of the words Kimiya, Sufi, Dervish and Qalandar," J. Univ. Bombay, 25:2, 1956, 124.
2. James W Redhouse, Turkish and English Lexicon. Beirut, rpt. 1974, 1890.
3. Habibullah Amozkar, Farhang-i Amozkar. Tehran, 1352 Fasli.
4. J Shakespear, Hindustani and English dictionary, Calcutta, 1849.
5. J T Platts, "Urdu, Hindi, English Dictionary, rpt., 1968, 1911.
6. Nayar Kokorvi Nurul Hasan, Nurul Lugath, Lucknow, 1924.
7. C H Fenn, The five thousand (word) dictionary (of Chinese), Shanghai, 1932.
8. H A Giles, A Chinese English dictionary, 1892.
9. Peter Mayne, Saints of Sind. 1956, p. 4.
10. The New Encyclopedia Britanica, 1973, vol. VI, p. 482.
11. "Chinese origin of the Indian terms for Climate, and of the Arabic word for magnet" Pak. J Sci., 8 (1956) 127-133.
12. Syed M Zauqi, Sirr-i Dilbaran (Urdu), Karachi, rpt. 1371., p. 306.
13. 'Legend of golden man' (in press)
14. D C Gruner. "Avicenna, a treatise on the canon of medicine", 1930, p. 14.
15. B Karlgren, Analytic dictionary of Chinese, Paris, 1923. p. 198.

Revised and edited; originally appeared in Islamic Culture October 1979.

4

The Doctrine of Sluk: Its Chinese Origins

S. MAHDIHASSAN

Deals with the idea of a path, or sluk, in trance. Sluk or way towards the friend is a borrowed concept, from Chinese.

Sufism is a cult of immorality while Islam is a perfect religious system. Religion establishes proper human relationship leading to larger integration of human beings. The ascetic, who was exiled to live as a solitary being, was absolved from following any tenet of religion and in the eye of the law, he was no better than a deer of forest. Solitary life requires no religion whereas ideal religion aims at the commonwealth of mankind. Confucius had entertained such an ideal and his philosophy would accordingly be religious. Lao-tze, a little earlier, tried to purify the individual who automatically becomes the desirable unit in any gregarious form of life. Whereas the Confucianist mocked at asceticism, the same being discouraged in Islam, the/ Taoists, who followed Lao-tze, concentrated on individual purification. Looking at these two systems of thought, religion, promoting communal life, offers enough opportunities for making life noble. By benevolence, charity and performing social service man can remain happy. And when death comes he can reasonably hope to acquire immortality in post-mortem existence. No religion then condescends to assure its followers of future immortality. However, there is an innate urge in-man to know life after death, which takes to mysticism, of which Taoism in China and Sufism in Islam are the cults of immortality. In mysticism the individual is the sole concern and he has to purify himself enough to be able to realize that man in reality is immortal. He has to undergo spiritual gymnastics by which the material nature of his corporeal system becomes soul-like. Thus purified he becomes supernatural and sees for himself that he is immortal. To be able to do so, or better transform himself into a supernatural being, the time and energy required make him an ascetic, if he is not already one. Such sacrifices are again beyond human nature which explains how even in the past there have been but a few real sufis. Briefly it can be stated that religion promises immortality but does not assure it, while mysticism promises that the seeker of immortality can assure himself of it before he dies. Thus arises a cult of immortality as an additive to religion. In China alchemy has two phases, exoteric and esoteric, each aiming at immortality. The exoteric system made drugs of immortality and the initial substance was called kim-iya in a Chinese dialect; this means gold-making-herbal juice.[1] It enters Arabic as *Kimiya*. In esoteric alchemy the Guru is called Sz-Fu, Master-Father, which became Sufi in Arabic[2] and the master could make man immortal. Thus both alchemy and Sufism came together and are Chinese in origin.

In Sufism the most important doctrine is that of Sluk. Redhouse[3] (1074) translates the word as, "Following the path of godliness; keeping to any road." In this connection the term, Ahl-i Sluk, is rendered as "a Devotee, a Dervish." To many the translation, though correct, is not enlightening in any way. Zauqi [4](199) explains, "Sluk as the way leading to God by direct revelation and not by indirect means of deduction or inference." To make a drug that can transform a mortal into an immortal, or to resort to spiritual exercises which can do the same, energy is required. No one talks of the active principle of elixir of gold or of elixir of life. Likewise we do not know how man becomes sublime enough to see for himself that he is immortal. This requires Creative Energy, an all changing power. It suffices for us to call it Soul. The ordinary soul is separable, it has to be replaced by one which produces impact upon the material nature of the corporeal system and makes it soul-like and enters into union with it as the opposite. Fung Yu-Lan[5] (269) writes that "to begin with there was Thai-

Chi, the Supreme Ultimate. Through movement it produces Yang (or positive phase). This having reached its limit (in a circular movement) is followed by Quiescence, or Yin (the negative phase). When Quiescence has reached its limit there is a return to Movement. These two alternate and become the source of the other and the two forms, Yin and Yang, stand revealed. By the transformations of the Yang and the union with Yin the five cosmic elements water, fire, etc., are produced." And with these the entire universe is constructed. Prof. Legge[6] (26), the Sinologist, translates Thai-Chi as "Original subtle matter" and Gruner[7] (126) likewise renders it as "Primordial Substance, Prime Matter." Then its cyclic movement generates creative energy which partly freezes and produces the five cosmic elements which Gruner correctly looks upon as Yang and Yin the forerunners of Jalal and Jamal, active and passive, the ascent (being called `Uruj in Persian) and the descent Nuzul together constituting the pulse of life (p. 127). What is important is the Gruner explains that the power the cosmic element possesses, of forming the universe, "was given to them by the Elemental Matter," Thai-Chi. This is Chinese would be the Supreme Ultimate or more precisely the same generating cyclic movement of Yin and Yang. Thus arises the importance of cyclic movement which donates the cosmic elements the formative powers they possess. Before we proceed further it may be pointed out that Gruner had fully realized the identity of the 'Uruj-o-Nuzul of the doctrine of Sluk, with Yang/ Yin of Chinese cosmogony. In one case the generated creative energy produced the universe, in the other the immortal.

The classical Chinese symbol of the source of the universe is a circular disc divided into two halves, black and white, as Yin and Yang. There have to be two entities as opposites, for it is union of opposites that generates creative energy. A simplified Chinese symbol is reproduced in Mr. Akhtar Ahmad's recent book. With union of opposites, as the motif, several modifications of the symbol have appeared. Inasmuch as alchemy also depends upon creative energy it reveals many such symbols. The classical symbol in alchemy is the Ouroboros, a serpent biting its own tail, when head and tail represent the opposites, and the act of biting union between them.

Zauqi (5; 20) however offers a simple explanatory diagram without any superfluity. The central disc is partitioned into two halves while the broken partition line signifies that they are parts of one whole. The candidate of immortality starts from station A. He represents the corporeal system which is mortal. The soul is imprisoned in the material or corporeal vehicle and station A is labelled *taqayyid*, literally, "paying attention, care." From A starts the path of ascendance, *`uruj*, which is Chinese would by Yang. The path leads to Fana or annihilation. This means de-individualization and not biological destruction of life. It corresponds in alchemy to calcination which is not cremation. The base metal is thereby purified so that a neutral, non-specific form of metal is left, to offer vacant possession to creative energy which would induce growth to perfection as gold and the same also vivified as ferment (which is something living) when he product becomes ferment gold. The seeker of immortality subjects himself to annihilation in order to start with a "clean slate" and imbibe creative energy which would make him immortal. When he has thus lost all qualities specifying himself he cannot recognize himself and all he can now know would be God. This station marked B is called *ahdiat* which Redhouse renders as "Unity, Unity of God." Now begins the Descent leading back to station A as the automatic result of cyclic movement. THe de-individualized system accepts divine emanation when it acquires Baqa, which Redhouse (4: 373) translates as being "eternal with God." Now such a definition is beyond common sense, in not being visualizable. Nor can we tolerate introduction in our explanation of an anthropomorphic divinity. While the resultant of Fana is conceivable the one as "eternal with God" is not. Here comes the responsibility of the commentator to make things clearer than existing in the original itself. If the resultant of Fana is a de-individualized being, then that of Baqa is one owning a Resurrection Body. *Baqa is the quality while Resurrection Body is the reality*. And this idea is also found in alchemy. A base metal is calcined to leave a neutral metal, prime matter. It is made to accept a herbal principle when it is resurrected as a live metal which is ferment gold. Now ferment gold is capable of growth and also capable of inducing other metals to grow into gold like itself. All the means that the quality corresponding to Baqa is present in ferment gold, an everlasting entity. The base metal was killed and resurrected and what is resurrected becomes sublime in form and eternal as well. As Radhakrishnan (176) correctly observes: "Resurrection is not a mere revivification of a corpse." And the The Chinese alchemists also believed a drug-made-immortal ascended to heaven just as Jesus did. Such a scene from the Chinese was reproduced before by me and is also available in Needham's classic on Chinese civilization. Once we qualify Resurrection Body with "Baqa" we have shortened all further discussion. To repeat again after calcination base metal became a living and ever increasing substance as ferment gold and after Fana or annihilation a mortar became immortal with a corporeal system now sublime as Resurrection Body. Perhaps just for this reason Sufism has taken Jesus as a model since his case is well known. Historian of Sufism not recognizing the importance of Resurrection Body have not appreciated the position of Jesus in Sufi thought.

We now come to core of the problem, to the source of energy for any transmutation, be it from metal to live-gold or of a mortal system into a Resurrection Body. There must be two entities and they must be opposites when these would automatically enter into union and thereby generate creative energy. We start with pure energy. Its one property would be movement in all directions or expansions. When expansion is rapid it brings about condensation of some energy which becomes matter or at least "corpuscular energy" with particles of different categories. In fact no energy due to its self-expansion can remain absolutely pure. Even light is corpuscular. Correspondingly soul is conceived as the gaseous replica of the individual when soul as substance becomes dust-fine matter like smoke. Thus energy creates its opposite as matter and soul is assumed to create body as its opposite. And union between body and soul results in life as energy. Above is the explanation of the genesis of opposites. In fact we partly define opposite as the creation of its progenitor. This idea is clearly presented by the legend which depicts Adam, before he was actually born, as having produced Eve when the two were born practically like twins. Adam and Eve exemplify progenitor and issue and yet opposites. Such would be corpuscular bodies or matter created by energy. This theory applied to creation assumes God the creator, and His opposite, creation, and the two as co-existent. Even logically speaking, how can there be a creator when there was no creation? Here the trouble lies in out maintaining the concept of time. Since we assign creator priority with respect to time, at the earliest stage there can be no creation. God however would be left in a vacuum. But ignoring time creator and creation would co-exist from the very beginning. However, we have to define opposite as the creation of its progenitor.

Let us now consider a slow expanding energy which which would not cause condensation of any energy. It would expand as uniform growth without producing any opposite. Then to produce the opposite energy has to be intense. And this gives us the clue to the final acquisition of immortality. Annihilation has to be at its maximum when the resultant entity would be purest. Thus energized it would inverse itself and create its opposite when union with it can easily follow. What then is the energy and candidate of immortality has to exploit? Now nothing is dearer to man than life and the intrinsic force responsible for its maintenance is love of life. Love like any force is bipolar just as magnetism is. Love is the positive pole and compassion is its negative. They are the Yang and Yin of life. Self-love pushes one forward and makes a hero. Self-compassion preserves life against misery of every kind. Now self-love has to expand and become universal love. Being powerful this would inverse to give rise to self-sacrifice or devotion whence arise the opposites, universal love and self-sacrifice of a devotee. Universal love now qualifies volunteers serving mankind as devotees. Further come two kinds of devotees, one stationary as dervishes, who would be approached to be relieved of misery and suffering. Buddha would be the ideal of such a stationary devotee. The other kind would make himself mobile curing everywhere the sick and the infirm otherwise unable to contact any benefactor. An ideal of the mobile benefactor would be Jesus. Even in Hinduism there is vanavasi, the ascetic living a secluded life in a forest, and a sannyasi, who is ever wandering. Likewise, among the Sufis, the Chishthiya order represents stationary devotees, while that of Shurawardiya, of mobiles ones. As long as they remain devotees they can prove to be benefactors factors by thought or by deed, as stationary or as mobile. Anyone can acquire salvation by service to mankind called karma yoga in Hinduism. And here Prof. Mahadevan explains that "salvation by service comes on doing good without regard to reward" and a devotee excelling others in this respect, according to him, would be "Perfect Man, who alone is the benefactor of the world." The term "Perfect Man" is easily Chinese is origin. It is Chen-Jen, the True Man, which is as connotative as Perfect Man. The Arabic translation of Chen-Jen is Insanu'l Kamil and in Greek Antropos teleios. Thus wherever mysticism has migrated the term for the immortal also appears as its different synonyms. However it is the path, called Sluk in Sufism, which leads one to become Insanu'l Kamil. To recapitulate what has been discussed, self-love is to expand as universal love. This is inversed as self-sacrifice to become its opposite. Union between them means love of humanity to the neglect even of self-compassion. Then personifying such concentrated love of mankind there follows the path of descent when the individual becomes conscious of himself as the incorporation of universal love. He now becomes "Perfect Man." For Muslims the Prophet is the ideal Perfect Man, or Humanity Personified. Perfect Man is the immortal who has acquired immortality by loving mankind. We have here to differentiate between God and Mankind. Oswald has remarked that matter is what we know and energy what we think. Likewise mankind is what we know and God what we think. To love mankind keeps one in the world of reality, and to think one is serving mankind is to enter into unity with God. To speak merely of unity of God without considering service to humanity is poetry, but not practical Sufism.

The discussion further extended to the origin of Sufism must take us to time and place with universal love reaching its highest water-level mark ever recorded anywhere. It is China where Mou-Tzu (468-376 B.C.) preached "the doctrine of universal love." To quote Wing-Tsit Chan (118) "The Moist school puts its ethics on a religious basis. He had 300 followers (who) were ascetics." Thus arose the doctrine of universal love with its foundation members as ascetics, or wholetime devotees. Moreover, Smith (61) quotes as authority Hui-nan-Tzu maintaining that "those who followed Mou-Tzu were 180 men (but) all of whom he could have made to enter fire and whom death would not have prevented from following one another." And a twentieth century Chinese philosopher, Hu Shi, writes that "Mou-Tzu was the only Chinese who may be said to have founded a religion." Such then has been the religion of universal love in China and the source to which Sufism, as cult of immortality, can be traced. The Master professing universal love was addressed as Shih-Fu, Master-Father. Arabicized as Sufi and his title itself became a charm, a magical term. The product of exoteric alchemy was ferment-gold, in Chinese Chin-Tan, Golden drug of immortality. The resultant of esoteric alchemy was Perfect Man, in Chinese Chen-Jen, who himself became the donor of immortality. As such he was deified and to his disciples none was greater on earth than their Guru. When Sufism was absorbed in Islam the Prophet became the Perfect Man, who could transform mortals into immortals. Inasmuch as Sufism incorporates universal love this is found purest or as the sole tenet of Moist religion in China. Moist asceticism then finally appears as Sufi asceticism. On being adapted in Islam it has undergone modifications but the original traits continue to persist in various degrees in the different Sufi orders.

Summary

Chinese alchemy is exoteric and esoteric with each phase aiming at immorality. Using kim-iya, gold-making-herbal juice, it made golden drug of immortality. Kim-iya was Arabicized as *kimiya*. By spiritual exercises esoteric alchemy made Perfect Man, in Chinese Chen-Jen, translated into Arabic as Insanu'l-Kamil. He was immortal and could make others immortal. As preceptor he was called Shih-Fu, Master-Father or Guru and was Arabicized as Sufi. The words Kimiya and Sufi testify alchemy and Sufism to be Chinese in origin.

Immortality depends upon creative energy and this is generated by union of opposites. Esoteric system of acquiring immortality starts with self-love which is extended to universal love. Man now loses all signs of individuality and cannot know himself. This is called Fana or annihilation of individuality. What he can now know would be Humanity. Now what we know is mankind and what we think is God. Thus annihilation means forgetting self and remembering God Universal love begins by loving the Preceptor, the personification of universal love. As the opposite the disciple makes himself volunteer slave when Master and Disciple become opposite and the disciple forgets himself and remembers his Master. This is looked upon as union between them as opposites. Here ends Fana. The path leading to it is Uruj, in Persian, corresponding to Yang in Chinese. It is the ascendant path. Movement being cyclic ascent automatically leads to descend. If the former is Fana/Annihilation, its opposite, as descent, would be Baqa/Eternity. With Fana individuality had been reduced to non-entity or to an embryonic from of personality. It is now to bloom into a personality as one is its own right having now acquired Baqa or Eternity. Admitting there was a destruction of individuality its revival means resurrection which is more than mere return to the original. Man was mortal which means his body was material. He would now become immortal and his corporeal system would be constituted of matter which the ideal was owned by Jesus. Resurrection Body is Immortal Body. Annihilation had made the disciple an "embryo" within the system of his Preceptor, like Eve in that of Adam before both emerged as adults. Incidentally, it means that to become immortal man has to be born again as the New Testament words it. Such emergence is relatively easier than achievement ending in Fana and the descent is called Nuzul, in Persian, and corresponds to Yin in Chinese. Having assimilated the blessings of the Preceptor he is charged with the power of serving humanity by thought or by action, in any case dedicating the future life to service and personifying himself as universal love. The impact of such power upon matter makes it soul-like and the disciple completes his circular path with the acquisition of a Resurrection Body, which is immortal body.

We realize that self-love is inherent in human nature but universal love, as ideal, must be powerful enough to produce its impact upon a seeker of immortality through service of humanity. Now nowhere in the world universal love has been preached and practised, at least for some time, so well as in China. This school of thought was founded by Mou-Tzu (479-381 B.C.) who is pronounced to be the sole thinker who founded a religion in China. There were ascetics before but Mou-Tzu produced ascetics whom we can look upon as archtypes of Sufis.

REFERENCES

1. My article "Alchemy in the light of its names in Arabic, Sanskrit and Greek," Janus 49 (1961) 79-100.
2. Another article of mine "Alchemy, with Jinn, Sufi andSuffa, as loan-words from the Chinese," Iqbal (Lahore), 7 (1959) 1-10.
3. James W Redhouse. Turkish and English lexicon. Beirut, 1970 rpt, 1890.
4. Shah Syed M. Zauqi. Sirray-Dilberan in Urdu: Secrets of lovers (Devotees), AH 1371/19581.
5. Fung Yu-Lan. Short history of Chinese philosophy. 1958, p. 269.
6. Paul Carus. Chinese Philosophy. 1902, p. 26. as quoted by Legge.

Revised and edited; originally appeared in Islamic Culture, October 1978.

5

Sufi Orders in Islamic Religion and Society

AKHTAR QAMBER

The chain of followers in a Order, call it Silsila or Tariqqa, is assessed as regards its history and growth. Also under study is the role these orders play in religion and Muslim society.

1. Introduction

In the history of Islam, hostility more than hospitality to Sufism has been a traditional feature of orthodox Islam. Since the begining Sufism had to face opposition from the Ulama and the rulers. Even under the Abbasids, especially under the enlightened al-Ma'mun, the Sufis did not escape censure from the 'Ulama' of Fiqh and Usul al-Din (Islamic Jurisprudence and Islamic Theology, respectively). Worse than censure some of the eminent Sufies have stood trial and suffered martyrdom. Too well-known are the highly tragic cases of Ibn Mansur al-Hallaj (d. A.D. 922) and 'Ain al-Qudat al-Hamadani (A.D. 1098-1131), both for views which were interpreted to look like heresies. Al-Suhrawardi al-Maqtul, the Illuminist philosopher, was put to death in A.D. 1191 at the early age of thirty-one.

Especially formidable was hostility from the Ulama of Iran with the coming to power of the Safavids in A.D. 1501 and the proclamation of the Shi'ah creed as the authorized creed of the kingdom. Fervent and active in their persecuting zeal were some highly respected divines such as Shaikh Baha'i Amuli (d. A.D. 1621) patronized by Shah 'Abbas (A.d. 1586-1629), and writers and historian like Mir Baqar Damad (d. A.D. 1631) and Muhammad Baqar al-Majlisi (d. A.D. 1699). Still another adversary, Aqa Muhammad 'Ali, gained the title of "Sufi Kush" (Sufi-killer) for "the hard line he took with Sufis."

The charges against the Sufis were that they "preferred a state of Grace" to devotion and obedience to the Twelve Imams; that they gave greater importance to the Shaikh than to the *Mulla* (religious teacher); to *Dhikr* than to the observance of *Salat* (the daily ritual prayers); to the Sufi *Tariqah* or Path than to *Shari'at* (Islamic Law); fellowship with the brethren than to fellowship with the people of the Faith and that they depended more on personal *Ma'rifat* (Gnosis) than on Prophetic revelation.

Sunni resistance was not absent. Fortunately it took a moderate form. Muslim divines like the renowned Ahmad ibn Hanbal (d. A.D. 855) admired a Sufi like al-Muhasibi (d. A.D. 857) but could not understand him, says Shafiq Gorbel. They spoke different idioms. Other denounced Sufis for their belief in mutual love between the Creator and the creature (developed first by Ma'ruf al-Karkhi), and were shocked by the amazing arrogance or plain stupidity of the idea. Still others criticized Sufi philosophical concepts such as those advanced by the philosopher-Sufi Ibn 'Arabi, especially the doctrine of "Wahdat al-Wujud," construed by critics and commentators, perhaps erroneously, as Monism or as Pantheism or as something else not intended by that Sufi master and not acceptable to islamic sensibility, which was heavily slanted towards transcendental monotheism. Probably the greatest stumbling block was the secret nature of the mysteries and the rare epiphanies of "Tasawwuf" (Sufism) which sustained the Sufis but which baffled and perplexed the rest. Hence a feeling of resentment at being left out! "But the common man incapable of comprehending the mystic principle at a higher level readily accepted its ceremonial aspect." Decidedly the Sufi orders had triumphed!

The challenge of opposition together with its own vigour and stamina enabled Sufism to hold its own over centuries. In fact its role in society, particularly that of the Sufi orders, apart from the purely mystical contribution, represents a grand vindication of the Sufi way of life.

2. The Role of the Sufi Orders in Islamic Religion

The role of the Sufi orders in Islamic religion and society is tied up with the larger impact of Islamic civilization on world communities, each with its own indigenous culture, in Arab lands, southern Spain, Sicily, Africa, Egypt, Turkey, Iran, India and further afield in the East.

The following observation apply in general to the influence of the *Silsilah-Tariqah* institution on religion, life and society in extensive and diversified nature of the Islamic dominions, which yet present an over-all unity.

The classical Sufism of the early Brotherhoods was strong on simple, straightforward faith in Islamic theology, personal devotion to God and trust (*tawakkul*) in Him under all conditions, personal loyalty to the Prophet of Islam and allegiance to the *Qur'an* and the *Shari'at*. The faith was accompanied by the practice of a well-controlled ascetic life and in many cases meant renunciation of the World. Then followed the Khanqah stage and concentration, between A.D. 1100 and 1400, on the creation of the *Silsilah-Tariqah* system, its organization, its rules of conduct and the writings of handbooks both on esoteric doctrine and on the Sufi path. During its historical development it gathered elements and characteristics from the intellectual and cultural climate of the region concerned which transformed it into a bourgeois and later a mass movement of wide acceptance.

Parallel to this over the centuries Sufi thinkers came up with mystical insights based on the unsuspected inner meaning of the Qur'an, and on inspiration from older philosophic traditions, Greek, Egyptian, Hebrew, Christian, Zoroastrian and Buddhist.

I shall take off with a quotation from A.E. Affifi: "Neither the philosophers nor the theologians nor the canon lawyers have contributed so much as the mystics towards deepening of the meaning of their religion and enriching its teachings."

Shafiq Gorbel writing on the same subject in the same book observes that since the middle of the ninth century "Sufis have shaped Islamic belief and practice." Undoubtedly the ideas and beliefs of humble or renowned Sufis and of the many Sufi orders have permeated every social stratum and exercised widespread influence in all fields of life and given to the Muslim character and outlook a certain uniformity and spiritual kinship.

The impact of Sufi philosophy cannot be assessed too readily. Naturally, passion for ideas was limited to the select few, born into the aristocracy of intellect and spiritual sensibility. But the impact of the Sufi order was unmistakable. Sufi spirituality and Sufi piety spread rapidly through the example of saintly Shaikhs of great spiritual stature and the teachings of their dedicated *murids* (disciples). Thousands who stood on the "outer fringes of the Orders," observes one writer, "sought guidance on matters of voluntary worship over and above the obligatory practices of Islam." Every *tariqah* acquired its own collection of litanies, invocations and prayers to offer to the spiritual suppliant. Through such books and through the beauty of the day-to-day life of Sufi Shaikhs and their inspiring discourses "the Sufi orders reach the outside world of Islam and other religious traditions as nothing else does."

In addition to the committed Sufi aspirants, others from all ranks of society were enthusiastically associated with Sufi houses without being formally initiated into an order, periodically participating in the annual *'Urs* and *Milad Sharif* celebrations, *Dhikr* sessions, sermons, *Sama Mahfils* and community *langar* at a *dargah.* It has been a common practice among some Muslims of all ages and countries to be connected with some religious order or other and accord special homage to a living Shaikh or departed Saint without in any way abdicating their normal worldly pursuits and professions, thus affirming a point of conviction and of pride that in Islam there has never been sharp demarcation between life in the world and a life of contemplation, as is exemplified by the Prophet's life and symbolized beautifully in his experience of the *Mi'raj*—his ascent to heaven and his return to the earthly condition. Kings and courtiers, scholars, poets, intellectuals and men in business and other professions joined or patronized their favourite Sufi order as well as engaged fully and whole-heartedly in the necessary temporal concerns without which the world's merry-go-round could not go on. The ascetic ideal of detachment held, to a lesser extent and perhaps only theoretically, a lure, at best a fascination for some, if only momentarily, if only romantically envisaged.

Popular expressions of Sufism among humbler folk can be gauged by the fact that village after village in Islamic lands has a patron saint and his *mazar* (shrine) if not always a mosque. Sometimes it might turn out to be a pseudo tomb, but it is always associated with the name of an authentic *pir*. Laleh Bakhtiar speaking of a typical shrine in Kashan, Iran, says that people are content to pass by this *mazar* as "a gateway to something greater than themselves" during their pressing daily rounds. "Some," she adds, "are awakened to further possibilities of Way."The mazar of Maula Ali in downtown Calcutta is a typical example of mazars in the cities of India. In the heart of the city, it is reported, Maula Ali, attracts devotees irrespective of caste and creed to pray for health, wealth, sons and cure for disease. On Thursday evenings it is customary for devotees to repair to some nearby *dargah sharif* or *mazar sharif* (the revered place of visitation) of their favorite saint in a village or a city to make their offerings taking with them flowers, sweetmeats and a lighted *chiragh* (an oil lamp). These modest and charming tributes are paid in the implicit belief that their gifts will be accepted and their prayers heard.

The beneficial and versatile role of a living Shaikh cannot be over-estimated. Visitors of all sorts brought problems, spiritual and secular, and the Shaikh was confronted with a wide range of questions for solution—illness, livelihood, dispute, marriage of daughters, etc. It was not within the power and scope of mystics to satisfy these needs, but no one, it is said, went away disappointed from a khanqah. The Shaikh, observes K.A. Nizami, could control, direct and understand not only the spiritual needs of his *murids*, but with his special gift of *nafs-i gira* (intuitive intelligence) had a deep insight into human psychology and could lend a healing to wounds just by laying his hands upon the sufferer or breathing upon him or teaching him some formula from the Qur'an or by writing the formula on a piece of paper for him to wear round his arm in a *ta'wiz* (amulet).

Work among the down-trodden, especially in the Indian class-conscious society, was a marked feature of khanqah social concern and care. In a khanqah the lower sections were made to feel no kind of discrimination at all. Among the initiates there were "no Turks and non-Turks, no caste or casteless people. All lived and slept and ate together." What is more, the Qur'an was open to all. As K.A. Nizami says popular religion, social uplift and khanqah life go together. Sufis turned from high mystic contemplation to the needs of the destitute, the chance wayfarer, the sick in body and mind, and helpless women and children who were seldom absent from the environs of a khanqah. Sufis have always had a sensitive social conscience and have rebelled against tyranny, oppression and social disparities. In this respect great Sufis have espoused progressive humanist ideologies.

3. Sufis, Rulers and Governments

The part that Sufi orders have played in the field of politics among men of worldly preoccupations and power is truly astounding. Many orders and many individual Sufis have show a rare gift for being found in the thick of political life while at the same time being in retreat from it. It would be interesting to study the relationship of Sufis with the court of Mahmud of Ghazana, with the Seljuq Amirs of Konya like 'Ala' al-Din Kaiqubad, the Ayyubid dynasty of Egypt, the Sultans of the thirteenth and fourteenth centuries of the Delhi Sultanate, the Safavids of Iran, and the Mughals of India. Links between kingly courts and Sufi Khanqahs, for better or for worse, are by no means rare.

Some of the Sufi Shaikhs not only won the allegiance of kings and princes but themselves came to royal families or were associated with royal houses before they took to the Sufi way of life. One of the earliest of these was Ibrahim ibn Adham of the eighth century, king of Balkh, who renounced princely pomp for a life of poverty. For some random examples from India the present writer is indebted to one or two books in Urdu and one in English.

Sultan Shams al-Din Iltutmish (d. A.D. 1237), who ruled India with "glamour and eclat," was a friend of Sufis and a mystic at heart (Nizami). Originally from Bukhara, he travelled to Baghdad and was enlightened by the discourses and teachings of masters like Shihab al-Din suhrawardi and Mu'in al-Din Hasan Chishti. Iltutmish established personal relationship with Shaikh Baha' al-Din Zakariya of Multan and bestowed on the Shaikh the title and office of "Shaikh al-Islam." Later, Iltutmish became a fervent *murid* (disciple) of Hadrat Qutb al-Din Bakhtiyar Kaki (d. A.D. 1235). At the death of his beloved *pir*, Iltutmish was given the privilege of washing the *pir's* corpse.

The debonair courtier, poet, mystic Khwaja Amir Khusrau (A.D. 1224-1325) came of a learned and wealthy family and was intimately connected both with the court of Delhi and with the Chishti Khanqah at Ghiyathpur (Nizam al-Din). A man of Sufi inclinations he was a much cherished *murid* of Hadrat Mahbub-i Ilahi.

By and large the Mughals of India had more cordial relations with Sufis than the Sultans of the Sultanate period in Delhi. Emperor Babar had already come into contact with Sufism in his home town of Farghana. The Emperor Akbar used to make an annual pilgrimage to Shaikh Salim Chishti's *mazar*. He paid homage also to the other more well-known Chishti *Pir*, Khwaja Hadrat Mu'in al-Din Hasan Chishti, whose dargah at Ajmer attracts thousands of pilgrims on the occasion of the annuals *'Urs* of the Saint. Prince Dara Shikoh (d. A.D. 1659) was not only a friend of Sufis, but an ardent member of the Qadiriya *silsilah*-

tariqah. His book *Safinat al-Auliya* in Persian bears witness to his devotion to the Sufi ideal.

It is common knowledge that Shaikh Shihab al-Din Abu Hafs 'Umar al-Suhrawardi (A.D. 1145-1234) favoured good relations with rulers. The Suhrawardi Khanqah at Multan followed the Suhrawardiya precedent elsewhere of accepting royal "jagirs" and subsidies for their khanqahs. Suhrawardi Shaikhs freely entered politics, held important government offices and wielded political power in the state. Shaikh Shihab al-Din served as a most successful diplomat for the Abbasid Khalifah al-Nasir of Baghdad at the Ayyubid courts of Egypt and Syria and the Seljuq court of Rum. On the whole, the Suhrawardiya khanqahs and zawiyahs were grand institutions maintained on a lavish scale. It is said their granaries were always well stocked and their coffers full of treasure. The Suhrawardi Sufis had well-furnished rooms which presented a striking contrast to the bare cells of the Chishtiya order.

Some Sufis, of course, categorically eschewed the patronage of kings and courts. Hadrat Nizam al-Din Auliya' is reported to have said: "It the King enters by the one door I make my exit by the other" (Khwaja Hasan Nizami Thani). Hadrat Shah `Abd al-`Aziz Muhaddith Dehlawi left instructions that his "Namaz-i Jenazah" (funeral service) should take place outside the city wall and that the king should not accompany the procession of mourners.

Many Sufi Shaikhs patronized by the royalty gave rulings on matters of statecraft. Shaikh Nasir al-Din Chiragh Dehlawi (d. A.D. 1274) of the ruling family of Bukhara, for instance, played an important part in seating Prince Firoz Shah Tughlaq on the Delhi throne and entreated the Sultan to rule justly. Patronage was often a matter of policy with royal families because of the influence Sufis and Sufi orders wielded over men in all walks of life. But as Sufi teachings and the Sufi outlook on life often held a genuine appeal for men so densely involved in secular affairs and government, the intermittent association with Sufis kept the door open for experiences of expanding spiritual horizons, however temporary or insufficient they might have been.

4. Intellectual and Educational Contribution of the Sufi Orders and a Word on Aesthetics

The intellectual and educational contribution of the Sufi *silsilah-tariqahs* to society covers a vast and engaging range. When at their best, religious traditions aim at the inclusion of the whole of society for regeneration and reform. So too is the case with Islamic mysticism and the Sufi orders. Their enterprise might go under the comprehensive term "spiritual culture," which, in addition to the cultivation of the non-worldly and purely mystical sense, includes those aspects of personal culture which are geared to man's life in society. What, in Sufi terminology, is called "Adab-i muridin" (etiquette for disciples) and illustrated in Shaikh Abu al-Najib al-Suhrawardi's *Kitab Adab al-Muridin*, is extended generously to those who are inclined towards the khanqah ideal and would avail themselves of its benefits.

It is interesting to note that in his *Kitab Adab al-Muridin* Suhrawardi often quotes Sufi masters who had lived before his time in order to highlight his own teachings. Recourse to past authority also shows that Sufi etiquette for *murids* had formed, and still does, an important part of Sufi discipleship.

Quoting Abu al-Rudhbari, Suhrawardi writes to "act aggressively against one who is above you is impudence, against one who is your peer, bad manners, and against him who is below you, weakness."

Quoting al-Tustari the author counsels "abstain from retribution...have compassion for him who wrongs you."

In another context al-Suhrawardi says: "If he (*murid*) travels in company he should walk at the pace of the weakest and stop when a friend stops."

Regarding nice manners with guests, al-Suhrawardi lays down priorities—first of all greetings, then expressions of respect, then offering of food, and finally conversation.

"When the Prophet was eating in company, he would be the last to finish."

"It is better to sit alone than with an evil companions, and it is better to sit with a worthy companion then to sit alone."

Al-Suhrawardi recommends respect for the Shaikh, intimate friendship with peers, kindness to servants, respect and honour to visitors, obedience to rulers (typical Suhrawardiya attitude) and compassion for wives and children. (Some Sufis badly neglected their families!)

Specifically in respect of Sufis al-Suhrawardi refers to Prophet Muhammad's (p.b.u.h) injunction: "There are four things which are of this world and yet are not of it—a piece of bread to satisfy your hunger, a piece of cloth (*khirqah*) to cover your nakedness, a house to shelter you from the cold and the heat and virtuous wife whom you can trust."

The appeal of such discourses heard from the lips of respected Shaikhs for visitors to the periodical assemblies at khanqahs must have been immediate and universal, especially those visitors who had aspirations for a refined and well-shaped personality. At their most sensitive levels Cardinal Newman's "Idea of a Gentleman" and the Japanese concept of social courtesies inculcated by the Tea Ceremony bear strong resemblances to what Shaikh Suhrawardi had in mind by way of education in ethics, good manners and social graces. For the *Sufi murid*, in particular, this education was accompanied by ascetic disciplines in preparation for the receiving of the mysteries of *Tasawwuf.*

The specifically intellectual work of the medieval madrasahs and of the learned doctors of Fiqh and Usul al-Din, the best of which has stood the test of time under a variety of civic and spiritual conditions, was supplemented by Sufi thinkers, philosophers and poets. Writings on Sufi doctrine and metaphysics by such men as al-Hallaj, Ibn 'Arabi, al-Suhrawardi, al-Maqtul (the Ishraqi exponent), 'Ain al-Qudat, Farid al-Din 'Attar and Rumi, to name only a few, present an imposing body of Islamic philosophy and literature. For instance, Gesu Daraz, a noted Indian Chishti Sufi writer and commentator, wrote exhaustively upon the works of Arab and Persian Sufis, notably Ibn 'Arabi and Farid al-Din 'Attar. About the year A.D. 1400 Gesu Daraz wrote a commentary on the book *Tamhidat*, which, it is said, contains brilliant but heterodox insights on mysticism by that rare genius, scholar, poet, Sufi 'Ain al-Qudat of Hamadan mentioned earlier. Sufism and the Sufi *silsilah-tariqahs* have engaged the attention of Western (European) critics, and translators of Sufi works into English, French and German have made the Western world acquainted with Sufism. They have promoted good critical studies, some objective and impartial, others charmingly but genuinely enthusiastic. A new trend in scholarship includes modern Persians, Arabs, Indians, and Turks associated with western universities who have written in English or French or whose works have been translated into English or French or other languages such as, E. Affifi, Sayyed Hossein Nasr, Shafiq Gorbel, Saiyid Athar Abbas Rizwi, Khaliq Ahmed Nizami, M.M. Sharif, Abul Hasan 'Ali Nadwi, A. Reza Arasteh, and Laleh Bakhtiar.

Sufis also addressed themselves to the equally important but humbler task of simply promoting literacy, inculcating the moral sense and imparting elementary religious education, partially conducted also by the *maktabs* connected with local mosques. The classical languages of the Islamic world, Arabic, Persian and Turkish, could convey complicated and profound philosophical concepts or express, not infrequently in poetic terms, mystical experience too elusive for any language at all. But it was the non-classical language used outside the Arab and Persian-speaking countries that received a boost from Sufi Houses in their process of linguistic development and growth. The Sufi message could reach the market square and the countryside only through what are known as regional languages.

Moreover, translations from the classical languages, Arabic and Persian, of Sufi treatises and manuals required careful study to ensure exactness and fidelity to the original sources. This proved extremely beneficial for the chiselling and strengthening of a language. In this exciting exploration the part played by poets, makers of language, and philosophers all over the Islamic world is truly great and indispensable. Especially did the poets work miracles in adorning and extending the scope of the language they used. Not that they always necessarily coined new words, they also employed existing vocabulary and phrases in more than one way and often assigned to them meaning other than what the dictionary connotes, in order to express concepts and mystical states which they had experienced directly, in the first instance, without the aid of words. Some words, when used for mystical experience, became, by implicit consent, standard terms for purpose of communication without which Sufi teaching could not have reached those who had had no such experience themselves. For instance, the single word "`Ishq" was enough for expressing non-mystical love relationship (though love remains in any case a mystical and non-explainable relationship). But when Sufis wished to talk about Divine Love they had to define the difference between "`Ishq-i Majazi" (earthly love) and "`Ishq-i Haqiqi" (Love of God). What better way was there to know the love of God except by what experience of earthly love could teach and what other recourse for communicating it to others than the secular and literary phraseology available to them at that time, or for that matter at any time?

It is interesting to make note of some of the phraseology used pre-eminently by Sufis and Sufi-poets and harnessed in the service of "`Ishq-i Haqiqi" also taken over by poets of "`Ishq-i Majazi," thus giving to both groups the mutual advantage of extended meaning and double and treble suggestive interpretations. Here are some typical examples relating to Divine Love—"Wisal" (union of lovers), "Hijr" (separation flight), "Fana" (annihilation), "Baqa" (an abiding in Allah), "Hijab" (veil or covering), "Kashf" (manifestation, revelation, unveiling), "Tajalli" (beatific vision, epiphany), "Be-khudi" (self-annihilation, the opposite of consciousness of the self), "Kaif" (ecstasy, intoxication), "Wajd" (rapture, transport, ecstasy), "Khilwat" (retreat, withdrawal from the world), "Zuhd" (asceticism, renunciation), "Hal" and "Maqam" (states in and stations on the Sufi Path), "Muraqabah" (vigilance), "Qurb" (nearness, approach), "Uns" (intimacy), "Nafs al-Ammarah" (ardent desire). On the other hand, there were terms used pre-eminently by non-Sufi poets which the Sufi poets appropriated for their mystical domain. Here are some random examples: "Mahbubi," "Sanam," "Dost" (all meaning friend or beloved), "Dilbar" (Charmer), "Shama`-o-Parwanah" (the light and the moth), "jam-o-badah" (goblet of wine), "Maikhanah and Kharabat" (tarvern), "Pir-i Mughan" and "Pir-i Kharabat" (tavern keeper), "Saqi" (cup-bearer), "Badah-Farosh" (wine-seller), "Butkhanah" (temple of Idols). So the Sufi borrowed from the poets and the poets saw new meanings in what the Sufi had found.

Furthermore, Sufi poets employed every literary device at their disposal—tale, fable, dream, dialogue, symbol, simile, and the realm of the subconscious—and every poetic form from the long "mathnawi," "qasidah" and "marthiyah" to the short "ghazal" and the "ruba`i" for Sufi teachings. Whereas philosophers made near incomprehensible doctrines and ideas accessible to the mind, poets found their way into the hearts of men and women with passionate songs and moved them to states of rapt contemplation, spiritual excitement and beatific vision, when glimpses of mystic realities might be possible. Poetry was an important and vivid means of popularizing Sufi teachings, attitudes and the Sufi outlook. Even esoteric doctrines were communicated in simple words and appealing rhythms and imagery.

Learning to read was followed by learning to write. Penmanship is an age when there were no printing presses was a highly prized and skilled art. Copies of the Qur'an and other sacred writings had to be made by hand. The Arabic script lent itself to artistic and decorative purposes in mosques, madrasahs, khanqahs, dargahs, mausoleums as well as palaces and forts. Verses from the Qur'an and sometimes Arabic and Persian poetry in Arabic script "nas-ta'liq" and "thuluth" were dexterously intertwined with floral and leafy patterns and intriguing geometrical symbols. The typical structure of calligraphy with vertical and horizontal strokes presents a fine representation of the principle of polarities, the masculine and the feminine, the active and the passive, the transcendental and the immanent believed to be found in all created beings. The mystic sees in calligraphy and arabesque "his inner complementary opposites," and meditates on their resolution into a harmonious relationship. At times the sense of union, if not unity, is so over-powering that the vertical and the horizontal movements in a design merge and flow into a circle, a symbol of completeness and oneness without beginning and without end. For illustration of calligraphy and symbolic content see the following:

The Land of Kings (Ministry of Information, Iran, 1974), p. 237. This is a reproduction of a painting by Zenderoudi where the calligraphical design has almost come full circle. Why the artist did not round up the circle may suggest that completeness and perfection in human life are never attainable and that may must merely suggest and try for the ideal, in this case the ideal unity.

The frontispiece of *The Sufi* by Idries Shah carries a reproduction of a very striking ship-shaped calligraphy—the horizontal, slightly circular movements meeting vertical strokes of lettering represent a shipload of pilgrims to Mecca.

A most attractive design of calligraphy in Martin Lings' book, *A Sufi Saint of the Twentieth Century, Shaikh Ahmad al-'Alawi,* is a reproduction of a Moroccan woodcut entitled "The Supreme Name: Allah surrounded by other Divine Names and verses for the Qur'an."

A reproduction of a thirteenth century Near Eastern Qur'an called "The Sura of Brightness (Suran al-Duha)" on p. 39 of Stoddart's *Sufism* is very striking.

The impact to Sufi ideals was also felt, if not indirectly, in the province of architecture. Sufis borrowed the generic forms of Islamic architecture, its dimensions, proportions and designs, for khanqahs, mosques, mazars and dargahs. Then they endowed the outward form with meaning. So the design and the meaning merged together unconsciously in the mind and presented rare mystical avenues for contemplation. Set in a garden with flowing water and recalling Paradisial fountains *Kauthar* and *Tasnim* (water being a symbol of life, or flux and change and most of all of purification and refreshment), the Khanqah suggested the concept of an earthly paradise where might grow the cosmic tree of knowledge. Here kindred souls meet in pursuit of spiritual experience. A Sufi might well look upon the gateway as an entrance upon the Sufi path with the "Iwan" (porch) offering a place of waiting, perchance of catching the light before entering the "hayat" (courtyard). The "gumbad" (dome) in its reposeful sitting-down position on a spacious high plinth became an archetypal symbol of the sphere or circle inherent in creation representing "the Divine spirit encompassing the Universe" eternal, timeless. The vertical dimensions, on the other hand, of the two slim flanking, upright "minars" (minarets or towers), sometimes disappearing in the haze into the distant horizon, were apt metaphors for man's upright soul soaring towards the transcendental origin. Facing the worshippers at *namaz* was "mahrab" the niche in the mosque which points the inward gaze towards the Ka'bah at Mecca. The "chahar taq" (a dome resting on a square base), open arches and lattice-work hinted at possibilities of the soul's windows being flung open to light and air and vast space. There was then the enclosure where the saint's earthly remains rested and the cells of the living *murids* were not so open. The sacredness and the mystery of the departed *pir* and the mental concentration of the living *murid* were enhanced in the dim enclosed, intimate atmosphere. Thus, by endowing architectural feature with archetypal correspondence the Sufi enriched the quality of his mystical contemplation and also contributed meaning to aesthetic form.

Even the image of the architect who is known as the

"muhandis" is made significant in his triple function of geometer, artist and builder rolled into one. He harmonizes diverse elements like space, line and material whether it be brick and mortar, wood or marble. Whenever this outward harmony is seen in terms of an inner harmony there comes about a point of inner concentration when a human soul might draw near to the Universal Soul—perhaps in mutual fascination, love and spiritual or mystic union.

So too with *Sama'* and *Raqs*. Music, melody and rhythmic bodily movements have figured prominently in the career of some Sufi orders, whether it was in relation to their role in mystical experience or in the controversy they generated.

Not all Sufi *tariqahs* favoured *Sama' mahfil*. Many Sufis were apt to look upon music as a hindrance in the way of mystical attainments. Early Sufis, notably those of the Chishtiya *tariqah*, had to enter into endless dispute and debate with those holding the Baghdadian tradition of al-Junaid. It was with difficulty that the sponsors of *Sama'* were able to establish the legitimacy of music as a useful experience in mystical discipline. Al-Suhrawardi approved of *Sama'* as *rukhsah*, "relaxation after certain ascetical pressures." A *dhikr majlis* might well lead the *Sama'* recitals and the singing of choruses and antiphonal compositions. These is turn might lead to moods of lyrical ecstasy and sense of selflessness. The Chishti Pir, Khwaja Qutb al-Din Bakhtiyar Kaki, was intensely moved by music and is said to have remained in a state of spiritual rapture once leading to state of unconsciousness for days under the influence of singing by a certain *qawwal* of his time. Only at prayer time would be come to himself. Sometimes he would reach such a state that he would begin dancing in the courtyard.

Sama' mahfils became a regular feature of Sufi activity in some khanqahs and zawiyahs. Especially popular were *Sama'* sessions on the occasion of annual Islamic celebrations such as *'Urs*. Among the Shi'ahs the most passionately moving exercise is *Marthiyah-Khwani* (singing of elegies) during the month of Muharram when the martyrdom at Karbala of Hadrat Imam

Husain is commemorated. *Qur'an Khwani* (reading of the Qur'an in a musical and rhythmic voice) is used both for special occasions and for routine services of devotion such as the opening and closing of religious assemblies. Some modes of music became associated, especially in the Indian sub-continent, with Sufism such as "Qawwali" (antiphonal choral singing of rousing kind). Both vocal and instrumental music was popular. Amir Khusrau is credited with the composition of as many as thirteen "Rags" (melodies). He is said to have introduced in musical circles different types of singing such as "Qaul", "Qawwali," "Khayal," "Qalbana," "Nigar", etc.

The sufi contribution in this field lay precisely in the synthesis that was initiated under Amir Khusrau's auspices between Indo-Islamic musical traditions which have grown steadily thus promoting a lasting feeling of cultural kinship between the major communities of India whatever be their religion. Music is universal language!

Raqs (dance) did not gain the same degree of importance and popularity among the Sufi orders. The Maulawiya *silsilah-tariqah* of Shaikh Jalal al-Din Rumi of Konya is associated with the dance of the whirling dervishes. This Sufi dance was no mere matter of bodily movements. The symbolic content of circling, whirling and leaping is quite elaborate.

Through art, architecture and music and the beauties and wonders of well-ordained Nature with its unchanging, reliable laws and processes, "the Sufi invokes the divine order as it resides in a hidden state within all forms" and presses every means in the service of mystical awareness when glimpses of the Truth might be vouchsafed to him.

5. Mystical Doctrines and Experiences are Supra-Religious

They transcend time, place, history, race and culture. Were there the remotest chance of any religious traditions arriving at a common meeting point it would be in terms of and at the level of mysticism. Wherever Islam went Sufism followed and drew men by its strong irresistible appeal. The Rishis of the Upaṇishad period, Zoroastrian and Greek seers and hermits, Tantra and Zen ascetics, Hebrew Hasidim, Christian mystics, the Bhaktas of Medieval India and the Sufis of Islam are citizens of the same mystic city, and would recognize immediately a kindred soul were they given the chance of meeting. Especially were medieval Bhakta saints like Chaitanya, Ramanuj, Kabir, Nanak and Dhanna and the Sufis of Islam akin to one another in their intoxication of the love of God. In fact this invisible bond has existed between mysteries of all ages in all places. Both "Tasawwuf" and institutionalized Sufism have shown a commendable flexibility to accommodate a diversity of mystical inheritances and temperaments in bringing together people of different faiths and cultures in friendly coexistence and rapport.

These are no mean achievements by any standard even if we stop at this juncture, which is to say that there is more, much more to explore and evaluate.

There is much more to explore also in term of decline of so great and magnificent a movement in Islamic history as the Sufi *Silsilah-Tariqah* and Sufism in general.

6. The Decline

The mystical impulse began to show signs of exhaustion from the seventeenth century onwards. It seems to have declined in most parts of the Islamic world by the middle or end of the nineteenth century. Sufism came in for its inevitable fate which is was to share with other religious faiths in the wake of events, ideas and movements beginning with the Industrial Revolution and leading eventually to our twentieth century technological, rather soulless civilization. Ideologically, the change in outlook was seen in the latter half of the nineteenth century and was initiated by the scientific and other discoveries of intellectual giants like Darwin, Freud and Marx. Especially did Darwin's view of man in scale of creation prove disturbing to religious belief--much more so than the Marxist Socio-economic revolution and the Freudian psychology of the subconscious and sex.

The scientific Humanism of the twentieth century, different in some important respects from the Humanism of the Ancient Greeks and that of the sixteenth century European Renaissance, relegated the spiritual sphere and its values to the shadow of doubt and scepticism. Sherrington's portentous dictum "The only friend of man is man" sounded a characteristic note of our times and introduced a mood of loneliness and melancholy in a world which was to be without God, a shattering prospect for Sufis whose best friend is God.

And, life without God many did accept—some at the lofty plane of secular existentialist philosophy like Sartre, others with high ethical and social values and substitutes for religion. Still others found compensation in the gleaming dogmas of materialism and better standards for living on earth. Some few still prayed, for as Iqbal says "prayer is a yearning of response in the awful silence of the Universe." More than one author on Sufism has pointed out that Islamic societies did not escape the prevailing rationalistic postures and secular trends inimical to mysticism in general. Sufis, the Sufi orders, and non-Sufis alike came under the all-dominant sway of modernistic city civilizations and the dream of endless progress had inhabited the aspiration of the soul.

The inner causes of the decline of Sufi orders were intimately connected with the old Sufi style of life. For instance, many Sufi *tariqhas* had enjoyed royal patronage which was increasingly withdrawn at one point or another in the course of history. Taking an example from the Indian scene, a king like Sultan Muhammad bin Tughlaq wanted Sufis, writes K.A. Nizami, either to join service under him or to leave Delhi. This was a tricky dilemma. Courageous Shaikhs like Chiragh Dehlawi and Qutb al-Din Munawwar could comply with neither condition. They refused to leave their khanqahs in the capital and allow them to run to seed. Other Shaikhs could not withstand political pressure and lost their freedom. Politics, therefore, was the undoing of many khanqahs as it had formerly been the making of them.

The weakening of the mystical impulse came as such from within. After all, Shaikhs are human beings and human beings are sources of infinite good-ness and infinite corruption. The Shaikh concept underwent big changes.

To begin with the hereditary principle in some orders as regards the appointment of the Shaikh posed a serious threat to spiritual excellence. The *barakah* (esoteric spiritual power) officially remained in the family of the incumbent Shaikh, but was no guarantee that all the succeeding Shaikhs would be genuine "Walis". Some Shaikhs ceased to be engrossed in mystical avocation and became flourishing members of society living with their large, prosperous households in rich *zawiyah* complexes. Not that Sufis in the past had not married or did not have families or did not enter politics or accept "jagirs" and endowments for their khanqahs, but now there was a marked difference in their attitude to wealth, marriage and politics. They had lost the independence of early Sufis who truly transcended kinship, family, position, riches, society and its conventions, or despite these had been able to engage in the pursuit of spiritual conditions so dear to their hearts.

Moreover, ritual purity gained over spirituality. On the popular level a superstitious devotion to saints, their power for intercessory prayer and for working miracles gave rise to the tomb cult and replaced the former personal attachments to and fellowship with living dynamic personalities. The tomb of the saints became a focal point. Collective *dhikr* and other collective activities came to have more importance than meditation and personal communion with Allah. The Shaikh came to be looked upon as a representative of God on earth "a kind of portage of Allah" rather than Allah's friend. With the disappearance of genuine Shaikhs at whose feet *murids* had received their spiritual disciplines and spiritual culture referred to earlier the *Tariqah* also disappeared. The succession in the *Silsilah* remained a monopoly in some single family and fell in the lot of some Shaikh who had no Sufi inclination or aptitude for a responsible Shaikh's avocation.

7. New Trends

Where the Sufi impulse was still strong it was channelled by some Sufi *silsilah-tariqahs* into other directions such as the fundamentalist movements beginning around the eighteenth century or as intensely patriotic political freedom movements or social and economic reform movements of the twentieth century.

The typical Arab reaction to the new age, it has been observed by historians, was conformist—back to the pristine purity of Islam--which first appeared in the less enlightened Arab lands and then spread to North Africa and to other lands in a modified form through the zeal of the Sufi orders. Iran presents the most recent spectacle in the regard. In general, it is seen that some of these modern movements are more a revival of Islam, some with a political slant, than a recreation of Sufism. Some of these stem from the orthodox traditions of Shaikh Ahmad ibn Hanbal or the ninth century and Shaikh Ibn Taimiyah of the fourteenth century culminating in the nineteenth century Wahhabi movement with its centres in Najd and in Hijaz. This movement stressed the importance of returning to the Qur'an and the Tradition. On the other extreme was the rise of rationalistic trends such as those that transformed Turkey into a modern State on the model of secular European States.

But neither straight conventional religion nor rationalism and science could satisfy all communities in the Islamic world. This is testified by the rinse of the Muhammadiya type of *tariqahs*, such as the Ahmadiya, Sanusiya and Tijaniya founded about the eighteenth century and popular mostly in Africa. The Khalwatiya, a more intellectual order, was founded in Egypt and Turkey. The Muhammadiya order, a branch of the older Naqshabandiya order, for instance, subscribed to fundamentalists beliefs as the basis of mystical experience. The mystical impulse, by no means diminished, found what is considered a more modern and enlightened expression. The chief exponents of the Muhammadiya order are well-known figures like Khwaja Nasir 'Andalib and his illustrious son, Khwaja Mir Dard, the mystic Urdu poet of the eighteenth century. This

Tariqah lays strong emphasis on the person of the Prophet of Islam and on his teachings as found directly in the Qur'an and the Shari'at. The Sufi doctrine, philosophy and activities are all centred in the Prophet's teachings and personality. Concentration on his attributes and virtues and on the pattern of his life was a necessary prelude to mystical knowledge and experience. In this pursuit sobriety was better than state of intoxication and living in the world in a controlled, dutiful manner better than ascetic isolation. Theirs was an "interior" kind of mysticism free from excessive outward rituals which had become empty of meaning. The Muhammadiya like its parent Naqshabandiya appealed to hard-working merchants, professional classes. Intellectuals, men of learning and craftsmen. The *Tariqah* inherited other characteristics from the Naqshabandiya, among them interest in statecraft and responsibility for social concerns. In general, then, the Muhammadiya order was both fundamentalist and reasonably political.

The Sufi orders that displayed both fundamentalist and politically militant tendencies were popular in countries dominated by European imperialist powers. The Sanusiya, the Tijaniya and one branch of the older Shadhiliya order of Egypt originating in the Maghrib were heavily motivated by political ambitions and "Sufis gripped by zeal for Islamic political independence" (B.G. Martin) engaged in the noble task of liberating oppressed and subject Muslim communities from foreign rule, chiefly that of the English and the French. These orders, it is observed, gained control over whole communities. The North African orders have attracted Europeans also. In the Sudan and the Dutch Indies "Maulanas" (learned men) usually belong to one or the other Sufi order. Muslim communities in Bulgaria, Greece and Yugoslavia patronize the Malamati order founded in Macedon. The Malamati *silsilah-tariqah* is known for its indifference to outward observance and is marked by a liberal outlook. It helped to foster the Turkish Revolution under Kamal Ata Turk when the Sufi orders along with the old Ottoman Empire were swept off the board.

8. Final Remarks

However, individual Sufis of exceptional mystical gifts and "spiritual eminence" (Martin Lings phrase) are to be found in every age. Some while still fulfilling the obligations of the world are mystics in the real sense of the word and continue to hear the call. Martin Lings writes of a few Sufis who, he says, "recall the golden age of Medieval mystics" like the twentieth century Shaikh Ahmad al-`Alawi (d. A.D. 1934) and his own immediate teacher Muhammad al-Buzidi. Shaikh `Alawi's generosity of outlook and imaginative sympathy can be measured by his own words: "If the grace of ecstasy is beyond you, it is not beyond you to believe that others many (sic) enjoy it." Besides such great Sufis, there are poets, intellectuals, peasants, and artisans who still continue to derive solace from the Sufi ideal not merely by way of an escape from the harsh realities of life, but as a meaningful way of living in society, *Khalwat dar anjuman*.

But let the critics last word. In the magnificent opening of chapter V of the *Reconstruction of Religious Thought in Islam*, Sir Muhammad Iqbar brings out in a telling manner the distinction between the prophetic and the mystic types of consciousness by quoting 'Abd al-Quddus of Gangoh: "Muhammad of Arabia ascended the highest heaven and returned. I swear by God that if I had reached that point I should never have returned." The Prophet's "Mi'raj," says Iqbal, "leads to the transformation of mankind" and creates "another type of manhood." Had the mystic returned to earth "it would not mean much for mankind!" Iqbal singles out asceticism and the other worldly outlook (not mysticism, not "Tasawwuf") as one of the causes that led to Islam's stagnation during the last five hundred years.

The second score on which a critic speaks is "Tasawwuf" itself and its esoteric nature. It will not be out of place to end this article with part of a paragraph quoted by Lings in his book, *What is Sufism*?. This passage contains advice by an early nineteenth century rector to students entering the Azhar University of Cairo.

"The love or Sufism falls into two categories. One of them is concerned with disciplining the character and investing it with all the spiritual courtesies... This lore...is within the grasp of anyone who has the slightest application to learning. In the order category the masters of Sufism are concerned with mysteries being unveiled and with direct spiritual perceptions... This lore is too abstruse for anyone to understand who has not shared their experience in some degree. Moreover it may happen that their manner of expression does not adequately convey their meaning, and if taken literally it may conflict with all logical evidence. It is therefore better not to pry into it, but to leave its masters to enjoy their own privileged states."

This sums up courteously, with a touch of gentle scepticism, the typical modern attitude to Sufism and, by extension, to the Sufi *silsilah-tariqahs*.

REFERENCES

1. Encyclopaedia of Islam.
2. K A Nizami, Some aspects of religion and politics during the thirteenth century, p. 62.
3. Islam the straight path, ed. Kenneth W Morgan (New York, Ronald Press, 1958), p. 167.
4. Ibid., Chapter by Shafiq Gorbel.
5. Martin Lings, What is Sufism?, p. 119.
6. "Urs," - anniversary of saint's death or literallly, his wedding feast when he is united with God, his beloved. "Milad" -anniversary of the Prophet's birthday. "Sama Mahfil" spiritual concerts, musical gatherings for devotion. "Langar" meals served at the khanqa.
7. Laleh Bakhtiar, Sufi: Expression of the mystic quest, pp. 94-5.
8. Ibid., p. 95
9. K A Nizami, Medieval Indian history and culture, pp. 92-93.
10. Sufis of Bijapur by R M Eaton is one such study in a localised setting (Bahmani Sufis by M Suleman Siddiqi, is also a similar study: ed.).
11. Bazm-i-Sufiyah, Sabah al-Din `Abd al-Rahman, Dar al-Musannifin, Azamgarh, 1971 (in Urdu).
12. 'Jagir' is a piece of land given by the government as a reward.

13. A Sufi rule for novices, ed. and trans. by Menahem Nelson (Harvard Univ., Press, 1975), p. 51.
14. Ibid., p. 37.
15. Ibid., p. 53.
16. Ibid., p. 54.
17. Ibid., p. 58.
18. Ibid., p. 45.
19. Ibid., p. 82.
20. Contribution to Islamic jurisprudence, for instance to the Indian Civil Code, is by no means small.
21. Laleh Bakhtiar, op cit., p. 103.
22. Ibid., pp. 39, 54-55.
23. Idries Shah, The Sufi, London, 1964.
24. Martin Lings, A Sufi of the twentieth century, Sheikh Ahmad al-Alawi, London, 1973.
25. William Stoddart, Sufism, p. 39.
26. Symbolical interpretations of architecture are partly suggested by Laleh Bakhtiar.
27. 'Sama' spiritual concert, `raqs' dance.
28. Raja Sultan Maqsood, `Music: Khusrau, the innovator' in Amir Khusrau critical studies (Lahore, 1975), p. 83.
29. Laleh Bakhtiar, op cit., p. 6.
30. K A Nizami, op cit., pp. 92-93.
31. Sir Muhammad Iqbal, The reconstruction of religious thought in Islam, pp. 92-93.
32. B G Martin, Muslim Brotherhoods in nineteenth century of Africa.
33. For this information the author is indebted to B G Martin, Martin Lings, and Annemarie Schimmel.
34. Martin Lings, op cit., pp. 120-126.
35. Muhammad Iqbal, op cit., p. 124.
36. Ibid., p. 126.
37. Martin Lings, op cit., pp. 117-18.

6

Sufi Interpretation of the Qur'an: Al-Ghazali as a Proponent

MUHAMMAD ABUL QUASEEM

While interpretation of Quran has been done by various schools, the Sufi interpretation agitated many, including jurists, traditionalists, and others. This essay is one attempt to highlight al Ghazali's defence of the Sufi interpretation.

Although the orthodox form of sufism [1] had its roots in the Qur'an and the Sunna and although it pursued an excellent aim of purification of the soul from vices and its beautification with virtues[2] so as to ensure the highest happiness in the Hereafter,[3] it was condemned, sometimes very strongly, by three classes of Muslim intellectuals, namely, jurists (*fuqaha'*) and traditionists (*muhaddithun*) in general, and Hanbalites in particular. This condemnation started from the second half of the second century of the *Hijra*, and it was based on several grounds of which the following three may be regarded as fundamental: Existence of weak (*da'if*) and spurious (*mawdu'*) Traditions in the writings of most orthodox sufis[4]; interpretation of many Qur'anic verses by these sufis which is repugnant to the usual exegesis[5]; and unbalanced ecstatic utterances of certain eminent sufis, such as al-Bistami (d. 261 A.H.), ash-Shibli (d. 334 A.H.), al-Kharraz (d. 286 A.H.), and al-Hallaj (d. 309 A.H.), expressing their relationship with God, which are atleast apparently in sharp contradiction with the teachings of the Shari'a—utterances referred to in sufi literature as the *shatahat as-sufiyya* or paradoxical utterances of the sufis[6]. The second of these serious accusations against orthodox sufism constitutes the subject-matter of this article.

Sufi interpretation is part of the characteristically mystical emphasis upon the inward consideration of matters. This consideration is done at two different, but closely related, levels: practical and cognitive. The former means emphasis upon acts related to man's inward self (*al-a' mal al-batina*) so that it may be purified from vices and beautified with virtues; this emphasis, however, does not in the least require the disregard of acts related to his outward self (*al-a'mal az-zahira*). Inward consideration at the cognitive level means to look for the inner, deep, hidden meanings (*al-ma'ani al-batina*) of intellectual matters in certain cases but not in all[7]. This is course must not be taken to be identical with Shi'a Batinites' belief that the literal meanings of texts of the Qur'an and radiations are only symbols for inward meanings which are radically different and which are really intended[8]; in fact the sufis condemn this belief of the Batinites as false[9]. When understanding the Qur'an the sufis sometimes pass from its outward meanings on to the inward which are different greatly or to a little extent from the outward; they hold that divine words have deep, hidden meanings—a thing which was recognized by those companions of the Prophet who were considered great scholars of the Qur'an, e.g. 'Ali[10] and Ibn Mas'ud[11]—and that these meanings are revealed to those who have purified their souls through self-training (*riyada*) and mortification (*mujahada*).[12] These inner meanings form the basis of sufi interpretation of the Qur'an. Just as this interpretation (*ta'wil*) is different from the Batinite interpretation, so also it is different from philosophic and Mu'tazilite interpretations which are made in an effort to establish harmony between reason (philosophy) and revelation (religion)[13]. Samples of this are interpretation of the verses.[14-18]

This type of interpretation appeared earliar as independent books in a few cases, but mostly scattered in various works of the sufis. Of these independent works composed before al-Ghazali are *Haqa'iq at-Tafsir* of as-Sulami and the *Lata'if al-Isharat* of al-Qushayri. As-Sulami wrote on Tradition, Qur'an-interpretation and sufism; although he spent a great part of his life on Tradition and although his *Haqa'iq*[19] constitutes a prime sources for the exegesis of early sufis, it is mainly on his work on sufism proper that his fame rests. His

Haqa'iq does not contain his own views especially; it is rather a collection of interpretations by other sufis:[20] this method of writing is in accordance with the special characteristics of the Khurasanian school of sufism. These writers usually concentrate on citing the views of others rather than giving their own opinions. This is unlike the Baghdadian school of sufism headed by al-Junayd where sufis usually cite first their own views and then the views of others in support of them[21]. The method of writing al-Sulami adopted in his *Haqa'iq* and also in his *Tabaqat as-Sufiyya* is identical with that of his Shaykh as-Sarraj, in his *Kitab al-Luma'*. As-Sulami's disciple, al-Qushayri, followed this method to a certain extent. All these sufis belonged to the Khurasanian school of sufism.

Sufi interpretation presented in the forms mentioned above was condemned by exegetes from among the literalists (*ahl az-zawahir*). One of the earliest critics of sufism was Imam Ahmed Ibn Hanbal (d. 241 A.H.), a jurist, traditionist and an ascetic of high rank, who was convinced that in the Sunna lay the essence of Islam and who was opposed to all other elements, whether theological, philosophic or sufistic. He was against great sufis of his time, such as al-Muhasibi and Dhun-Nun (d. 245 A.H.)[22]. His follower, Ibn Taymiyya (d. 728 A.H.) later attacked sufism more bitterly. The bitterest attack, however, was made by the Hanbalite Shaykh Ibn al-jawzi (d. 597 A.H.), who, in his *Talbis Iblis*, pointed out, without hesitation, all that he considered wrong in ascetics and sufis including al-Muhasibi, as-Sarraj, al-Qushayri, al-Isfahani (d. 430 A.H.), al-Makki, and al-Ghazali. He condemned as-Sulami's *Haqa'iq at-Tafsir* as infidelity and nonsense consisting of a collection of sufis' oral discourses and not authentic[23]. Imam al-Wahidi remarked: If he (*i.e. as-Sulami*) believes that (*i.e. Haqa'iq*) is really an interpretation of the Qur'an, he has committed infidelity."[24] The celebrated historian adh-Dhahabi (d. 748 A.H.), criticized as-Sulami's *Haqa'iq* even more severely.[25] As-Suyuti (d. 911 A.H.), a noted scholar of Qur'anic studies, considered it "not commendable."[26] As regards al-Qushayri's work on interpretation, Ibn al-Jawzi criticized it as more peculiar than his *Risala*.[27] These criticism apply equally to all other mystical understandings of the Qur'an.

Al-Ghazali, in whom the orthodox sufism of the medieval times culminated, studied the Qur'an-interpretations of his sufi predecessors[28] and was perfectly aware of the criticism of them made by their opponents. Although he did not compose any independent work on exegesis, he mystically interpreted many Qur'anic verses in the greatest work, the *Ihya'*. An example of these interpretations is his view that in the verse the word *asnam* means "gold and silver," i.e. wealth, because the rank of prophecy is too exalted to be afraid of idol-worship; so idol-worship must mean here love of wealth.[29][30] No outward exegete has ever given such an interpretation of this verse. In his *Jawahir* al-Ghazali insist upon understanding the deep, hidden meanings of the Qur'an and minimizes the importance of outward exegesis.[31] To the end of the eighth `book' of *Ihya* consisting of twenty-two large pages devoted to the problem of Qur'an-recitation, he has added one complete chapter consisting of five large pages dealing with Qur'an-explanation by personal opinion (*Tafsir bi-r-ray*). His main aim in this chapter is to defend the sufi interpretation[32] to people with purified souls are especially important; this contradicts the Tradition which prohibits explanation of the Qur'an by personal opinion[34]; have attacked those sufis whose interpretations of certain verses are different from those of Ibn 'Abbas[35] and other traditionalists; thus the problem of interpretation by personal opinion deserves serious consideration.

Al-Ghazali then considers this problem through several stages. First he establishes the existence of secret meanings of the Qur'an apprehendable by men of understanding, by citing verses, traditions, opinions of the companions and of scholars of early period, and by mentioning the nature of the Qur'an as containing the core principles of all forms of knowledge.[36] The conclusion he arrives at is: "...in the understanding of the meanings of the Qur'an there are wide range and excessive width and that outward exegesis which has come down by tradition is not the end of the understanding of the Qur'an."[37]

At the second step al-Ghazali considers the statements of the Prophet, Abu Bakr[38] and other companions, and some others on the prohibition of Qur'an-explanation by personal opinion. He proves, in four ways, that the purpose of this prohibition is not to teach that one should confine oneself to that understanding of the Qur'an which has come down by tradition (*manqul*) and which is heard (*masmu*) from authorities on exegesis and that one should abandon the eliciting of meaning from the texts of the Qur'an (*istinbat*) by one's own effort.[39] The conclusion al-Ghazali Qur'anic interpretation. Rather it is lawful for everyone to elicit meanings from the Qur'an commensurate with his understanding and the limit of his intelligence."[40]

At the third step al-Ghazali determines the positive reasons for prohibition of personal opinion. Two such reasons are determined[41]. One is: "The intended meaning of `personal opinion' would be the corrupt personal opinion suitable to one's passion and not correct personal effort. Personal effort includes that which is valid and that which is corrupt, and that which is suitable to passion is sometimes specified with the name of personal opinion."[42] The gist of the second reason is that "one who hastens to explain the Qur'an by considering the outward (i.e., the rules) of the Arabic language, without knowing by heart what was heard (and transmitted from authorities) in the case of those verses which are related to strange words of the Qur'an (*ghara'ib al-Qur'an*) in the case of those verses in which ambiguous terms and substitute words occur, and in the case of those verses in which are to be found conciseness omission, suppression of words understood the shifting (of a word from its proper place) and putting a word at a place later (than the appropriate one). One who, without being prudent at outward exegesis, hastens to elicit deep meanings by mere understanding the (rules of the) Arabic language makes many mistakes and is included in the group of those who explain the Qur'an by personal opinion."[43]

According to al-Ghazali transmission from authorities and direct hearing from them are necessary for outward exegesis in those cases where mistakes are likely to be made. It is only after mastery over outward exegesis that one may be able to elicit deep meanings of the Qur'an. Al-Ghazali cites a number of strange words of the Qur'an which can only be understood by hearing from authorities, and emphasises that it is not possible to neglect the memorization of outward exegesis first.[44] Knowledge of outward meaning of the Qur'an is a precondition for knowledge of its deep meanings. Then he elaborately deals with six Qur'anic subjects in which transmission and direct hearing from authorities are necessary.[45] He believes that whoever is content with understanding the rules of the Arabic language and hastens to explain the Qur'an without knowing by heart the direct hearing and transmission in these six and other similar subjects, is designated as a man who explains the Qur'an by personal opinion. When direct hearing from authorities is achieved in these subjects, one has known the outward exegesis which is the translation of its words. This, however, is not sufficient for understanding the real meaning of the Qur'an. Al-Ghazali explains the distinction between the reality of meanings of the Qur'an and its outward exegesis by examples.[46] In his opinion sometimes in apprehending the real meaning of verses assistance needs to be sought from the vast ocean of different forms of knowledge obtained through mystical intuition; mere outward exegesis is of no avail; after the clarification of many obscure matters through mystical intuitions the real meaning is unveiled. A full study of the real meaning of every verse needs much time. Part of the secret meanings of the Qur'an is certainly unveiled to those established in knowledge, in proportion to the abundance of different forms of their knowledge the purity of their souls from vices, fullness of their motives for pondering over the Qur'an, and their isolation for seeking its meanings. For each of those established in knowledge there is a limit in rising to a grade higher than his. As for the full unveiling of all secret meanings, this is a goal impossible to achieve. From this perspective men differ in understanding the secret meanings of the Qur'an after sharing in the outward exegesis, and it is necessary to achieve the outward exegesis first.[47]

To illustrate the unveiling of hidden meanings al-Ghazali cites the unveiling of the meaning of a tradition to the mind of a certain sufi[48], Al-Ghazali concludes his discussion by clearly stating the relation between deep meanings and outward exegesis: Deep meanings cannot be reached by outward exegesis; they do not oppose it; rather they complete it and constitute the means of reaching the pit of the Qur'an from the external aspect.[49]

With this brief outline of the contents of the last chapter of the eighth 'book' of the *Ihya*, its English translation with notes is given in the following pages so that the reader may know al-Ghazali's views in full. Care is taken to make the translation very close to the original. The matter in square brackets provides the meaning; and round brackets are translations of the original. Since the *Ihya'* has not yet been critically edited, variants in its different printed texts have not yet been brought to light. The present translator has at hand eight printed texts: (1) the text published by the Lajna Nashr ath-Thaqafa al-Islamiyya, Cairo, 1356-57 A.H. (abbreviated here as LN), (2) the text published by al-Maktaba at-Tijariyya al-Kubra, Egypt, n.d., (3) the text published by al-Mataba's al-'Uthmaniyya, Egypt, 1933/1352, (4) the text published by Dar ash-Shu'ab, Egypt, n.d., (5) the text published by Mu'ssisa al-Halabi, Cairo, 1967/1387 (abbreviated as MH), (6) the text published by Dar al-ma'rifa, Beirut, n.d., (abbreviated as BE), (7) the text shown by az-Zabidi in his *Ithaf as-Sada al-Muttaqin bi-Sharh asrar Ihya' 'Ulum ad-Din*, Cairo, 1911 A.H. (abbreviated as ZT), and (8) the text published on the margin of az-Zabidi's *Ithaf* (abbreviated as ZE). Five of these printed texts have been compared by the translator, and the variants are pointed out in footnotes. The obvious misprints are, however, disregarded. The numberings of all references of the *Ihya'* in this article are, as in the BE. The Qur'anic verses and suras are numbered according to the official Egyptian edition of the Qur'an.

Understanding the Qur'an, and its Explanation by Personal Opinion Which has not Come Down by Tradition

You may perhaps ask: In the preceding section you have magnified the matter concerning the understanding of deep meanings of the Qur'an (*asrar al-Qur'an*) and concerning those meanings of it which are unveiled (*yankashif*) to people possessed of purified souls (*arbab al-aulub az-zakiyya*); (288) how can this be praiseworthy seeing that the Prophet (may God bless him and greet him!) has said, whoever explains the Qur'an by his personal opinion (*bi-ra' yihi*) shall take his permanent seat in Hell"[50] (Because of his prophetic tradition) people expert in the outward exegesis of the Qur'an (*zahir at-tafsir*) have reviled the sufis, i.e. those exegetes who subscribe to sufism, and who[52] interpret (*ta'wil*) certain Qur'anic sentences contrary to the explanations given by Ibn 'Abbas and other exegetes; the revilers maintain that these interpretations (lead to) infidelity. If what the proponents of outward exegesis have said is correct, what is the meaning of understanding the Qur'an without memorizing their exegesis? If (on the other hand), what they have said is not correct, what is the meaning of the Prophet's statement, "whoever explains the Qur'an by his personal opinion shall take his permanent seat in Hell".

(In reply to your question) know that the man who imagines that the Qur'an has no meaning except that which the outward exegesis has translated (and described) is acknowledging his own limitations; he is right in his acknowledgment (because he knows only this measure and is not aware of that which lies beyond this), but is wrong in his judgement which places all other people on the same level as himself.

The truth is that traditions (*akhbar* and statements of the companions and of other pious Muslims in early Islam (*athar*) prove that for men of understanding there is wide scope in the meanings of the Qur'an. Thus 'Ali[53] said: ".... except the God bestows understanding of the Qur'an upon a man."[54] If there is no meaning other than that which is related (from Ibn 'Abbas and other exegetes) what is that understanding of the Qur'an (which is bestowed upon a man)? The Prophet (may God bless him and greet him!) said: "Surely the Qur'an has an outward aspect, an inward aspect, a limit and a prelude." This is also related by Ibn Mas'ud[55] on his own authority and he is one of the authorities on Qur'anic explanation. (If there are no meaning of the Qur'an besides the outward ones), what is the meaning of its outward aspect, inward aspect, limit and prelude? 'Ali (may God show regard to his face!) said: "If I so will I can certainly load seventy camels with the exegesis of the Opening Sura of the book (*Fatihat al-Kitab*)," What then is the meaning of this statement of 'Ali, when the outward exegesis of this sura is extremely short[56] (and can be set forth in a few pages)? Abu d-Darda'[57] said: "One cannot (fully) understand the religion until one sees the Qur'an from different perspectives." A certain scholar said: "For every verse there are sixty thousand understandings (comprehensible to man). The understandings of it which remain (incomprehensible to man) are (even) more than these in number." Another scholar said: "The Qur'an encompasses seventy-seven thousand and two hundred forms of knowledge, since every Qur'anic sentence constitutes one form of knowledge. This number is multiplied by four times, since each sentence has its outward aspect, inward aspect, limit and prelude. Repetition of the verses, "In the name of God, most Gracious, Ever Merciful,"[58] by the Prophet twenty times could not have been for any reason other than that he was pondering over its deep, inward meanings; otherwise its translation and its outward exegesis are so obvious that one like the Prophet would not be in need of repetition. Ibn Mas'ud said: "One who intends to acquire (the core principles of) the knowledge of the ancients and the moderns should ponder over the Qur'an." This knowledge is something which is not achieved by its mere outward exegesis.[59]

In short, all forms of knowledge are included in the works of God and His attributes, and in the Qur'an there is an explanation of His essence, attributes and works. These forms of knowledge have no end, but in the Qur'an there is an indication of their confluence. Penetrating deeply into the explanation of the Qur'an by stages amounts to the understanding of the Qur'an; mere outward exegesis[60] does not lead to that. The truth is that to everything pertaining to reflective and intellectual matters which had become ambiguous to men of reflection and in which people have differed, there are indications and implications in the Qur'an which can be grasped by men of understanding. How can these indications and implications be completely conveyed by the translation of its outward meanings and by its (outward) exegesis?

This is the reason why the Prophet ordered: "Read the Qur'an and seek to know its (deep), strange meanings (by eliciting and understanding)." He also said "Surely my community will be split up into seventy-two sects all of which are misguided[61] themselves and misguide others by calling them to Hell. When this state of affairs comes about, you must adhere to the book of God, for in it lies the message concerning those who were before you and the message concerning what will happen after you, and the judgement of all that happens among you. Anyone of (even) the most powerful men who contradicts it is severely punished by God (great and mighty is He!), anyone who seeks knowledge from a source other than it is led astray by God. It is the strong rope of God (which man should grasp firmly), His clear light (in which man should walk in all aspects of his life), and His useful means of healing (of man's spiritual diseases)[62]; it is a protection for one who holds fast to it, and a (means of) salvation for one who protection for one who holds fast to it, and a (means of) salvation for one who follows it; it is not distorted so that it needs to be set aright, nor has it deviated so that it needs to be brought to its normal state; its wonders are never exhausted, nor does much-repeated recitation of it make it old." (289).[63] In another Tradition [64] it is mentioned that when the Messenger of God informed him of the disagreements (among Muslims) and their splitting into sects which would occur after his time, he said: "I enquired, `Messenger of God, what do you command me to do should I meet with that (unfortunate state of affairs)?' He replied: `Learn the Book of God and act in accordance with its teachings. This is the way of escaping from that (state of affairs).'" Hudhayfa said, "I repeated that question to the Prophet thrice, and the he replied thrice by saying: `Learn the Book of God and act in accordance with what is taught in it, for in it lies salvation.'[65]

'Ali said, "One who understands the Qur'an can thereby explain the totality of knowledge." By this statement 'Ali indicated that the Qur'an implies the confluence of all forms of knowledge. ('Abd Allah) Ibn 'Abbas said, in the explanation of the words of God, "Whoever is granted wisdom has indeed been granted abundant good,"[66] that "abundant good" means understanding of the Qur'an. God said: "We gave Solomon the right understanding of the matter, and upon each (of David and Soloman) We bestowed wisdom and knowledge.[67] Here God had called what He bestowed upon both Solomon and David "knowledge and wisdom," but the prudence which He gave Solomon alone He explicitly mentioned as "right understanding" and mentioned it before "wisdom and knowledge."

The matters (mentioned above), then, prove that in the understanding of the meanings of the Qur'an there is a wide ranged, an excessive width and that outward exegesis which has come down by tradition is not the end of the understanding of the Qur'an.

As for the saying of the Prophet, "Whoever explains the Qur'an by his personal opinion...," and his prohibition of this kind of Qur'anic explanation, the saying of Abu bakr, "What earth will bear me and what sky will overshadow me if I say anything by my personal opinion when explaining the Qur'an?" and other traditions and statements of the companions and of others in early Islam on the prohibition of Qur'anic explanation by personal opinion these were intended (a) either to confine the understanding of the Qur'an to that which has come down by tradition (*naql*) and to that which is heard (from authorities on exegesis) (*masmu'*) and to abandon the eliciting (of meanings from the Qur'an) (*istinbat*)[68] and independent understanding (*istiqlal*), or (b) to be something different. It is certainly wrong to believe that the purpose was to limit our understanding of the Qur'an to only that which one hears (and receives) from an authority; and (this is wrong) for several reasons:

First, it is as stipulation that it should be heard from the Messenger of God, and be supported by a chain of narration going back to him, but this is something which applies only in the case of (a small) part of the Qur'an. As for that (explanation of the Qur'an) which Ibn 'Abbas and Ibn Mas'ud give from their own understanding, it should not be accepted and should be called 'an explanation of the Qur'an by personal opinion,' because they have not heard this explanation from the Messenger of God. (The same is true of other Companions: They too gave explanations of certain Qur'anic words, without hearing them from the Prophet; so their explanations should also be regarded as explanations of the Qur'an by personal opinion).

Second, Companions of the Prophet and exegetes (who flourished after them) disagreed over the explanation of some verses; they gave such varying explanations of them that it is impossible to reconcile them. It is impossible that all these conflicting explanations were heard from the Messenger of God; if one of them was in fact heard the rest (which are contradictory to it) must be rejected. Thus it is definitely clear that on the meaning (of words of the Qur'an) every exegete came to his own conclusion through his eliciting, (investigation and personal effort), so that they gave seven different opinions concerning the letters at the start of some suras which arè impossible to reconcile. Thus a certain exegete said that *alif lam ra'*[69] are letters from the word *al-Rahman.* Another said that letter *alif* stands for *Allah*, the letter *lam* for *latif* and the letter *ra'* for *Rahman*; other exegetes gave other explanations. Since reconciliation of these explanations is impossible how can they all have been heard from the Prophet?

Third, the Prophet prayed for Ibn 'Abbas, saying: "God, bestow upon him the understanding of the religion and teach him the interpretation (*ta'wil*) of the Qur'an." If interpretation of the Qur'an is something which is heard (from the Prophet) like revelation and which is preserved the way revelation is preserved, what is the sense in specifying Ibn 'Abbas in this case?

Fourth, God said. "...those of them who are adept at eliciting the truth would know its (real nature)"[70.] In this verse God affirmed the validity of eliciting meaning by learned. It is well known that the eliciting of meaning is something beyond hearing (from an authority; it has to do with one's knowledge and understanding). The totality of the statements of the Companions and other pious Muslims in early Islam on the understanding of the Qur'an which we have quoted (above) contradicts this opinion. Thus it is false that hearing (from an authority) is a stipulation for Qur'anic interpretation. It is lawful for every-one to elicit meaning from the Qur'an commensurate with his understanding and the limit of his intelligence.

As for the prohibition of explanation of the Qur'an by personal opinion, it is for one or two reasons. One of them is that the person giving an explanation has an opinion (of his own) on a matter, and this opinion is influenced by his nature (*tab'*) and passion (*hawa*). So he interprets the Qur'an according to his opinion (*ra'y*) and passion in order that he may adduce an argument in favour of his purpose—if he did not have that opinion and that passion that meaning would not appear to him from the Qur'an. (This happens in different conditions). (a) Sometimes it happens despite knowledge (of the Shari'a), as in the case of a man who adduces an argument from a certain Qur'anic verse for validating his heresy (*bid'a*) knowing (well) that this is not intended in the verse, but by doing his he seeks to confuse his opponent.

(b) Sometimes it happens to a man ignorant (of the basic principles of the Shari'a). But since a verse can be interpreted (from two or more perspectives) his understanding inclines to that perspective which (290) suits his purpose and that aspect is given preponderance by his own opinion and passion. Thus it turns out that he has explained the verse with his personal opinion, i.e. his personal opinion is that which had led him to that explanation. If his own opinion did not exist the perspective (which suits his purpose, and not the other) would not bear such weight with him.

(c) Sometimes a man has a valid purpose for which he seeks a proof from the Qur'an, and he adduces a proof for that purpose with[71] a verse in which, he knows, that purpose is not intended[72]. An example of this is a man who invites people to pray for forgiveness of God just before dawn and who adduces an argument for this from the words of the Prophet. "Eat a meal just before dawn for there is blessing in this meal."[73] He gives the impression to people that the intended purpose of this saying of the Prophet is remembrance of God just before dawn,[74] knowing (well) that the purpose really intended by this saying is to eat food (just before dawn). Another example is a man who invites people to strive hard against hardness of the mind. He says that God ordered (Moses), "Go to Pharaoh; he has certainly transgressed grievously,"[75] and, hinting at his own heart, says: `This is what is meant by Pharaoh (in the verse)'. This kind (of Qur'anic explanation) is sometimes employed by some religious preachers for good purposes by embellishing their speeches and encouraging their audience (to these purposes), but this is forbidden. Sometimes Shi'a Batinites employ this (kind of explanation of the Qur'an) for corrupt purposes in order to deceive people and to invite them to their false school of thought and practices (*madhhab*). To support their (corrupt) opinions and (false) school, they bring down the Qur'an to certain matters, knowing definitely that these matters are not meant in the Qur'an.[76]

These (three) kinds of explanation, then, constitute one of the two reason for prohibition of Qur'an-explanation by personal opinion. The intended meaning of 'personal opinion' would be the corrupt personal opinion suitable to one's passion and not correct personal effort (*al-ijtihad al-sahih*). Personal effort includes that which is valid and that which is corrupt and what which is affected by passion is sometimes specified with the name of personal opinion.

The second reason (for the prohibition of Qur'an-explanation by personal opinion) is that (this prohibition applies to) one who hastens to explain the Qur'an by considering the outward aspect (i.e. the rules) of the Arabic language without knowing by heart what was heard (and transmitted from authorities), in the case of those verses which are heard (and transmitted from authorities), in the case of those verses which use strange Qur'anic words (*ghara'ib al-Qur'an*), in the case of those verses in which ambiguous terms and substitute words occur, and in the case of those verses in which are to be found conciseness, omission, suppression of words understood, precedence (of a word from its proper place) and putting a word at a place later (than the appropriate one). One who, without being prudent a outward exegesis, hastens to elicit deep meanings by mere understanding the (rules of) the Arabic language makes many mistakes and is included in the groups of those who explain the Qur'an by personal opinion. Then transmission (from an authority) and hearing (from him) are necessary for outward exegesis first, so that the exegete may, by them, be safe in places where mistakes are likely to be made. After this, understanding will be wide the eliciting of deep meanings will be possible.

The strange words of the Qur'an[77-124] which can only be understood by hearing directly (from authorities) are many. We should like to indicate a number of them so that one may seek information about this type and know that it is not permissible to neglect the memorization of outward exegesis first. There is no coveted object in reaching the inward (knowledge) before being prudent at the outward. One who claims to possess understanding of the deep meanings of the Qur'an, without being prudent at its outward exegesis, is comparable to a man who claims to reach the upper part of a house without crossing its door, or claims to understand the purposes of the Turks from their speeches whereas he does not understand the language of the Turks. (This is) because outward exegesis occupies the place of learning the language which is needed for understanding the meaning.

This and the cases similar to their are included in those Qur'anic subjects in which only transmission and hearing (from authorities) are of avail. The Qur'an, from its beginning to its end, is not devoid of this kind of thing, because it was revealed in the language of the Arabs and so it included various characteristics of their speech, such as conciseness, prolongation, suppression of words understood, omission, substitution of one word by another, and occurrence of a word before or after its proper place, so that it may be able to silence the voice of the Arabs against it and be fully eloquent to them. Anyone who is content with understanding the outward aspect (i.e. the rules) of the Arabic language and who hastens to explain the Qur'an without knowing by heart the meaning transmitted (from the authorities) in these Qur'anic subjects, is designated as 'a man who explains the Qur'an by his personal opinion.' Such an explanation is: He understood the best known meaning of the term *umma* and so it naturally inclined to this meaning (when he finds the word used in a verse); but when he finds it is another place he is inclined to this well-known meaning which he heard (and understood from authorities) (292) and abandons a thorough study of the transmission of its many meanings. Perhaps this is what is prohibited (by the Prophet) and not the understanding of deep meanings of the Qur'an, as has already been discussed. When hearing (from authorities) is achieved in (these and) similar Qur'anic subjects, then one has mastered the outward exegesis of the Qur'an which is (merely) the translation of its words. This, however, is not sufficient for understanding the reality of the meanings of the Qur'an.

The distinction between the reality of the meanings of the Qur'an and its outward exegesis can be understood from an example: God (great and mighty is He!) said: "You (i.e. Muhammad) did not throw (the handful of gravel at the infidels' faces) when you threw it, but God threw it."[125] The outward exegesis of the verse is clear. Its real meaning, however, is obscure, because it affirms throwing and negates it (at the same time), and these appear contradictory unless it is understood that he (i.e. Muhammad) threw from one perspective and did not throw from another and that from the perspective from which he did not throw, God threw. Likewise God said: "Fight them; God will punish them at your hands."[126] When it is they (i.e. believers) who are the fighters how can God be the one who inflicts punishment? If God is the one who inflicts punishment by moving their hands what is the sense in commanding them to fight? The real solution to this problem receives help from a vast to fight? The real solution to this problem receives help from a vast ocean of forms of knowledge obtained through mystical intuition (*`ulum al-mukashafat*); outward exegesis is of no avail. This solution consists in knowing (first) the mode of the linkage between man's works and the power created in him and (then) the mode of linkage between this power and the power of God, so that, after the clarification of many obscure matters, there will be unveiled to him the truth of His words. "You did not throw when you threw, but God threw."

If one's entire life is spent seeking the unveiling of secrets of this meaning and that which is linked up with those matters which precede and those which follows it, one's life will perhaps be exhausted before fully knowing all[127] that follows that meaning. A study of the real meaning of every sentence of the Qur'an needs a duration like this. Part of the secret meanings of the Qur'an is certainly unveiled to those established in knowledge, is proportion to the abundance of different forms of their knowledge, the purity of their souls (from vices), the fullness of their motives in pondering (over the Qur'an), and their isolation for seeking (its meaning). For each of those established in knowledge there is a limit in rising to a grade higher. As for the full unveiling of all the secret meanings, there is no coveted object in it. 'If the ocean were to become the ink and trees the pens (for transcribing) the secrets of God's words which have no end, all the oceans would be exhausted before the words of god come to an end'[128]. From this perspective men differ in understanding (the secret meanings of the Qur'an) after sharing in the knowledge of outward exegesis, and it is necessary to understand first the outward exegesis.

An example of this is the understanding of a certain sufi, (*ba'darbab al-qulub*) from the words of the Prophet during his prostration. "I seek the protection of Your pleasure from Your displeasure; I seek the protection of Your forgiveness from Your punishment; and seek the protection of You against You. I am unable to praise You; You are as You have praised Yourself". The Prophet, being commanded by God:" Prostrate and (thereby) achieve nearness to me, (prostrated) and when he attained this nearness during prostration, considered divine attributes and sought the protection of an attribute from another—pleasure an displeasure are two divine attributes. Then, when his nearness to God increased including in itself the first nearness, he rose to divine essence and said: "I seek the protection of You against You." Then, when his nearness to God increased further as a result of a thing of which he felt ashamed, i.e. to seek protection being on the bed of nearness, he look refuge with praise, saying: "I am unable to praise You." Then when he realized that this was a shortcoming he said: "You are as You have praised Yourself."

These are thoughts exposed to those possessed of purified souls, i.e. perfect sufis. They have further depth which consist in understanding the meaning of nearness to God and its specification with prostration, and understanding the meaning of seeking protectionwith one divine attribute from another and the meaning of seeking protection with him against Him. There are many secrets here, but outward exegesis cannot guide us to them. They are not opposed to external exegesis; rather they complete it and constitute the essence of the Qur'an from its external aspect. They from that which we arrive at for understanding the internal meanings, not that which oppose the external meanings. God knows best.

REFERENCES

1. Orthodox sufism is very close to Quran and Sunna, whose exponents included al-Junayd, al-Muhasibi, as-Sarraj, al-Makki, and al-Ghazali. Unorthodox sufism had Ibn al-Arabi and others. For the meaning of terms like orthodoxy, sunnism, etc., in theological context, see W Montgomery Watt, The Formative Period of Islamic thought, Edinburgh, 1973, pp. 3, 5f.
2. Ibn al-Jawzi, Talbis iblis, ed by Khayr ad-Din Ali, Beirut, n.d., p. 183; al- Ghazali, Ihya Ulum ad-Din, Beirut, n.d., III, IV.
3. See my article "al-Ghazali's conception of happiness," Arabica, XXII, 153-61.
4. Talbis, pp. 183, 184, where Abu Talib al-Makki is accused, 186 where al-Ghazali is charged. Also see my other work, The ethics of al-Ghazali, 2nd ed., New York, 1978. pp. 30f. 39.
5. See infra, pp. 3f.
6. Talbis, pp. 187, 190ff, 407, 418, 421, 423; and my forthcoming work "al-Ghazali's evlauation of Abu Yazid al-Bistami and al-Hallaj", where shatahat are discussed.
7. Thus, for most Verses and Traditions on faith, Sufis accept the outward, literal meanings. They allow interpretation to this category of verses and traditions, if acceptance of literal meaning becomes impossible (Ihya, I, 115). Asharites agree with this, but Mu'tazilites and other philosophers donot.
8. See Talbis, p, 111.
9. See infra, p. 16.
10. See infra, p. 10, n. 53.
11. See infra, p. 10, n. 55.
12. Ihya, I, 284.
13. Al-Kindi, Risala fil-ibana an-sujud al-jirm al-aqsa wa ta`atihi li-Allah, in Rasa`il al-Kindi al-Falsafiyya, ed. by Abu Rida, Cairo, 1950-53.
14. Quran, 87:6
15. Quran, 7: 169.
16. Quran, 50: 37.
17. Abu Nasr as-Sarraj, Kitab al-Luma, ed by R A Nicholson, London, 1963, pp. 84.
18. This phrase is the title of as-Sulami's work on the sufi interpretation .
19. As-Sulami seems to have composed firs his Haqaiq then his Tarikh as-Sufiyya and then his Tabaqat as-Sufiyya. The Haqqaiq was written in the seventh decade of the 4th century AH.

20. Cf. Haji Khalifa, Kashf az-Zuman, ed. Flugel, Leipzig, 1835-58, III, 79; as-Subki, Tabaqat ash-Shafiyya al-Kubra, Cairo, 1324, III, 62.
21. Another significant feature of the Khurasanian school of sufism mentioned in al Junayd's statement, "Syria is the home of chivalry, Iraq of eloquence and Khurasan of sincerity." See al-Qushayri, Risala, Cairo, 1346, A.H., p. 103.
22. Talbis, pp. 186f.; Subki, Tabaqat, II, 39; Khatib al-Baghdadi, Tarikh Bhagdad, Cairo, 1931, VI, 214; Ibn Khaldun, Wafayat al-Ayan, Cairo, 1299, I, 158.
23. Talbis, 185.
24. Haji Khalifa, Kashf az-Zunun, II, 339, 79.
25. Adh-Dahabi, Tarikh al-Islam, MS. no. 392 (Tarikh), Dar al-Kutub al-Arabiyya, Cairo, XXI, 221; Siyar Alam an-Nubala, MS. no. 12195, Dar al-Kutub al-Arabiyya, Cairo, II, Pt. i, p. 56.
26. As-Suyuti, Tabaqat al-Mufassirin, Leyden, 1839, p. 31.
27. Talbis, p. 185.
28. Al-Ghazali, al-Munqidh min ad-dalal, Cairo, 1309 A.H., p. 20 where in he says that he read the works of eminent sufis of past and present.
29. Quran, 14: 35.
30. Al-Ghazali, Ihya, III, 235.
31. My another book, The jewels of the Quran: Al-Ghazali's theory, 1977, pp. 19f., 36f.
32. See Infra, p. 10.
33. Third chapter of eight book of Ihya, has nine large pages. It deals with mental tasks (al-a`amal al-batina) involved in reciting Quran.
34. At-Tirmidhi, Sunan, Tafsir, 1.
35. See Ibn Hajar al-Asqalani's al-Isaba, Egypt, 1358/1939, II, 322-26. (refer Abd Allah Ibn Abbas).
36. Infra, pp. 10-13.
37. Infra, p. 13.
38. For Abu Bakr's biography, see Ibn Qutayba, al-Ma`arif, ed. by Tharwat Ukasha, 2nd ed., Cairo, 1969, pp. 167-168.
39. Infra, pp. 13-15.
40. Infra, p. 15.
41. Infra, pp. 15ff.
42. Infra, p. 165.
43. Infra, p. 17.
44. Infra, p. 17.

45. Infra, pp. 17-23.
46. Infra, p. 24f.
47. Infra, p. 25.
48. Infra, p.p 25f.; s sufi interpretation of this Tradition was also cited by as-Sarraj in Luma, p. 112, al-Ghazali seems to have been influenced by this.
49. Infra, p. 26.
50. At-tirmidh, Sunan, Tafsir, I.
51. BE and MH.
52. Eg., as-Sulami, as-Sarraj and al-Kashani. see az-Zabidi, op cit., IV, 256; Supra, pp. 3f.
53. Ali Ibn Abi TAlib's biography can be seen in Ibn Abd al-Barr, al-Istiab in Ibn Hajar, op. cit., III, 26-27.
54. Ihya, I, 283.
55. Abd Allah Ibn Masud 's biography can be seen in Ibn Abd al-Barr, op cit., II, 308-16; Ibn Hajar, op cit., II, 306ff.
56. LN
57. Abu Darda's biography can be seen in Ibn Hajar op cit., III, 46.
58. Quran 1:1.
59. BE
60. BE.
61. LN
62. Cf. Quran 17:82.
63. At-Tirmidhi, Sunan, Imam 18: Abu Dawud, Sunan, Sunna, I; Ibn Maja, Sunan, Fitan, 17 (with variation).
64. Hudhayfa ibn al-Yman, a Companion known as `possessor of secret knowledge of the Prophet', see, Ibn Hajr, op cit, I, 316, Ibn Abd al-Barr, op cit, I, 336ff.; Abd ar-Rauf al-Munawi, al-Kawakib ad-Durriya, ed. by Mahmud Hasan Rabi, Cairo, 1357 AH. I, 50f.
65. Abu Dawud, Sunan, Sunna, 28.
66. Quran, 2:269.
67. Quran, 21: 79.
68. Cf. Quran 4: 83.
69. Arabic letters occuring at the start of five Suras - 10, 11, 12, 14, 15.
70. Quran, 4: 83.
71. BE.
72. Check MH

73. An-Nasai, Sunan, Siyam, 18, 19; Ibn Maja, Sunan, Siyam 22; Ibn Hanbal, Musnad, II 377, 477, III, 32, 99.
74. God's rememberance before dawn is praised, Quran 3:17.
75. Quran 20:24.
76. Al-Ghazali wrote several works in full or part against Batinites or Talimites who were identical with Ismailites, exposing their heretical beliefs. See my work, Jewels, p. 39.
77. There is much work on this, (az-Zabidi, op cit, IV, 529), The best is ar-Raghib al-Isfahani's al-Mufradat fi Gharib al-Quran.
78. Quran 17:59.
79. See BE and MH.
80. Quran 2: 93.
81. Quran 17: 75.
82. Quran 12: 82, see ZE.
83. See BE and ZT.
84. ZE
85. Quran 7:87.
86. 56: 82.
87. Quran 3:194.
88. Quran 97:1
89. Quran 38: 32. ; see also 38: 31-34.
90. Quran 39:3.
91. Quran 4: 79-80.
92. MH
93. Quran 4: 79.
94. ......95:2
95. ......37:130
96. MH
97. Quran 10:66
98. BE, MH.
99. Quran 7:75
100. ......20:129.
101 ......7:187.
102. .....8:4-5.
103. ......8:1.
104. ......60:4

105. ......16:75.

106. ......16:76.

107. Al-Khidr is generally believed to be a saint. (al-Bukhari, Sahih, Ilm, bab 16, 19, 44, Anbiya, bab 27; Muslim, Sahih, fadail, trad. 170-174; at-Tirmidhi, Sunan, Tafsir, sura 18, bab 1); Quran 18:65; 60-82; A J Wensink, `al-Khidr', SEI, pp. 232-35.

108. Quran 18:70

109. BE and MH

110. Quran 52: 35. (see also Ibn Jarir at-Tabari, Tarikh al- umam wal muluk, Egypt, n.d., I, 188-94.

111. Quran 50:23

112. ......50:27.

113. ......28: 23

114. BE and MH

115. Quran 16:120.

116. ......43: 22.

117. ......11:8

118. ......12: 45; 12: 21-101.

119. Zayd ibn Amr ibn Nufayl died five years before the advent of Islam. See Ibn Qutayba, al-Ma`arif, pp. 59, 154.

120. Quran 100: 4-5

121. ......7: 57.

122. ......2:185

123. ......44:3

124. ......97:1; 97:3-5

125. ......8:117, on Battle of Badr; see also 8:1-50 .

126. ......9:14.

127. MH

128. Cf. Quran 18: 109.

(Revised and edited, originally published in Islamic Culture, April 1979).

7

Tasawwuf: Its Doctrine and Practice

KUTPI IBRAHIM

Deals with the rise and early development of sufism, beginning with its institutionalising phase to the sufi way, to the emergence of an orthodox sufism and a clear sufi theosophy.

Origins: Prophet Muhammad's consciousness was founded upon very definite, vivid and powerful mystic experiences briefly described or alluded to in the Qur'an (17: 1; 50: 1-12 and 13-18; 81: 19-25). These are all Meccan; in the Medinan era we have a progressive unfolding of the religio-moral ideal, and the foundation of the social order for the newly instituted community but hardly any allusions to inner experiences. This is in consonance with the orientation of the Prophetic consciousness for which the spiritual experience is not for its own sake but is primarily meaningful for action in history. Indeed, even the allusions in the Meccan period are not in Qur'an for the sake of pure description but to support the truth of the mission (see verses 53:11-12, and 81: 22-23).

But when action began and the community came into being, the need for this infact disappeared and so did allusions to experiences; mysticism was fulfilled in prophethood. Nor did the Companions ask many questions about the nature of these experiences. For one thing, they were being trained for a moral purpose on a religious basis and their activism probably made them disinclined toward an inquiry into the metaphysical secrets of spiritualism. They were interested in divine commands, not in the Sufi mysteries. Besides, they must have thought that these spiritual fights were characteristic of the Divine

Messenger and that their duty lay in believing and in carrying out what they believed (which itself was, as history knows so well, a formidable task) with an intensity of faith and a deep sense of purpose.

What Islam inculcated among its early followers, in varying degrees, was a grave sense of responsibility before the justice of God which raised their behaviour from the realm of worldliness and mechanical obedience to the law to a place of moral activity. The keynote of this piety is *'Fear of God'* or responsibility to the moral ideal. Among the Companions, there were some with whom this sense deepened into a special degree of inwardness of actions, or the introspection of the moral motive. This is exemplified by men like Abu Dharr al-Ghifari, who formed the nucleus of Medinian piety after the Prophet. This became the foundation stone of Muslim asceticism that developed rapidly during the later 1st/7th century and the 2nd/8th centuries.

This ascetic pietism received a further stormy impulse from two sides: the environment of luxury that prevailed in the Muslim community with the establishment of the vast new empire, and especially as a sharp reaction to the secular and none-too-pious and attitude of the Umayyads at their court. At this stage, the protest of the pious nucleus of the Community is still undifferentiated; the 'Ulama' and the ascetics are identically the same persons, with varying degrees of emphasis on personal piety and abstinence. This protest asserts that the ruling group should accept, observe and enforce the Shari'a rather than make their own will and expediency the law of the state. Should this come to pass, the pious hoped that the original spirit of Islam would be reinforced to its true life. Thus, the trend in this period (late 1st-early 2nd/early 8th century) is purely ethical with a deepening of the inwardness of the ethical piety, the most famous is al-Hasan Basri (d. 110/728) who not only won the recognition of his contemporaries but who exerted after his death one of the most powerful influences for posterity. Secondly, the Sufi impulse undoubtedly fed on that isolationism which set in as a tremendous reaction to Kharijism and the political controversies that it raised. This isolationism, which is preached side by side in Hadith literature with Ijma', teaches that men should desist not only from politics but even from administration and public affairs, and much Hadith seeks, indeed, to preach that a person should retire toa cave and leave others alone.

During the 2nd/8th and the 3rd/9th centuries, the Muslim religious intelligentsia tended to become divided into two groups; the 'Ulama' or theologians and legists on the one hand, and those who gave to religion a more personal basis in religious devotion on the other. Among the sciences of the religion, the first to develop was the law . The legists themselves endeavoured to give their system as much of inner life as possible. The legal life must, however, by its very nature, remain impersonal. It was as a reaction against this legal formulation of Islam—which was also its first formulated expression—that the early pietistic asceticism changed definitely into what is technically known as Sufism with its proper ethos. The Qur'anic concept of trust in God (*tawakkul*), as already stressed by pietism in an ethical sense, was developed in certain circles into an extreme doctrine of renunciation of the world and a vindictive independence from nature 'causes', al-though on its precise meaning difference of opinion has always existed among the Sufis, typified in the following story: Malik ibn Dinar and Muhammad ibn Wasi', two Sufis of the 2nd/8th century, differed over the question of possession of means of subsistence. Malik would prefer to have a piece of land on which he could live and be independent of men, while Ibn Wasi' would rather be a man who, if he had a meal, knew not whence his next repast would come.

This development of the doctrine of *tawakkul* directly led to the central Sufi concepts of the relationship between man and God—the twin concepts of love and grace fused into one sentiment. The famous woman saint, Rabi'a al-'Adawiya (d. 185/801), sings of the pure love and grace in the oft-quoted verses:

> I love Thee with two loves, love of my happiness,
> And perfect love, to love Thee as is Thy due.
> My selfish love is that I do naught

But think on Thee, excluding all beside;
But that purest love, which is Thy due,
Is that the veils which hide Thee fall, and
I gaze on Thee.
No praise to me in either this or that,
Nay, Thine the praise or both that love and this.

Ma'ruf al-Karkhi (d. 200/816), is reported to have said, 'Love is not to be learnt from men, it is a gift of God and comes of His grace.'

Such was the Sufi challenge of love and pure devotion to the legists' concept of obedience and observance of the Law. There was as yet not open friction except for an uneasiness on the part of the legists who contended that the *law* of Islam could only legislate for external behaviour and could not deal with the inner tribunal of Conscience or the state of the agent's heart: a worry that harked back to the old Kharijite doctrine which drew perilous conclusions about a man's inner faith on the basis of external acts; only now it was the other way round: whereas the Kharijites made a man's faith suspect because of his actions, the Sufis called actions into question on grounds of the quality of faith, something which is was impossible to handle legally.

Considerable debate has gone on the nature of sufism, how far it is 'genuinely' Islamic and how far a product, of outside influences, particularly Christian and Gnostic. So far as the ideas of trust in and love of God arer concerned, their rise to prominence is a result of the developments within the intellectual and spiritual life of the community. This idea of 'trust in God' is prominent in the Qur'an, although there it does not exclude, and is not opposed to, God's working through 'causes'. Similarly, the ideal of love of God, if necessary, at the sacrifice of all worldly possession, is put forward by the Qur'an repeatedly, although again, love is there not the name of a pure emotion, only inwardly cultivated, but has a decisively activist tendency. In the new Sufi context, on the other hand, both have shifted their emphases remarkably. But this purely introverted attitude of emotional idealism is a response to an inner situation, viz. a this-worldly realism, political activity, civil wars, and the development of legalism. Outside influences must have supervened upon an initial native tendency. Nor is this the only phenomenon of this type in the early development of Islam. This case, within its own special terms, bears a striking resemblance to the early theological controversy between the Mu'tazila and the Hanbalites. Just as there the Mu'tazila espoused the justice of God to the exclusion of His omnipotence and were diametrically opposed by the Hanbalities, so here Sufi 'inwardism' arises as a direct challenge to the external political and legal developments in Islam. The point of peril is reached in modern scholarship when, on the basis of this division, one is tempted to characterize the pre-differentiated Islam, and pass one-sided judgments on the prophet or the early Community. The situation resembles an undifferentiated central nucleus which expands and develops new cells, but does not and cannot exclude outside factors although it cannot be intrinsically explained in their terms.

One fact stands out plainly in the life of the Prophet: that he practised rigorous realism with (and we believe that this was *because of*) an intense spiritual life. Devotional prayers and solitary nocturnal vigils were a normal part of his life. It would be astonishing indeed—even if there were no historical evidence—if this had not affected his followers in varying degrees. This point of view must throw light also on the Islamic attitude to the much discussed question of celibacy which certain Sufis began to practise in the 2nd/8th century (although married life remained the normal practice of Sufis down the ages). The Qur'an had undoubtedly encouraged marriage but it has no left it for an exceptional intelligence to guess why it did so. Man's nature normally seeks sexual companionship and, indeed, the Qur'an declares this law to be true of the universe in some sense: 'And of everything we have created pairs' (LI, 49). The Qur'an recommended matrimony, either for the protection of women (3: 3) or for the general purpose of chastity (*tahassun*), i.e. to avoid an unregulated sexual life. If follows therefore, that *the Qur'an discourages celibacy* as an *institution*. In its critique of monasticism (57: 27), it does not condemn it morally, but criticizes it *as an institution that failed of its purpose*. On monks individually the Qur'an is full of praise at several points as embodiments of saintliness and as the opposites of conceit and pride.

Beginnings of Institutional Sufism

For the first two centuries· Sufism remained a spontaneous individual phenomenon but, with the development of the formal disciplines of Islamic law and theology, and the gradual emergence, with them, of the class of 'Ulama', it rapidly developed into an institution with a tremendous mass appeal. The beginnings of the movement are connected with the activity of a class of people who themselves had arisen from the ranks of earlier ascetics variously called 'ascetics' (*zuhhad*), 'reciters' (*qurra' — scil.* of the Qur'an) who 'wept' as they recited and preached (*bakka'un* 'weepers'). These popular preachers, also known as *qussas* or 'storytellers', exerted a powerful influence on the masses by enlarging Qur'anic stories with the aid of materials borrowed from all kinds of sources, Christian, Jeswish, Gnostic and even Buddhist and Zoroastrian, indeed, anything that would make their sermons persuasive and effective. As the Sufi way of life became common as a recognized type, and term Sufi slowly replaced the older names *'zuhhad'* and *'nussak'* applied to this class of men (and women). The name 'Sufi' seems to be originally derived from *suf* or wool, the coarse material these people used for clothing as a sign of ascetism and renunciation. Other etymologies suggested either by later Muslim writers, for example, that 'Sufi' comes from the root *safa*, 'to be pure', or from *Suffa,* i.e. the raised platform in the Prophet's mosque in Medina where poorer people used to sit and exercise devotion, or as suggested by some moderns authors, that the word is derived from the Greek *sophos*, have little reliable foundation.

The earliest beginnings of Sufi organization are indicated by informal and loose gatherings for religious discussions, and spiritual exercise, called 'circles' (*halaqa*). The repeated recitation of the religious formula, called *dhikr*, can take place anywhere, including mosques, which fact shows that still at this stage (first half of the 3rd/9th century) Sufi practice was not, and was not regarded as, a rival growth challenging the formal disciplines of Islam. But later on, as we shall see, the simple practice developed into elaborate spiritual concepts with the introduction of music and dancing and threatened the position of the mosque as the centre of religious service.

Through the activity of the popular preachers and the pious mass orators, a number of ideas were introduced into Sufism and thence into popular Islam. These ideas, as we have said, originated from heterogeneous sources, but the chief impact made on Sufism seems to come from the Shi'ite sources which themselves were under the influence of Christianity. The most important of these importations is the eschatological doctrine of the Mahdi ('The guided one of God'), a spiritual personage who will appear at the end of time and restore the supremacy of justice and Islam over ungodly forces. The Shi'a, already sometime during the latter half of the 1st/7th century, had developed the idea of the 'awaited Mahdi', after their attempts failed to control the course of Muslim political life. Among the 'orthodox' or Twelve Shi'a, this personage was identified with the 'hidden Imam' who would effect the victory of the Shi'a political faith. The fusion of this Messianic doctrine with the Christian doctrine of the Second Advent of Christ was a natural development. In Sunni Islam itself, where a deep-seated consciousness existed of the failure of political and public life to meet the standards of the Islamic ideal, such ideas found a ready place in the hearts of the frustrated and disillusioned public through the effective mediacy of the preachers. And although the doctrine of the Mahdi was never formally included in Sunni theology, it has always weighed heavily with popular orthodox Islam. To this field of activity also belongs the overwhelming influx of late Jewish and apocryphal Christian ideas that found their way into the commentaries of the Qur'an and against which later Muslim critical theologians and doctors raised their protests (carried on into modern Islam as well), stigmatizing them as 'Isra'iliyat' or 'of Jewish lore and legend.'

With the growing inner rupture between Sufi practice and its implicit ideology on the one hand and the emerging orthodox system on the other, a new body of 'hadith' also comes into existence. The Sufis, in order to justify their stand, formulated (i.e. verbally invented) statements, sometimes quite fanciful and historically completely fictitious, which they attributed to the Prophet. These exaggerate the frugality of the Prophet into extreme renunciation and asceticism (very soon this was also applied to 'Ali, through the mediacy of Shi'i propaganda). The anti-Sufi Hadith is general reproves excessive asceticism, the especially monasticism and withdrawal from the world, besides emphasizing the superiority of a scholar to an ascetic. But although both sides of this type of Hadith may be regarded, in so far as their verbal formulations are concerned, as inventions, there is no reason to reject either side as being substantially untrue in the sense that they attribute to the Prophet things that were entirely foreign to him. The so-called this-worldly Hadith, stressing the actual implementation of the moral ideal realistically in the social context, belongs patently to the spirit of the Qur'an. But the Sufi Hadith also, once divested of its excessive and fanciful drapery, equally exemplifies the life of the Prophet and the teaching of the Qur'an in stressing the purity of the heart and inner life.

The disturbing feature, however, was the exclusive character implicit in this situation which once more compellingly reminds us of the Mu'tazilite-Hanbalite dichotomy in theology. Especially unacceptable to Islam was the negative attitude to this world that seemed to develop among the Sufi with alarming alacrity. Hence it rightly deserved the rebuke administered to it in the famous Hadith, 'there is no monasticism in Islam' with the further commentary, 'the monasticism of this Community is the Holy War.' These efforts saved Sufism from the further step of establishing completely monastic orders; otherwise, with its popular character and mass appeal, the whole fabric of Islam would surely have been destroyed.

As the rift threatened to widen, however, a number of eminent representatives of orthodox Islam set themselves the task of saving the situation. From the 3rd/9th century onwards there arose a whole series of important orthodox Sufis who both by their practice and teaching sought to integrate orthodoxy and Sufism and from then on the central spiritual history of Islam can be viewed as a continuous tension between these two streams and progressive attempts at integration and the resolution of this tension. This was because

Sufism, on its side, continued to absorb ever novel ideological modes and heterodox elements while formal religious disciplines continued as before.

The first great name among this succession of orthodox Sufis is that of Harith al-Muhasibi (d. 243/857) who, after a moral conversion from rational theology to Sufism, devoted himself to establishing orthodox religion on an intense inner life of the conscience. Like al-Ghazali, two and a half centuries later (for whom he seems to have served as a model), he summed up the pietistic legacy of the early Sufis in order to base upon it and enliven the external life of religion with its law and ritual. The essence of his teaching consists not in the renunciation of the outer life but in a ceaseless vigil on the purity of motive and in perpetual self-criticism, especially with regard to self-deception and inner self-righteousness and pride. This concentration, he taught, generates a succession of moral 'states' of conscience, progressively deepening the purity of motive.

The Sufi Way

But Sufism could not stay content for long with its simple piety and its gospel of love. Once it won converts to its general point of view from among the respectable members of the orthodoxy, it soon evolved the methodology of its 'inner way', its 'spiritual itinerary' to God. Its impulse to do so probably quickened with the charge of the 'Ulama' that, should the Sufi claims be granted, a door would be opened to spiritual anarchy because of the impossibility of regulating, controlling, and indeed, predicting the course of the 'inner life'. Dhu'l Nun of Egypt (d. 245/859), who is generally credited by the Sufis with having classified the 'stages' of spiritual development, was actually charged with heresy at Baghdad in 240/854. Besides, the Sufis themselves were in need of developing some method of control and criticism in order to standardize and, as far as possible, to objectify their experience.

If this doctrine of the stages or 'stations' (*maqamat*) of the Sufi itinerary was generally stated in religio-moral terminology, borrowed on the whole from the Qur'an (it usually includes such terms as 'repentance', 'abstinence', 'patience', 'gratitude', 'trust' and 'pleasure' (in God's Will), it also celebrated a theory of psychologico-gnostic 'states' (*shwal*) through which the Sufi passed. By the middle of the 3rd/9th century this development became definite, and led to the doctrine of 'absorption' or 'annihilation' (*fana'*), i.e. replacement of the human attributes by the Divine. This doctrine is traditionally associated with the name of the famous Sufi Abu Yazid al-Bistami (d. 260/874), to whom are attributed certain ecstatic utterances such as 'Praise be to me; how great is my majesty', 'I am your Lord' and 'my banner is greater than that of Muhammad'.

Such ecstatic statements, which multiplied among the Sufis and were called *shatahat*, were explained away as 'non-responsible' utterances spoken in the 'state of intoxication'. But the whole method of the Sufis created a problem of the utmost gravity for Islam. With the emergence of the Sufi doctrine of the spiritual itinerary, there arose the problem of the Sufi goal defined in terms of 'annihilation' of the human into the Divine attributed and qualities. With this the concept of sainthood, *wilaya*, was elaborated with an appeal to the use of the term *wali* ('friend of God') in the Qur'an, but with a peculiar Sufi content borrowed from the mysticism of EAstern Christianity, Gnosticism and later on from Neoplatonism. The question then arose as to how sainthood is related to Prophethood and the saint to the Prophet. That in the concept of sainthood Sufism saw a parallel to prophecy, and a rival to the religion instituted by the Prophet, became clear already in the 3rd/9th century when, in contradistinction to the concept of the 'Seal of the Prophet' (a term applied by the Qur'an to Muhammad indicating the fulfillment of prophecy in him), the idea of the 'Seal of the Saints' was introduced. In a book by the Sufi al-Hakim al-Tirmidhi (d. 285/898), the greatest Sufi authority on doctrine and systematizer of the 3rd/9th century, such questions are treated as: 'who deserves the title of the Seal of the Saints?' and 'how is a saint related to a Prophet?', etc.

Sainthood also brought with it the doctrine of a hierarchy of 'preserving' saints, most probably a Sufi parallel to the Shi'a doctrine of the Imam. The beginning of the teaching were in the 3rd/9th century, but it became a definite part of Sufi doctrine in the following century. According to this doctrine, the world is kept intact, thanks to the existence of a network of invisible saints of different ranks. The successive rungs of this ladder are constituted by 'successors' (*abdal,* plural of *badal'* a substitute' or 'a successor'), 'pets' (*awtad*), 'pillars' (*'ama'id*), etc., and end in a 'pole' or 'axis' (*qutb*) around which the whole universe rotates. But for this spiritual structure, the universe would go to pieces. A special place in the Sufi hagiarchy is occupied by an invisible figure called al-Khadir or al-Khidr (literally 'the Green') who, like the Phoenix, ever recreates his youth, is immortal and whose chief function is to guide those who lose their way in the wilderness (both physical and spiritual). Many eminent Sufis claim direct discipleship of al-Khidr from whom they have received investiture for the spiritual guidance of mankind. (The orthodox identify him with the 'Servant of God' on whom; according to the Qur'an, XVIII, 65, God bestowed special knowledge and who is represented there as a spiritual guide of Moses).

So much for the invisible realm. In the visible world, Sufis or rather those among them who were credited with sainthood, were invested with miracles or special divine graces and favours (*karamat*) which constituted signs of their sainthood. Special theories were constructed to distinguish scrupulously between these miracles and those of the Prophets, lest the two should the regarded as rivals. When thus qualified, orthodoxy felt no qualms about accepting the doctrine into its system.

But from the 4th/10th and 5th/11th centuries onward there emerged a new doctrine, completely opposed to the spirit of orthodox Islam, but which nevertheless became the first article in the constitution of Sufism as it launched itself in an organized fashion. In this respect the contrast, not only with orthodox Islam but even with the early Sufi practice, is remarkable. Whereas during the first three centuries, seekers of the Sufi path displayed a striking independence of spirit, resourcefulness and creativity, later on a rigorous discipline was imposed and an absolutely unquestioning submission tot he spiritual dictatorship of the Shaykh or the master. And whereas in the 3rd/9th century Junayd of Baghdad taught that a seeker should behave, *vis-a-vis* God, as a puppet, it was now said that he should be in the hands of his preceptor as 'a dead body in the hands of its washer'.

In the meantime, efforts had already begun in the 3rd/9th century within the Sufi told to bridge the gulf between orthodox Islam and Sufism and to keep the latter within reasonable limits. We have already studied the case of al-Muhasibi. After him came al-Kharraz (d. 286/899) and that great critical spirit in early Sufism, the formulator of orthodox Sufism, Junayd of Baghdad (d. 298/911), who is said to have been a pupil of al-Muhasibi. The result of this movement, the development of an orthodox Sufism, we shall study below. We end by mentioning the price Sufism paid in the execution of one of its great representatives in the 3rd/9th century, al-Husayn ibn Mansur called al-Hallaj ('the wool-carder'). Al-Hallaj, who had been a disciple of Junayd but who was expelled by the latter from his circle, was charged with having identified himself with God in his saying, 'I am the Truth' (*and 'l-Haqq*) and with deceiving people by sorcery, and was condemned to death with the approval of eminent jurist of Baghdad. He was flogged in public, mutilated, hung on a gibbet, decapitated and burnt. Islam never forgot this event (although the Sufis themselves later devised formulas both to exonerate him from heresy and to excuse his opponents) and the name of al-Hallaj has become a legend across the centuries not only with Sufis but in popular folk-literature throughout the Muslim world.

The Emergence of Orthodox Sufism

The emergence of a Sufi reform movement aiming at integrating mystic consciousness with the Prophetic Shari'a has its origins in Sufism itself and started in the last half of the 3rd/9th century with the activity of men like al-Kharraz and Junayd. Al-Kharraz introduced the concept of 'subsistence' or 'survival' (*baqa*) a amend and amplify Bistami's doctrine of 'annihilation' (*fana'*) On account of the paucity of resources, it is not easy to say what 'subsistence' meant fully to al-Kharraz, although it is generally said that he meant by it something positive; whereas 'annihilation' destroy (the human defects), by virtue of 'subsistence' man 'subsists in' or 'survives with' God. What seems certain from the scanty words of the author of the doctrine is that 'subsistence' is a spiritual development whereby God bestows upon man a recovery of his self. By the 4th/10th century, the doctrine had come to be accepted by Sufism and al-

Kalabadhi (d. 385/995) quotes a Sufi authority (probably al-Hallaj himself) as saying:

'Subsistence is the station of the Prophet (in contradistinction to saints) who are invested (by God) with peace and integrity (*sakina*), for, whatever comes to them (by way of ecstatic developments) does not prevent them from carrying out God's duties.'

Junayd subjected Sufi claims to an acute criticism both in terms of their experiences and their external practices. He thus disallowed to the Sufi 'states' and objective validity and declared that Sufis, including Abu Yazid al-Bistami, had died prisoners of their imagination. He also sought to counteract the antinomian and latitudinarian trends in Sufi practice by enunciating the principle that 'knowledge (*'ilm*) has a priority over gnosis (*ma'rifa*) and prohibition has a priority over permission'.

As a result of this process, the Sufi doctrine evolved a multitude of partly antithetical, partly complementary pairs of categories to integrage and do justice to the mystic and prophetic consciousness, the inner life and experience of the spirit and the Shari' law as a social institution. We have already described the twin categories of 'annihilation' and 'survival'. The other major sets of categories are: (1) 'intoxication' and 'sobriety'; (2) 'unity' and 'difference'; (3) 'absence' and 'presence' (i.e. of the self before God in mystic experience). The difference between the mystic and the prophetic consciousness came to be located in the fact that whereas the mystic consciousness generally remains content with the first part of the experience described in each of the above-mentioned categories, in the prophetic consciousness it form only a moment in the total experience which exhibits a dialectical character between the two terms. Epistemologically this doctrine led directly to the doctrine, accepted very widely, that ecstatic statements uttered in the state of intoxication are invalid and that reliance may be placed only on statements when 'sobriety' supervenes, even though many Sufis contended that the state of 'intoxication' was the higher of the two and that the Prophet 'returned to sobriety' perforce and under the command of God.

Even though the Sufis were not able to formulate explicitly an organic relationship between their dialectical categories, nevertheless their doctrine contributed materially to salvaging their relations with orthodoxy and the disciplines represented by it. From the middle of the 4th/10th century there are visible signs of a movement for compromise between Sufism and orthodox theology. A well-known Sufi, Ibn Khafif (d. 371/981), rallied to al-Ash'ari's theology and was its noted defender. A curious example is offered by a brief credal exposition of strict orthodoxy, attributed to the theologian al-Maturidi (see above, Chapter V). This work, called *'An Epistle on the Creed'* (*Risala fi'l-'aqa'id*), though it cannot have been written by al-Maturidi himself (he died in 333/945), nevertheless cannot, it seems, be later than the second half of the 4th/10th century, for its terminology is primitive and pre-philosophical. The Sufi overtones of this otherwise strictly formal work are striking, even though these mystic traces are kept in check so that they do not fall outside the fundamental framework of *kalam*-theology. Thus, on the nature of Faith, we are told:

> Islam is the knowledge of God *simpliciter* (without asking 'how') and its seat is the breast; and faith is the knowledge of God is His Godhead and its seat is the heart which is inside the breast; and true knowledge (*ma'rifa—gnosis*) is the knowledge of God with His attributes and its seat is the centre of the heart (*fu'ad*) which is inside of the heart; and (recognition of) the unity (of God) is the knowledge of His (absolute) unity and its seat is the 'secret' (sirr) or the inner being which is interior to the centre of the heart. A parable of this is what God is Exalted has said 'the likeness of God's light is like a niche wherein a lamp', etc. (Qur'an XXIV, 35).

From the very beginning of its formulation at the hands of al-Ash'ari the possibility of non-prophetic miracles or 'signs of the righteous' was accepted by theology. This anti-Mu'tazilite doctrine was a major concession to Sufism, a concession that was made easier for the theologians by their atomic view of nature and the time. In the 4th/10th century, the acceptance of belief in the saintly miracles grew very wide and even a completely rationalist philosopher like Ibn Sina found a place for them in his anti-atomistic system, although he explained these miracles as 'natural' effects of the power of the mind over matter. Later orthodox text books of the creed invariably accepted the miracles of the saints, which were Community a particular saint belongs—an interpretation which the Sufism unanimously accepted:

A powerful instrument in the whole *rapprochement* were the new traditions put into circulation throughout the 3rd/9th and 4th/10th centuries with the double purpose of promoting the cause of Sufism and bringing it into the orthodox fold. In the last quarter of the 4th/10th century a number of men wrote books, like al-Sarraj's (d. 377/987) *Kitab al-Luma'* and al-Kalabadhi's (d. 385/995) *Introduction to the Way of the Sufis*, to plead the cause of a moderate Sufism with a structure of ideas consistent with and even lending support to orthodoxy. This activity was followed in 438/1047 by the famous 'epistle (*Risala*)' of al-Qushayri (d. 465/1073), a manifesto for a synthesis of Sufism and orthodox theology.

This movement culminated in the monumental life-work of al-Ghazali, who proved to be its genuine corner-stone. This greatest figure in medieval Islam proved decisive for the future development of Islam, not so much through what he thought as through what he taught on the basis of his personal experience. Endowed with a rare religious insight (developed through a series a spiritual crises and struggles that affected him even physically) and a keen and formulas of orthodox theology about the Divine Will, Power and Mercy into a living and moving personal reality that throbbed in his very veins (see Chapters V and VI). He called both the 'Ulama' and the Sufis to this in a philosophical language of remarkable clarity, incisiveness and irresistible persuasiveness.

The influence of al-Ghazali in Islam is incalculable. He not only reconstituted orthodox Islam, making Sufism an integral part of it, but also was a great reformer of Sufism, purifying it of un-Islamic elements and putting it at the service of orthodox religion. As such he represents a final step in a long developing history. Sufism received, through his influence, the approval of Ijma', or consensus of the community. Islam received a new vigour of life and a popular appeal which won large areas in Africa, Central Asia and India to the Faith (see next chapter). Henceforth, often a great theologian and a great Sufi were one and the same person, a development which, as we shall see presently, produced in due course a series of original thinkers ·who reconstructed Muslim theology on a new and more integral basis, than the old formal *kalam*. Two dangers, however, threatened the new synthesis from two sides, dangers which ultimately altered, to a large extent, the character of Islam between the 7th/13th and 13th/19th centuries and were responsible for much of the degrading beliefs and practices with which Muslim society became loaded. One of these dangers, the invasion of Islam by popular religion, we shall deal with in the next chapter. The second, the development of Sufi theosophy, we must discuss next, for, at the intellectual level, it was this that sapped the energies and almost unreservedly claimed the minds of men of the greatest ability and creativity.

The Sufi Theosophy

If the early ascetic piety, with its emphasis on the interiorization of the motive, was a reaction to the external development of the law, during the 3rd/9th and 4th/10th centuries Sufism developed a doctrine of Gnosis (*ma'rifa*), of an inner experiential knowledge which is progressively came to oppose to the intellectual knowledge (*'ilm*) of theology which developed during the same period. There is evidence that in the 3rd/9th century the Sufis, on the whole, were a special class of theologians, rather than being opposed to theology. The author of the earliest extant bibliography of Arabic works, *Kitab al-Fihrist*, treats of them as the fifth category of theologians, whereas he does not give a separate class even to the Ash'arites. To the *'ilm al-tawhid*, the 'science of the unity (of God)' as dialectical theology was called, the Sufis then opposed their *ma'rifat al-Tawhid*, the 'gnosis of unity'. This 'unity' of God was then transformed under the Sufi experientialism, into 'union' with God (the Arabic word *tawhid* means both 'regarding something as one' and 'unification of something with something else'.

The Sufis, then, soon arrived at the idea, encouraged most probably by influence from outside, that God alone is really existent and from there on to the doctrine that *God is the sole reality of everything.* When the new Sunni theology of al-Ash'ari and al-Maturidi came into circulation, declaring that the author of all acts is God alone (against the Mu'tazilites), Sufi theosophy readily clung to this dictum but interpreted it on its own characteristic principles: nothing *exists* except Allah. This is what the Qur'anic doctrine of the unity of God was transformed into through the experiential method of the Sufis.

Yet, more ever than any particular doctrine Sufism might put forward as the content of the mystic consciousness, it was the principle of gnostic knowledge with its self-righteous intuitive certainly and the infallibility of its specially privileged deliverances that was not and could not be admitted by the 'Ulama'. For with gnostic Sufism the case was very different from that of the early pietistic Sufism where it was a matter of merely emphasizing the purity of the conscience against external acts. The Sufis now claimed an incorrigible way of *knowing* which was supposedly immune from error and, further, whose content was utterly disparate in character with intellectual knowledge. The 'Ulama' resisted this claim not only because it threatened a body of doctrine they had evolved with great effort over the four centuries, but more fundamentally because of Sufi gnosis was not open to any check and control, being be definition incorrigible. Even after the revolution through al-Ghazali's labours, the 'Ulama' never admitted the objective validity of the uniquely privileged mystic knowledge.

Similarly, the 'ecstatic statements', despite the general acceptance of the principle that these were made in the state of 'intoxication' and were not valid, were nevertheless at the same time regarded as having a peculiar cognitive nature not open to the scrutiny of ordinary avenues of knowledge. The very doctrine of the 'states' of inner experience implicitly assumed the possession of an esoteric knowledge of a unique, irreducible type posited for the unquestioning recognition of the Faithful. Here is a brief early statements of this cognitive miracle attributed to al-Tustari (d. 283/896):

'Lordship has a secret which, is manifested, would destroy

Prophethood; and Prophethood has a secret, which is divulged, would nullify knowledge; and the gnostics have a secret which, if manifested by God, would set the law at naught'.

It is the same al-Tustari who is reported to have said: 'I do not discuss the sinners in the community of Muhammad, its evil-doers, murders, fornicators and thieves, but I disown those who lay claims to *trust* in God, *satisfaction* with Him, *love and desire* of Him'. Indeed, a peculiar mixture of extreme moral contrition (for developing which into a doctrine he was castigated by the 'Ulama') and hold theosophic claims exists in this personality. As a matter of fact, whatever the claims to esoteric knowledge, the Sufis were coming strongly under the influence of the Greco-gnostic concepts and Christian and Manichaean doctrines.

An early example of the intrusion into Sufism (later 3rd/9th century) of these Gnosis-Manichaean ideas was the doctrine of Muhammad as the Primal Light, the penultimate constituent of ontological reality after God, a doctrine which later became a centrally 'orthodox' doctrine of Sufism through the teaching of Ibn al-'Arabi (7th/13th century) who, as we shall see, made of this light God Himself. With the doctrine of Muhammad as the Primal Light in which all the Prophets were foreshadowed, including Adam, emerged the Hadith, largely accepted even by orthodoxy, which declared that 'Muhammad was a Prophet while Adam was still (in a state) between water and earth'. Orthodox did not accept the metaphysical implications of the Hadith but regarded it as a correct eulogistic statement of Muhammad's position *vis-a-vis* other Prophets.

In a passage attributed to al-Tustari but which represents probably a development of his doctrine by his followers are read: 'God created the Light of Muhammad from His own Light and He formed it and brought it out at His own hands. This Light remained before Him for a hundred thousand years, during which time He contemplated it every day and night seventy thousand times. Then He created from it the whole creation.' This philosophical trend was accelerated by the infusion of Neoplatonic ideas of emanation which exerted a powerful attraction on speculative Sufism. These ideas were formulated in a famous encyclopedia of popular character in the later 4th/10th century by an esoteric Isma'ili circle calling itself 'the Brethren of Sincerity'. This religio-philosophical work, *'The Epistles of the Sincere Brethren'* which circulated widely in the 5th/11th century, and upon which later Isma'ili theosophy drew as a source, held up before the seekers of the gnosis the goal of the Neoplatonic ascent or 'return' of the soul to the ultimate principle of Being and absorption of the former into the latter.

Such was the Sufi gnosis. It developed a peculiar doctrine of the relationship between the Shari'a and what is called the *haqiqa* ('inner truth'). Many Sufis came to hold that the seeker who arrives at this mystic truth goes beyond the Shari'a—the religious law of which he is no longer in need, and which is meant only for the masses and neophytes. Even those who held a less extreme view saw in the positive religion only a pedagogy, a ladder to be climbed and then discarded. Some, indeed, insisted that the law may not be transcended at any point. These were precisely the orthodox Sufis who developed the categories of the 'inner'and the 'outer' described in the previous section. But their reform was not enough; they did not develop any *organic and necessary* relationship between the Inner and the Outer, between the mystic experience and its cognitive content on the one hand and the Shari'a life and the discursive intellect on the other. If they had been able to do so, this might not only have averted the gravest inner conflict in Islam, but would have enriched it with an unprecedented creativity. As a result, these Sufis also left the impression that they were merely juxtaposing two irreconcilable currents out of hypocrisy and through fear of the 'Ulama'.

Yet Sufism exerted an irresistible pull on men's minds and during the 4th/10th and 5th/11th centuries won an increasing number of the ablest intelligentsia. The systems of the 'Ulama' had become rigid and their legal casuistry and empty theological pedantry drove the more serious-minded men of religion and originality into the Sufi fold. The 'Ulama' scoffed at the Sufi pretensions of possessing the unique cognitive avenues to God but they did not seem to understand the power and the depth of the genuinely religious demand represented by the tide of Sufism, and the ground was rapidly slipping beneath their feet. The more orthodox Sufis made the effort to come half-way, but the 'Ulama', as a whole, remained insensible. In the meantime, the more extravagant forms of theosophic Sufism were gathering momentum. Immediately before al-Ghazali, the great systems of philosophical mysticism elaborated by the philosophers al-Farabi and Ibn Sina gave a fresh impetus to and were exploited by this theosophic Sufism.

Al-Ghazali's mission, therefore, was welcome not merely as a reform or rather re-orientation of orthodox Islam but equally as a reform of Sufism. Philosophic enquiry into the ultimate nature of god had yielded him no results; hence he did not turn to Sufism to gain this knowledge in another way. He neither wanted nor hoped for any occult miraculous knowledge. His purpose was to live through the verities of the Faith and to test those verities through the Sufi experientialist method. He succeeded. The test confirmed his faith and he concluded (1) that it was only through the 'life of the heart' that faith could really be acquired and (2) (and what is of at least equal importance) that Sufism has no *cognitive content or object but the verities of the Faith*. He, therefore, disallowed the pretensions of theosophic mysticism and castigated the men of ecstatic delirium.

This was a remarkable lesson taught by a great mystic spirit, one of the most remarkable lessons, we venture to think, in the whole history of mysticism—viz., that mysticism is *not* a way of finding extra *facts* about Reality but is a meaningful way of looking at it, of looking at it as a unity. Further the unity of the mystic consciousness is *conditioned* by the factual content (however much it may try to transcend that content), which it tests and transforms by new *meanings*. This was an especially reassuring discovery for the position of the Shari'a, and it revolutionized the relationship of Sufism to the orthodox faith, producing in course of time men who worked out that relationship, as we shall see, and restated their faith in new terms.

But the critical, synthetic and reforming activity of al-Ghazali, at the same time, proved to be a great watershed in the spiritual history of Islam, and forced the currents of ideas in the Muslim community into both new divisions and new combinations. The most powerful and fateful for the future of Islam was the junction produced during the century after al-Ghazali between philosophical currents and Sufism at the level of doctrine, to which we have alluded in the previous chapter. Under the violent attacks of orthodoxy, successfully initiated by al-Ghazali, rational philosophy did not die but went underground, and avenged itself through its new guise of theosophic Sufism where it found a ready and secure home. It was, indeed, an almost unassailable citadel, for, whereas in its rational, purely philosophical form it could be criticized and its inadequacies exposed by an al-Ghazali, under its new Sufi form this theosophy claimed to be the product of infallible intuitions, immune from rational criticism. Thus, the formal structure of Sufi methodology advocated by al-Ghazali as outlined above and adopted by orthodox Sufis was set at naught by the new theosophy which increasingly attracted some of the best minds of later medieval Islam. In place of the moral, non-metaphysical mystic experience of orthodox Sufism, an out-and-out philosophical intuitionism was now substituted whereby men claimed to arrive at metaphysical knowledge.

The classic formulation of the new Sufi epistemology was worked out by Ibn al-'Arabi 9d. 638/1240), the apostle of theosophic mysticism in Islam. At the beginning of his *magnum opus* entitled 'The Meccan Revelations (*al-Futuhat al-Makkiya*)' he discusses the 'ways of knowledge' and concludes that intuitive revelation (*kashf*) is the highest and the only sure source of cognition. He criticizes the philosophers for their exclusive reliance on reason but he also admonishes the religious classes in the same work that not all philosophical doctrines are to be rejected as false. What really happened in the process was that the philosophical legacy was adopted and developed by Ibn al-'Arabic and his followers into a monistic doctrine, but instead of being given out as a product of reason it was issued in the name of mystic intuition. Subsequent mystic works of theosophic Sufis are full of criticism of 'rationalists' and of disparagement of reason over against intuition, and give the impression that the Sufi are the arch enemies of philosophy. Thus Jalal al-Din Rumi, the great Sufi poet-philosopher (d. 672/1273) says:

'Philosophers' legs are made of wood;
Legs of wood are infirm, indeed.'

The truth, however, it that this opposition is only methodological, and corresponds more or less accurately to al-Ghazali's opposition to the orthodox 'Ulama'. The content does not vary in this opposition; what is contrasted here is the form of experience with the process of discursive reasoning. Indeed, we find that later philosophers like Sadr al-Din (see the preceding chapter) also systematically adopt intuitive revelation as the highest form of knowledge in their epistemological framework.

So much for the epistemological challenge of Sufism to orthodox theologians. But even more grave was the content of the theosophy which is also essentially the product of Ibn al-'Aṛabi's versatile and imaginative genius. His system, which, for the speculative Sufis, came to supplant that of orthodox theology, is thoroughly monistic and pantheistic, the very reverse of the teaching of orthodox Islam. Briefly, Ibn al-'Arabi taught that the Absolute Reality is transcendent and nameless and its only attribute it self-existence. But the Absolute, by a kind of propulsion or process of 'descent' and 'determination' develops a state of being wherein it becomes conscious of its attributes, knowledge, power, life, creativity, etc. These attributes of perfection, however, exist only in its mind or consciousness. But it is also these attributes which constitute the stuff from which the word is made. The 'creation' of the world is nothing but the projection of these attributes from the Divine Mind outward into 'real existence' which is nothing but the existence of the Absolute Himself. The attributes or names of God, as they are in the Divine Mind prior to external existence, also constitute the essence of the 'created' World. The highest of these essences is the essence of Muhammad which manifested itself in the historic person of the Prophet Muhammad but whose transcendental state is to be fulfilled not in the 'Seal of the Prophets' but in the 'Seal of the Saints'. This 'Seal of the Saints' is not other than Ibn al-'Arabi himself.

Both these doctrines threatened orthodoxy directly. The second doctrine, which was a challenge to the status of the Prophet personally, lost its force because Ibn al-'Arabi's pretensions to be the 'Seal of the Saints' were not taken seriously, but even so the old controversy of pre-Ghazalian times as to the relationship of the saints to the Prophet was revived. But the more insidious effect of both doctrines was that the position of the Shari'a and its visible pillar, the law, was gravely endangered. A thoroughly monistic system, no matter how pious and conscientious it may claim to be, cannot, by its very nature, take seriously the objective validity of moral standards. 'All is He' (Persian: *hama ust*) was the inevitable conclusion. Jami, the 9th/15th century Persian mystic poet, teaches:

> The companion, comrade and co-traveller,
> All is He,
> In the mendicant's tattered robe and in the brocade of the regal dress, All is He;
> Whether in the display of variety or the privacy of unity—
> By God All is He! Again, by God All is He!

A remarkable feature of this literature especially in its poetic form, was the development of the images of earthly love and its employment to depict the spiritual passion of the seeker of God. Ibn al-'Arabi himself had composed his lyrical *Interpreter of Desires* inspired by a lady of parts in Mecca. Later he had to comment on this poem to show that his object of desire was spiritual. In general, para-sexual symbolizm abounds in his thought. Adam, he taught, was really the first female for Eve was born from his inside, an act repeated by the second Adam, Mary, in generating Jesus. In the subsequent Persian Sufi poetry that blossomed so brilliantly, amorous images are employed in stark realism and many poets have been objects of controversy as to whether they were singing of spiritual love or earthly passion. This imagery became the stock-in-trade of most Persian, Turkish and Urdu poetry, and so powerful was its charm that it is only during the present century that literary style has begun to move away from it.

We may end this chapter by noting the methods by which the orthodox forces set themselves to face this challenge. At the level of doctrine, orthodoxy, as we noted above, was unwilling to admit the objective validity of the Sufi insight or intuition, although certain later figures like al-Taftazani (d. 791/1389) concede that mystic intuition is authoritative for the experiencing subject himself even though it cannot claim validity beyond him. At the theological level (which, unlike the creed, is not the level of the masses but of religious intellectuals), however, chiefly due to al-Ghazali's influence, Sufi intuition began to be taken seriously although its claims to infallibility were not and could not be conceded. Indeed, the monistic theosophic content of Sufi doctrine was severely rejected by the majority of orthodox theologians.

It is this background which mainly set the field of activity of Ibn Taymiya and his disciples, primarily Ibn Qayyim, from the 8th/14th century onwards. Ibn Taymiya accepted the validity of the Sufi experimental method although he and his school relentlessly attacked the Sufi rituals and practices of tomb worship and the cults of saints. His pupil, Ibn Qayyim, showed himself even more tolerant in his language than his master. What Ibn Taymiya and his school insisted upon, however, was that Sufi experience had no exclusive and infallible validity and that in fact the validity of its content is to be tested with reference to the external world. Thus, Sufism might interpret and give new meaning to the Shari'a and the Revelation, but it cannot set them at naught. The doctrine of monism, they held, obliterates all distinctions in the real world which must serve as the touchstone for the validity of any proposition and thus destroys the Shari'a or the moral order. Monism not only fails to satisfy this criterion but negates the criterion itself. Hence the doctrine as a *moral* interpretation of the universe must be rejected. There is no doubt that the immediate object of Ibn Taymiya's criticism is the Sufi doctrine of the Unity of Being. But he goes back and attacks the philosophers whose doctrines had prepared the way for Sufi monism. And pushing his analysis back still further, the Ash'ari doctrine of the Will of God is found to be a great milestone in this monistic development. Ibn Taymiya felt it imperative, therefore, to construct a concept of the Shari'a which would synthesize a double but analogous duality between Mu'tazilism and Ash'arism and between Sufi monism and the reality of the moral law.

Ibn Taymiya's teaching aroused much bitter criticism even fwidely scattered throughout India and in Transoxiana. Confirming the teaching of Ibn Taymiya from the Sufi side, he taught that the Sufi 'Reality' (*haqiqa*), which was so commonly opposed to the Shari'a was really the life-foundation of the Shari'a itself from among the ranks of the 'Ulama', the chief reason for which was his rejection of the unquestioned acceptance of authority (*taqlid*) and his consequent fearless criticism of almost all Muslim sects, including the orthodox Ash'ari theology which he denounced in very strong terms as advocating anti-Islamic predestinarianism. Gradually, however, his message served as a leaven for subsequent religious developments and in the 12th/18th century burst out in the violent form of the Wahhabi reform. But the more hopeful and influential approach was to reform Sufism from within Sufism itself. Gradually recognized by the Ijma' of the Community after al-Ghazali, Sufism attracted many followers from the ranks of the 'Ulama' who realized that the only hope to rid Sufism of its medieval centuries of Islam, it came to be a normal procedure to combine the purificative and contemplative path of Sufism with the normal orthodox disciplines of Hadith, law and theology.

Excesses and aberrations was to take it seriously. In the later Criticism of extravagant intellectual and spiritual consequences of Ibn al-'Arabi's monistic doctrine had begun early even within Sufism. A notable Sufi, al-Samnani (d. 736/1336), had accused him of 'confounding God with the world' by identifying the Divine and the human. This movement culminated in the teaching of Ahmad Sirhindi (d. 1034/1625), an outstanding Indian theoretician of reformed Sufism. Sirhindi, a practising Sufi of the Naqshbandi order, declared that the experience of the Unity of Being, although real as an experience, does not represent the last stage of the mystic's development. He then constructed his own doctrine seeking to do justice to the reality of the moral distinctions in religion and propagated it through numerous letters to his disciples who were subcontinent and largely successful in counteracting the antinomian tendencies within the ranks of the Sufi adepts. Despite the efforts of this group, however, the attraction exerted by monism on many minds was irresistible. In India this was especially the case because of the Hindu pantheistic influences to which Islam was constantly exposed. It was partly these influence which had led the Mughal emperor Akbar to proclaim a syncretistic religion (*Din-i Ilahi*) in the 10th/16th century and to attempt to impose it as state religion (to which the Sirhindi-led movement was a successful reaction). The second Sufi movement, therefore, had as its objective to synthesize the monistic framework of mystic theosophy with the moral exigencies of the Shari'a. The most prominent exponents of this type of thought were the Syrian 'abd al-Ghani of Nabulus (d. 1144/1731) and Shah Wali Allah of Delhi (d. 1176/1762). A similar reinterpretation of the Sufi doctrine, breaking away vehemently from pantheism, was undertaken in the Malay Archipelago by Nur al-Din ibn Muhammad al-Raniri (d. 1077/1666). These Sufi theologians, in their general objectives, are comparable, from the Sirhindi's movement was of very considerably influence in the Sufi side, to the synthetic spirit of Ibn Taymiya at the orthodox scholastic level. A remarkable effect of these endeavours was to change the character of Islamic theology from its traditional scholastic mould to a more genuinely intellectual and speculative one. It was achieved by men who were processional Sufis but whose orthodoxy was equally indubitable. It provides us with a shining example of that fundamentally catholic genius of Islam—a panorama of continued tensions and challenges and of equally persistent efforts to resolve these tensions and meet these challenges in a process of modification, adaptation and absorption.

(Revised and edited: Originally appeared as Islam: Chapter eight, Sufi doctrine and practice).

8

Developments in Sufism in Safavid Persia

HOSSAIN MIRJAFARI

A gradual transformation in the meaning of Sufism took place in the Persian region during the rule of the Safavids.

Shaikh Safi-al-Din of Ardebil (650-735/1252-1334), the Safavid family was one of the greatest Sufis and gained considerable fame. Shaikh Safi was directed by Shaikh Zahid Gilani (d. 694/1296) to follow the Khorassani order of Sufism.[1]

Both Shaikh Safi and his son Shaikh Sadr-al-Din, as leaders of Sufism, were absolute followers of Sunni Fatih.[2] Khwaja Ali, Shaikh Safi's grandson, was the first in his family who showed a tendency towards Imamits and became a Shi'a, but his inclination to this faith was not very strong.

The followers of Khaja 'Ali, after Khwaja's death in palestine, in 831/1427, extended the concept of Shi'ism to the extreme, such that their leaders (Pear) were considered to be emanation of God, displaying God's attributes.

Under the influence of this extremism, the "Pears" began to treat those who believed in other religions, particularly Sunnits, very harshly, ordering *Jihad* against them, during which Shaikh Junaid and Shaikh Haydar. Shah Ismail's grandfather and father were killed as partisans. Shah Ismail, who spent his early years in concealment and had narrow escapes from death, was later recognized as the spiritual leader of the Sufis.[3]

When the Safavid clan accepted the Shia faith, Sufism lost its significance and was only used in it apparent and nominal sense. This was because the "Theory of the Unity of God and Man" which was the base of Sufism, is rejected by Shi'ism.

Those who followed Shaikh Junaid, Shaikh Haydar, constituting their armies, were called Sufis. Various historical sources indicate that Sultan Haydar had ordered his Sufi Trukaman artisans to wear scarlet caps (Tajs) with twelve grooves standing for the twelve Imams of Shi'a distinguishing them from others, and that they granted them the honourable name of Qizilbash (red head).

The historian of the Safavid period believed that, although the "Red Cap" was called "Taj-e-Haydari", there are proofs that a group of Sufis were using hats with twelve or twenty grooves, prior to the emergence of the Safavid Clan.[4]

It is understood that the twelve-grooved that to the Safavid time was not meant to be a hat or a sign of the twelve Imams, but was the symbol of those who were Sufis and who had isolated themselves from the material life. Therefore, the word "Kolah-e-Faqr or Kolah-e-Fakhr" meant really magnanimity or independence crown. If one wore the twelve groved cap, one was considered to have abandoned the material world and have reached the spiritual world. Being convinced of the importance of this symbolism, Shaikh Haydar reccommended all his followers to become Sufis and be none other than men of Truth.

Fazlullah Khunji-Isfahani (d. 926/1520), the historisan of the Aqquyunlu court, has several times indicated in his book "Tarikhi-Alam are-yi Amini" that the word "tark" means to give up all needs and desires for worldly wealth and physical welfare and to deprive oneself from the material life. He writes about his father. My father Roozbehan replaced (Magnanimity Cap), rejecting his ancestor's positions, and lived in isolation.[5]

Fazlullah has indicated in his book the abstemirousness and worship of Shaikh Safi, the leader of Safavid Clan, and recited the story of Sultan Muhammad Oljauto's invitation of the Shaikh to his feast, which was rejected by the latter as he criticised the Sultan' politics and acquisition of the wealth, and also his greediness for the Sultanite Crown instead of Taj-E-Tark (Magnanimity Cap).

The word "Taj" was defined in Taj-Nameh, written by Shah Nemattullah Veli as follows:

There are twelve grooves in each Taj, symbolisting twelve "abstentions" and twelve demands. A Sufi should avoid twelve "indecencies" and demand twelve "dececise".

The twelve "indecencies to be avoided are as:

(1) Jealousy (2) Spite (3) Anger (4) Rancour (5) Egotism (6) Cavil (7) Selfishness (8) Lasciviousness (9) Inhumanity (10) Gluttny (11) Sleepiness (12) Evils.[6]

After Shaikh Haydar's demise, the word Qizilbash was given to all his followers and the Sufis of the Safavid Clan, thus, the word Qizilbash became equilivent to Sufi.

It is understood from the sources that before Shaikh Haydar there were groups of people who had been wrapping a piece of red cloth round their heads. This caused fear in the heart of the onlookers. The first person who, in the Islam history, wore a red head band was said to be a man in the Ohod War and devoted his life to the Prophet Muhammad.[7]

Islamic sources record that Ali, the Son-in-Law of the Prophet Muhammad, wore a red head band in the Khaybar war, showing his preparedness and seriousness towards enemies and showing that he was ready to die, but not to escape. As a result of this seriousness Ali was successful in conquering the Khaybar Fort.[8]

Zia-Shakir, Turkish historian, acknowledging all above references, states that Shaikh Haydar followed Abu-Dajjaneh and Ali in wearing a red head band, saying that he will take revenge on his father's and grandfather's enemies and will gladly die for their cause. In order to create more bravery, belief and coordination in his army, Shaikh Haydar ordered everyone wear a red head band.[9]

Shaikh Haydar's reason for wearing a red head band for making his army wear it, was that, by these means he could create an increased spiritual power and faith in his army members and Sufis and show them the way Iman-Ali went.

At the beginning of his rule Shah Ismaul's followers and devotees were called Sufis. Consequently in European countries where Shal Ismail's name and fame had filled the political circles and also in other parts of the world where tourists and Ambassadors have spread information about Iran, Shah Ismail was called "The Grand Sufi". This name remained some how with all Safavid Kings till the decline of this dynasty.

At the time of Shah Ismail (907-980/1520/1524), all his followers and army members were called "Qizilbash" and the title of Sufi was given to a limited group of people and the famous as old Sufis and disciples of the Safaid Clan, so that the Sufis mostly were found in the tribes of Rumlu, Shamli and Qajar. The king was commander and leader and had the title of "Murshid-i-Kamil" (Great Leader).[10]

The head of each Sufi tribe was called "Khalifeh" and the chief of all Sufi tribes was called "Khalifeth-al-Kholfa". Because the chief was the deputy to the Murshid-e Kamel his position was considered to be both spiritually and secularty very important.

This position was mostly occupied by the leaders of the Rumlu Tribe out of whom Hussain-Gholi-Rumlu came to be named as Kalifeth-al-Kholafe of the Shah Tahmasb (930-84/1524-76) and Shah Ismail II (984-85/1576-77).[11]

After Hussain-Gholi-Rumli dies, a man named Bulgar-Khalifeh occupied the position of Khalifeh-al-Khulafa. The latter was said to be of the Rumbu Tribe. The other greats of the Rumlu Tribe holding the position of Khalifeh while having other military and governmental posts were:

Nur-Ali-Khalifeh-Rumlu,[12] Safian-Khalifeh-Rumlu,[13] Mahammad-Goli-Khalafah-Rumlu,[14] and Shah-Gholi-Kholafah-Rumlu.[15]

The basic condition for reaching the position of Sufi was unquestionably obey the orders of Murshid-e-Kamil (The Great Leader—Shah) and not to do anything against his willings sacrificing lives for the sake of Murshid-e-Kamil was the least and lowest possible degree of faith.

As a result of this deep faith and devotion to Murshid-e-Kamil or Shah, some of the Safavid Kings were reputed to have miraculous power.

Many European missionaries who visited Iran during the time of the Safavid's have recited stories about the supernatural power of the Safavid Kings, although they did not fully substantiate the sources of these beliefs. A Venetian contemporary who visited Iran at the time of Shah Ismail's emersion writes as follows; "de ceulx de sa cour et ses subjectz ilest ador (sic) comme prophete". That is "Those who were in Shah Ismail's court and all his men were treating him as a prophet".

A Venetian merchant who was in Tabriz in 1518, states that this Sufi—namely, Shah Ismail is loved and worshipped by the people of his country as God, and that his soldiers go to the warfields unarmed believing that they will be supported and watched over by their Master Ismail.[16]

Vincento D'Alessandri, Venetian Ambassador to Shah Tahmosb's court, states that the love and the faith people have towards the King is unbelievable as they worship him not as a King but as a God and beleive that since he is one of the grandsons of Hazrat Ali, he has the resurrection power.[17]

Jalal' al-din Muhammad, the Astronomist of Shah Abbas I, has mentioned in his book the miraculous power of Shah Abbas and writes as follows: "When Shah Abbas was a child he started to suck the milkless breasts of Ali-Golikhan's mother and suddenly the breasts were full of milk."[18]

Also in the same book he says that "When Muhammad Mumen-Ibn-e mirza Arab Mogalled Marvi, was disabled at the age of 5, his mother took him to the Shah and Shah touched his disabled foot with his hand and immediately he regained his power to walk."[19]

Furthermore, "When Shah Abbas had gone as a pilgrim to Shaikh Safi's speculcher in Ardebil in whichever look he touched in different parts of the sanctuary, it was opened immediately and this caused astonishment in the audience."[20]

All the beliefs regarding the Safavid King's miraculous find their origin in the deep-rooted faith in their spiritual and gnostic position. Those who lied to Murshid-e-Kamil or disobeyed him were sentenced to death by the Sufis. Bulgar-Khalifeh, Khalifeht-al-Kholafa of Shah Ismail II, (984-85/1576-77) had the same fate when he lied to the King and he was kicked to death by Sufis at the King's order.[21]

The position of and respect for the Sufis in the Safavid period gradually declined to a level where only a small and special group of people were called Sufis. They had a very simple administrative position in governmental offices in the time of Shah Abbas I (995-1038/158-1629.)

Safavid Kings have been choosing Sufis for the posts of Royal Palace guards. A group of Sufis were private guards of the King and always accompanied him and attened in his presence for the purpose of executing his immediate orders. Their number never exceeded 200-300 and their duty was to carry out the King's orders, executing those who were condemmed to death by the King.

The sufis killed their victims in Murshid-e-Kamil's presence with sword and battle-axe, or by kicking them to death. Sometime they ate their flesh after having murdered them.[22]

Shah Abbas I, hated the Sufis and did not trust them as they were disciples of his father Shah Muhammad Khodabardeh (985-95/ 1578-88) who was deposed (of his crown) by Shah Abbas.[23]

The attitude of Shah Abbas I, and his disrespect for the Sufis, reduced their credit and importance amongst people to a level that they were dismissed from their posts as guards of the King and Royal Palaces and were appointed as janitors of the buildings, watchmen and executioners.

Despite the above-mentioned treatment and disrespect, the Sufis never failed to hold their circle sessions on Friday nights and holidays, headed and led by Khalifath-al-Kholafa. Their food and lodgings were provided for at the order of Shah. Although the Sufis' respect and credit had declined to the extreme minimum, they were still considered the King's close men and by the majority of people they ware reputed for their spiritual sacredness and position. Some people believed that a bit of Sufis' food, was a cure and remedy for sickness and disease. Shah Abbas, however, was not on good terms with the Sufis and called them ungrateful and rogue, but apparently pretended to respect them.[24]

Some of the Safavid Kings insulted other groups of Sufis, besides disrespecting their own followers. J. Rypka recites in his book, named, "History of Iranian Literature" the following: "Religious orders died out under the pressure of Safavid policy and with them the Sufi conception and speculations, which were contested and suspected by the Majtahids with the most intense hatred. To keep Mowlavi's Masnavi in one house involved constant danger. Moreover, Tahmasb I (930-84/1524-70) has already driven the Mowlavis from Persia. The Sufis were persecuted in an even more cruel manner by the last real Shah of the Safavid dynasty.[25]

Minorsky, quoting from Sanson, who visited Iran during the last years of Sha Sulayman's (1077-1105/1667-94) reign, says that the Sufis who were once respected, had now lost their repute in the court and were appointed to the duties of watchmen, porters, horse grooms and farm care-takers.[26]

As results of the decline in the respect for and influence of the Sufis in the Safavid courts, Shi'a Mullahs were able to gradually extend their influence in the Safavid King's courts such that Sufis became to be considered the enemies of Safavid courts.[27]

Consequently, the policies of the later Safavid Kings, especially those of Shah Sultan Hassaub (1105-35/1644-1722) who was a very prejudiced Shi'a, were based on his personal hatred for the Sufis. The author of the history book "Tarikh-e-Tahmasiye" (on sheet 131 a) says that "Shah Sultan Hussian abolished the Sufis path which at the commencement of the Safavid Kingdom, was slogan. He also stopped holding any sessions or gatherings in the Sufis' circle "Towhid Khaneh", which was built next to the King's Palace, where every Friday night the Sufis circle was held and where the King and the high ranking officers of the government together with the Sufi leaders used to participate in religious ceremonies.[28]

All Sufi leaders were exiled from Isfahan and Mullah Muhammad Begher Majlis, the Shi'a great Majtahid spread and extended his religious influence and power across the country.

Reza Gholikhan Hedayat mentions in his book "Ravzat-al-Safaye-Naseri the exile of a Shi'a Religious leader from Isfahan who was accused to be a Sufi.[29]

It is astonishing that the Safavid Clan which was the founder and promoter of Sufism and which endeavoured towards extending and strengthening Sufism, finally decided to cause its decline and abolishment.

It is understood that Sufism was at the beginning a kind of spiritual and gnostic movement which directed the disciples to loving worship of God, frankness, innocence and which campaigned against any luxury, prejudice and illogical rules and regulations. But despite the Sufi leaders 'and disciples' willingness Sufism changed its nature from being a spiritual School of thought to becoming an official institution which caused its own downfall.

In conclusion, it is worth nothing that Sufism and gnosticism were inter-related with Shi'ism in the Safavid period. This caused a gradual disappearance of Sufism's apparent and external aspects and characteristics and resulted in the extension of its spiritual and gnostic aspects, but the interchanging enabled the interrelation of these two paths to remain constant and unchanged.

REFERENCES

1. J S Trimingham, The sufi orders in Islam, Oxford, 1971, p. 100; see also his pedigrees in the same source, pp. 30-31.
2. The first indication that Safi was a Shafei Sunni is cited in Hamdullah Mostowfi's Nuzhat-al-Quloob, Tehran, 1956, p. 92 written during his visit to Ardebil, five years after the demise of Shaikh Safi. He writes: The majority of the population of Ardebil are the disciples of both the Shafe`i school of the Sunni faith. Shaikh Safi on the same subject is also cited in : a) Ibn-Bazzar Ardebil, who himself was a disciple fo the Shaikh, states in his book "Safvat-al-Saf" (MS. Ayasofya Library, no. 2123, sheet 464), (b) Ahmad Karavi,Shaikh Safi and his clan, Tehran, 1948. (c) Z V Togan, Sur l'orgine de safavides, Melanges Louis Massignon, Dams, 1975. (d) Die Safaviden, Saeclulum. 1953.
3. Laurence Lockhart, The fall of the Safavi dynasty and the Afgan occupation of Persia, Cambridge, 1958, pp. 15-19.
4. Aref Ardebil, who wrote in the 14th century, during Sultan Owaise Jalayer's period, and who was invited to Shirvan, by Shirvanshah Kaykavoos Ibn Ghobad (744-45/1343-44) states in his work "Farhad Namesh" (the only Ms. in Ayasofya Library), that there were a group of people using Scarlet Caps with twenty grooves, viz., "Twenty Grooved hat on his head." "He has worn a beautiful ragged robe" (Muhammad Ali Tarbiat, Azarbaijan Scholars, Tehran, 1936, pp. 251-2).
5. Fazlullah Khurji-Isfahani, Tarikh-l-Aram-ara-yi. Amini, Reproduced copy, Faith Library, Istanbul, no. 4431, p. 89.
6. See "A research on Quizilbash", by Firouz Mansouri, Historical Researches (Bar' Rasihay-i Tarikh-i Tehran, no. 59, p. 148.
7. Ibn-al-Athir, Al-Kamil fi al-Tarikh, Egypt, 1938, vol 11, p. 106.
8. Ibid., vol 11, p. 148.
9. Zia-Shakir, Mezspeller Tarihi, Istanbul, (no date), p. 95.
10. Nasr Allah, Falsafi, Zindagani-yi Sheh Abbas-i Avval, Tehran, 195-62 (refered hence as Falsafi) 1,pp. 181-2.
11. Iskandar Beg Munshi, Tarikh-i Alam-ara-yi Abbasi, 2vols., Tehran 1955-56 (refered hence as TAAA), 1, p.11 (-201).

12. Hasan-i- Rumlu, Ahsanut-tevarikh (A chronicle of the early Safavids), Baroda, 1931 (refered hence as Hasan-i Rumlu), p. 134.
13. Hasan-i- Rumlu, p. 268-9.
14. TAAA, 11, p. 882.
15. TAAA, 1, p. 326.
16. A native of Italian travels in Persia. Trans. C Gray, London, 1873, 11, 203, and 8 and 206.
17. Ibid., p. 223
18. Jalal -i Munajjim, Tarikh-i Abbasi, Tehran, Makek Library, no. 3762, Sheet 2a.
19. Ibid., sheet 200a.
20. Ibid., sheet 238a-239b.
21. TAAA, 1, p. 153.
22. Seeing the body of Shaybak Khan, Shah Ismail hit it angrily with his sword and ordered the Sufis to eat his body (Rowzat-al-Safaviyyeh, Mirzabek Junabadi, Falsafi, 1, 184).
23. For more information on the enimity between Qizilbash leaders and Shah Abbas I, refer TAAA, 1, 184).
24. Falsafi, 1, p.186.
25. J Rypka, History of Iranian literature, Dodrecht, 1968, p. 292.
26. Tadhkirat-ul-Mulk, trans., and commented by V. Minorsky, E J W. Gibb Memorial series, new series. XVI, London, 1943, pp. 13-14.
27. J S Trimingham, The sufi orders in Islam, p. 99.
28. Klaus Michael RoohrBorn, Provinzen und Zentralgewalt Persiens im 16, und Jahrhun-dert Libertragen ins persische von K. jahan-dari, 1971, Tehran, p. 58.
29. Riza-Gulkhan Hedayat, Ravzat-al-Safay-e Naseri, 10 vols., Qum, 1960, VIII, p. 586.

Revised and edited; originally published in Islam and the Modern Age, vol. IX, No. 2.

9

Sufism and the Concept of Knowledge

S M RAHMAN & OTHERS

Sufism is simply one of the schools of Islamic life. And here knowledge is discussed as understood by sufis: Seeking ilm is an ordinance obligatory upon every Muslims.

Sufism: A cursory glance on the history of the great religions demonstrates, beyond doubt, that the prophets, the lawgivers, and the promulgators of the Faiths have invariably been beset with one very serious difficulty. It is the conflict between knowledge and ignorance, the heart and the head, science and superstition, which, at times, becomes irreconcilable. The up-ward and downward movement of thought has in its clusiveness, been the despair of many of these.

The educated, and the intelligentsia, struggle hard to raise the Faith to a higher pedestal of intellect, and endeavour to impart a philosophical setting to it, while the uneducated, equally persistently, try to drag it down to its pristine plane. No religion, known to history, has been immune from this "internal conflict". That Sufism, like all other philosophical and mystical schools of thought in Christianity, Hinduism and Buddhism, owes its origin to this universal tendency of the human mind, will be apparent if we study the genesis of this school of thought in Islam.

European writers, who always try to show that all good ideas emanate from the West, identify the word "Sufi" with *sophos,* a Greek word, meaning wise. In the earlier period the term Sufism connoted one whose clothes were of wool (Ar. Suf) i.e., coarse clothing, the cotton fabrics of Dacca and Calicut being the monopoly of the nobility in those days, and avoided every kind of luxury and ostentation. The name of "Pushminaposh" was, therefore, given to Sufis in Persia. Some feel that it is derived from the "Ahlu'l-Suffah," or the "people of the bench". However, the popular conception is that it is derived from "Safa," which means purity.

We know that the Prophet (peace be on him) preached the Creed to the simple sons of the desert, whose intellectual horizon was confined to the oases, dotted here and there in the midst of their parched homeland. They were a plain folk, real children of nature, who occasionally came in contact, in the course of their commercial peregrinations, with learned men among the Christians and the Jews inhabiting the fertile plains of Palestine and Syria. This contact had but helped to distort their notions of religion and confirm their faith in the worship of "Lat" and "Manat." That period was also an epoch of disintegration—national, social and religious. The never-ending wrangling of warring creeds and rituals had converted some of the simplest faiths into an eternal labyrinth of sacerdotal speculations. Never in the history of the world was there greater necessity for the promulgation of a simple creed. The message delivered by the Arabian Prophet was meant alike for high and low, peasant and prince, learned and unlearned, and, therefore, consisted of a set simple formulas that could be understood by the most ignorant. But the great Prophet fully realised that no faith can claim homage from the intellectual section of its followers unless it is given a philosophical turn. For this reason alone, to satisfy the cravings of the intellectuals, the school of Sufism came into existence.Though one of the four premier schools of Sufism traces its origin to Abu Bakr(R.A), there is a consensus of historical opinion on the point that Ali (R.A), alone, is the founder of all the four schools into which the Sufis are divided.

It will be abundantly clear from the above that Sufism is not a sect in Islam, but only a philosophical aspect of that great Faith. It has simply sought to interpret some of the most fundamental principles of Islam on the higher plane of thought, and is nothing but its intellectual foundation.

Knowledge, Love, and Renunciation, form the keynote of Sufism. Owing to the abstruseness of its principles, its teachings have always been kept exclusive, and the institution of the Preceptor and the Disciple has become its permanent feature. In spite of these precautions, the masses have always tried to abuse some of its most important precepts. Light, according to the Sufis, can only come with knowledge. Real knowledge is the knowledge of God, and knowledge of God connotes retirement into the innermost recesses of one's soul, which alone contains the Light. It further connotes, says the Sufi, complete surrender to God and—as its necessary concomitant—the shutting out of all knowledge except that of God. This process of concentration should, after laborious training, end in the extermination of the Self and complete absorption in the Light itself, in Him "Who dwells and works everywhere and Whose home is the human heart." This object (Fana fi'llah) home is the human heart." This object (Fana fi'llah) can be attained, first by the surrender of the Self to the Shaikh (Fana fi'sh-shaikh), and, then, surrender to the Prophet (Fana-fi'r-rasul). The shutting of the bodily eyes and the opening of the spiritual eyes was thus the be-all and end-all of a Sufi's life. This belief in the all-pervading God naturally originated the theory of the Universality of Love. If God is Omnipresence, the whole creation is nothing but the manifestation of Him. Therefore, the creation must be identical with the Creator. If the creation is believed to be identical with the nothing but love should pervade the creation itself. Everything in this universe should be loved, and by loving the handiwork of the Creator, we can love the Creator; and the complete surrender of Self is nothing but this Universal Love. The Sufis argued, that Love must be the First Cause, as it alone has real existence and is self-sufficing, whilst everything else is unreal and has only a dream-life. "O may God! I invoke Thee in public as Lords are invoked, but in private as loved ones are invoked. Publicly I say, 'O my Lord,' but privately I say 'O my Beloved," cries a Sufi-philosopher in ecstasy.

Once this doctrine had taken root, as against the schismatics, the Sufis began to believe that there is truth in every religion and, as truth is always originally one, all the religion were originally one. Only they were altered by men to suit their purposes. This attitude led to the sympathetic study of the different religions of the world, and the mystic teachings present in them did not fall on deaf ears. It should be remembered, however, that the Sufis never forgot to search for sanctions for their acts in the Quran and the Ahadith. This also inevitably led on to asceticism, self-sacrifice, or self-renunciation, and mortification of the flesh thus became one of the most important doctrines of their creed. The `ulama had become immersed in outward forms and practices. The conquest of the Middle East and Persian had opened the coffers of the "Kaisars" and glutted Arabia with untold wealth, which, in its turn, had given rise to untold evils. The Prophet himself and his immediate Companions lived a very simple and austere life. Asceticism, therefore, soon took firm root in Sufism. "Ahlu'l-bait," the members of the Prophet's family, were confirmed ascetics. The Caliph 'Ali, both by precept and practice, taught self-renunciation, without which salvation was not to be attained. We find from his famous sermons, collected by Imam Sharif Raza, in "Nahju'l-Balaghat, that complete abstinence is the only means of true Knowledge and Love.

The pure, we may say, the sublime and exalted side of this philosophy was subsequently developed by Ghazzali, Ibn Tufail, Jalaluddin Rumi, and Farid-uddin Attar, and, in course of time, certain platonic conceptions became a part and parcel of it. The doctrine of evolution and progressive development began to be adhered to most tenaciously. The doctrine may be summarised thus:

"In the region of existing matter, the mineral kingdom, comes lowest, then comes the vegetable kingdom, then the animal, and finally the human being. Above him is God. The lowest is linked by a chain of progress to the high-est. The human soul perpetually strives to cast off the bonds of matter, and, becoming free, it soars upwards again to God from Whom it emanated." The theory has found expression in the world-renowned Mathnavi of Maulana Rum, and the beautiful couplets are often recited by the Darvishes in their halkas, during transports of ecstasy. The incorporation of this philosophy in the Mathnavi, a book which is called the "Quran in Persian" by the Sufis, (Mathnavi-i-Maulvi-i-Manwi hust Quran dar zaban-i-phalwi) is an important landmark in the history of Sufism.

A comparative study of Sufism and Vedant brings into relief many striking points of contact, on account of which certain bigoted 'ulama have not been slow to pass strictures on Sufism and condemn it as an unwarranted innovation in Islam. They erroneously infer, from certain well-known affinities, that the doctrines of Sufism must have been borrowed from Vedant. Human nature being what it is, unconscious coincidence of doctrines is one of the commonest features of the development of the great religions of the world.

The idea got elaborated both in Sufism and Vedantism, that the spirit of man, when completely purified by contemplation, religious fervour and love, becomes that of God from Whom it is an emanation. One, who makes a deep study of contemplative and mystical theory and aspires to His Communion by spiritual means, is the Sannyasi of Vedantism and the Darvish of Sufism. Bodh of the Brahmin is Ilm (knowledge) of the Sufi. Both equally vehemently declare that the emancipation of the soul is impossible without knowledge. A class of laterday Sufis, the Baktashis, hold that the soul, after separation from the human frame, may enter into the body of an animal or a man. This belief, which is not shared by the generality of the Sufis, is, more or less, in conformity with the theory of Avagawan, or Transmigration of the Soul, and they call it Tanasukh. The Isma'ilis, the followers of the Agha Khan, had borrowed the doctrine from the Baktashis, before their flight from Persia, their homeland. Uppadhi is nothing but the nafs, and the 'Alam-i-Misal (the world of illusion) is almost identical with the Maya of the Vedantic philosophy.

These parallels between the Semitic and Aryan schools of contemplative philosophy, which could easily be multiplied, are the most enthralling study of the universality of the human mind, which is essentially one, despite the differences of creed, climate and country.

Sufism has undergone considerable deterioration, at the hands of self-seeking men, the bane of all religions. But even the most virulent critic of Sufism cannot gainsay the fact that this mystical and contemplative element in Islam has bettered the lives of thousands of devout Muslims, and has added a great idealism to their Faith. The idylls of that Universal Divine Love, which pervades nature from the lowest type of God's creation to the highest, sung in rapturous strains by Rumi and Attar, are among the most beautiful productions of our Prophet's followers.

The Sufi Concept of Obligatory Knowledge

It is well-known to Muslims, including the Sufi and orientalists that the Prophet Muhammad (may peace be upon him!) said, "To seek knowledge (*al- `ilm*) is an ordinance obligatory upon every Muslim." Although this Tradition (*hadith*) is not to be found in any of the six canonical collections of Traditions (*sihah sittah*) other than the *Sunan* of Ibn Majah, and although it is considered to be a 'weak' (*da'if*) Tradition, it is stated strongly by Muslims, including the Sufis, and often quoted by them in support of the view that Islam has attached tremendous value and importance to knowledge, education and instruction. They argue that weakness in the chain of narration of this well-known Tradition does not warrant its rejection, because its meaning and content are in full accord with many correct *(sahih)* traditions on the value of knowledge to be found in those six collections as well as in the reputed biographies.

The Prophet's attribution of great value and importance to knowledge is an explanation and elaboration of great value briefly attached to knowledge in the Qur'an. "Say: can those who know be like those who do not know?" 'He gives wisdom to him whom He pleases, and whoever is given wisdom has indeed been given abundant good." However, neither the Qur'an nor the Prophet has put forward a theory of knowledge, whether brief or detailed, although from a thorough analysis of their teachings on different subjects, including knowledge, relevant theories may somehow be formulated. Basically the Qur'an is not a work giving abstract theories and formulae, nor is the Prophet a theoretical man engaged in abstract thinking and armed-chair theorizing. The teachings of both the Qur'an and Prophet are fully practical in nature, aiming at providing mankind with guidance (*hidayah*) in all aspects of life.

Sometime after the Prophet, however, Muslim intellectuals started formulating theories of knowledge for reasons which need not be mentioned here. The jurists (*fuqaha'*) and the theologians (*mutakallimun*) discussed epistemological problems to a certain degree, but elaborate and comprehensive discussions of these problems were made by the philosophers and the orthodox Sufis of the medieval times in different perspectives. However, there were differences between the discussions made by these two groups of Muslim intellectuals. The philosophers' treatment of the subject is less comprehensive but much more abstract and theoretical in nature than that of the orthodox Sufis; their mainly theoretical motive is variously described by such phrases as 'satisfaction of intellectual curiosity,' and 'knowledge for the sake of knowledge.' In all this, as in their other theories, they are deeply influenced by Greek philosophers, especially Plato, Aristotle and the Nepolatonists, whose mainly theoretical motive of philosophizing is well-known. The orthodox Sufis, by contrast, are almost exclusively influenced by the teachings of the Qur'an and the *Sunnah*, and since these teachings are thoroughly practical in nature, the Sufis' treatment of the problem of knowledge has assumed the same practical character. The Sufis are not 'men of words' (*ashab aqwal*), on the contrary they are men of action, believing that knowledge which is not acquired for action is no better than ignorance. With such an attitude towards knowledge the Sufis have dealt with epistemological problems most elaborately, formulating theories on different aspects of cognition—theories which aim at providing Muslims with such knowledge as may really be useful to them.

Among those medieval Sufis who have discussed epistemological problems in detail the most prominent are the Baghdadian Sufi Shaykh Abu Talib Muhammad al-Makki (d. 386/996) and the great Imam Abu Hamid Muhammad al-Ghazali (d. 505/1111). The former is a Traditionist and Sufi and head of the theological school of the Salimiyah of Basra. He was devoted the 31st chapter of the first volume of his principal Sufi work, *Qut al-Qulub fi Mu'amalat al-Mahbub*, to a discussion of knowledge and the learned men. The chapter is divided into many sections dealing with different aspects of knowledge considered relevant to the contemporary Islamic society. The discussion starts with an enquiry into the knowledge which God, through His Apostle, ordered every Muslim to seek. Another independent work of al-Makki entitled *Kitab al-'Ilm* is devoted to epistemological discussions. In a whole chapter of this work the problem of obligatory knowledge is treated, but some parts of this treatment are more detailed than, while other are an abridgment of, their corresponding parts of the discussion made in the *Qut al-Qulub*. In this, as in many other aspects of Sufi doctrines and practices, his influence upon al-Ghazali has been tremendous—a fact which al-Ghazali himself states in his *al-Munqidh*. In view of the extreme need of knowledge for religio-mystical practices al-Ghazali deals with the problem of knowledge in the very first 'book' *(kitab)* of his magisterial *Ihya.'* He divides this book into seven chapters, the second of which is partly devoted to a discussion of the knowledge, the seeking of which is binding upon every individual Muslim. This paper aims at representing only the view of al-Makki on this knowledge, for it is complete in itself and has a strong influence upon subsequent Sufis. The theory of al-Ghazali which is even more complete may be considered in a separate article.

Shaykh Abu Talib al-Makki's treatment of the obligatory knowledge mentioned in the Tradition, "To seek knowledge (*al `ilm*) in an ordinance obligatory upon every Muslim." has two parts: on dealing with his own opinion, and the other considering the views of others, most of whom were his predecessors from different categories of intellectuals. He does not subscribe to these views wholly, although he appears to appreciate them. His own theory deserves consideration here first in view of the fact that it is subsequent, more developed, more correct and thus more important than the views of others.

Al-Makki's own opinion is that obligatory knowledge is the knowledge of those five actions on which Islam is based. They are; "the testimony (*shahadah*) that there is not god but Allah and that Muhammad is His servant and messenger, the performance of ritual prayer, the payment of *zakah,* the pilgrimage to the (holy) House, and the fasting during (the lunar month) Ramadan." To prove that knowledge of these five actions is binding upon every Muslim al-Makki argues as follows:

Only these five actions are obligatory upon Muslims—no other

> action is binding upon them; an action is correct if its agent has knowledge of it; so knowledge of these five actions must be obligatory.

This argument al-Makki explains:

> The first thing about an action is knowledge of it. Thus knowledge of an action becomes obligatory if the action is obligatory. Since only these five actions are obligatory upon Muslims, seeking knowledge of these five has become obligatory, for it is obligatory of the obligatory.

Al-Makki includes knowledge of Divine unity (*'ilm al-tawhid*) in the knowledge of the five basic actions, for the first concern of knowledge of Divine unity is with `the testimony that there is no god but God,' through the affirmation of the attributes attached to His essence, and the negation from Him of the attributes of other-than-Him. All this is included in the knowledge of 'the testimony that there is no god but God." Thus that part of Islamic theology (*'ilm al-kalam*) which deals with Divine unity is, in al-Makki's opinion, binding upon every individual Muslim.

Al-Makki also includes knowledge of sincerity (*'ilm al-ikhlas*) in the knowledge of the five basic actions, for sincerity is a stipulation for the correctness of one's Islam, as evident from a Tradition to the effect that one cannot be Muslim unless one performs devotional acts (*'ibadat*) sincerely for God. Sincerity is stressed in the Qur'an as well.

Aside from the argument stated above, al-Makki puts forward what he calls a "basic proof" by obligatory knowledge the Prophet did not mean knowledge of everything that is possible to be known, for there is a 'consensus of the Muslim community' (*Ijma' al-ummah*) that he did not mean sciences of medicine, astronomy, grammar, poetry and warfare, although the term knowledge is applicable to all these and their possessors are called knowers. There is also a 'consensus' that the Prophet meant neither the sciences of legal decisions and judgements, nor the science of different schools of

Islamic jurisprudence and different opinions on legal matters. None of these forms of knowledge is obligatory upon *all* Muslims according to the 'consensus,' whereas a grammatico-linguistic analysis of the Tradition under consideration shows that the Prophet meant in it a specific knowledge which is obligatory upon *all* Muslims. The analysis is: the word 'kul', meaning all, shows that the intended knowledge is binding upon all, not on some, Muslims; the term *al-'ilm*, a noun—made definite by adding the letters *alif* and *lam* to the word *`ilm*—shows that what is intended is something definite and already known, to which the word 'knowledge' is applicable. Since the possibility of the Prophet's intending sciences of medicine, legal decisions, etc., is thus absent it is correct to assert that what he intended by obligatory knowledge is only the knowledge of the five obligatory actions on which Islam is based, for without knowledge these actions cannot be correct.

To prove that only these five basic actions are binding, so that obligatory knowledge is only the knowledge of these five and not of any other, al-Makki cites a Tradition to the effect that once an *a'rabi* (villager) asked the Prophet about what God has made obligatory upon him. The Prophet replied: the testimony, ritual prayer, the fast of Ramadan, *zakah* and the pilgrimage. The *a'rabi* asked, "is any other action obligatory upon me?" The Prophet replied, "No. You may, however, perform supererogatory acts." The *a'rabi* said, "By God, I shall do nothing more not less than these five." The Prophet said," He shall succeed and enter Paradise if he is true." This Tradition proves that only these five actions are obligatory upon a Muslim. Since without knowledge no action is correct, knowledge of these five acts must be obligatory.

If knowledge of the five basic actions is what the Prophet meant by obligatory knowledge the question arises as to why he did not specifically say this. Al-Makki replies to this question, saying that God made acquisition of knowledge obligatory through many Qur'anic verses, seven of which he cites partly. Then the Prophet made five actions obligatory through the two Traditions quoted above. Then he briefly said, "Secking knowledge is obligatory." Then he emphasized this using the phrase, "on every Muslim." Thus the term knowledge here obviously refers to those five actions which have already been made obligatory; for the sake of brevity they are not mentioned again; instead of mentioning them again a noun with a definite article, i.e. *al-`ilm* (the knowledge), is used in order to allude to them. Thus an explanation of the Tradition is: seeking knowledge of those actions on which Islam is based is obligatory upon every Muslim because of their obligatoriness.

Knowledge in general, al-Makki says, cannot be obligatory upon every individual, because some forms of knowledge are not useful and some are even harmful, and ignorance is better than these kinds of knowledge. In support of this point al-Makki cites a Tradition that the Prophet regarded knowledge of poetry, genealogy and the days of the Arabs as not useful for action or for drawing man towards God, so that lack of this knowledge is not harmful. He cites another Tradition that the Prophet sought protection of God against a knowledge which is not useful. All this proves that knowledge in general cannot be regarded as binding upon every Muslim.

In the second part of al-Makki's treatment of obligatory knowledge eleven views are stated together with proofs and evidence. These views are held by his predecessors as well as his contemporaries from among Sufis, theologians, jurist, religious scholars and devotees. Al-Makki divides them into (a) those who are concerned with man's inward self (*ahl al-batin*), i.e. Sufis, and (b) those who are concerned with man's outward self (*ahl al-zahir*). The different views of the former group based on interpretation (*ta'vil*) of the Tradition on obligatory knowledge quoted above, are near to each other in meaning, though not in words. The latter group took the outward meaning of the Tradition and, accordingly, formed opinions on obligatory knowledge. These opinions are different from those of the Sufis, but not in conflict with them; rather these are complementary to them, as the body is to the soul. Al-Makki, therefore, evaluates the views of both groups as "good and possible" opinions, though he does not accept them wholly. Only a small part of them, i.e., the part dealing with Divine unity and sincerity, he incorporates into his own theory.

These eleven views need not be discussed here in detail, for these are not fully correct in the opinion of al-Makki. Their importance is mainly historical, and hence it will be sufficient here to mention them very briefly together with the names of those who held them.

	Scholars	*Views on Obligatory Knowledge*
1.	Sufi Abu Muhammad Sahl al-Tustari:	Knowledge of the state (*'ilm al-hal*) existing between man and God.
2.	Some gnostics (*al-'arifun*):	Knowledge of gnosis (*'ilm al-ma 'rifah*).
3.	Some scholars of Syria, e.g. 'Abd al-Rahman ibn Yahya al-Armavi and his followers:	Knowledge of sincerity (*'ilm al-ikhlas*), evils of the outward self (*nafs*) and its suggestions, guiles of the devil and his deceptions, and what causes good and bed deeds.
4.	Some devotees and Sufis of Basra, e.g. Malim ibn Dinar, 'Abd al-Vahid ibn Zayd and his followers from devotees (*nussak*) and their preceptor al-Hasan al-Basri:	Knowledge of the outward self and details of passing thought (*khavatir*).
5.	Devotees (*'ubbad*) of Syria, e.g. Ibrahim ibn Adham, Yusuf ibn Asbat, Wuhayb ibn al-Ward, and Habib ibn Harb:	Knowledge of what is lawful (*halal*) according to the *Shari'ah*.
6.	A group of gnostics:	Knowledge concerned with man's inward self (*'ilm al batin*).
7.	Devotees (*nussak*) of Basra:	Knowledge of the Islamic faith (*'ilm al-Imam*).
8.	Some righteous scholars of early Islam (*salaf*):	Knowledge of the most essential part of Divine unity (*'ilm al-tawhid*)
9.	Some jurists (*fuqaha'*) of Kufa, e.g. Imam Abu Hanifa, Sufyan al-Thawri, and their followers:	Knowledge of sales and purchase, marriage and divorce, etc., when intention is made to involve in these contracts.

10.	Some early scholars of Khurasan, e.g. Ibn al-Mubarak and some Traditionists:	Sometimes a man intends to do a religious deed, or a question concerning belief in God or worship of Him occurs to his mind. Seeking correct knowledge of this deed or correct answer to this question is obligatory upon him.
11.	Harith al-Muhasibi and those theologians who followed him, Abu Thawr Ibrahim ibn Khalid al-Kalbi, Dawud ibn 'Ali, and al-Husayn al-Karabisi:	Knowledge of those things or deeds about the lawfulness of which there is doubt (*shubahat*); and knowledge of those actions or affairs, on the lawfulness of which it is difficult to decide (*mushkilat*).

As to the methods of seeking obligatory knowledge al-Makki states different opinions held by scholars just mentioned. Thus some of them maintained that this knowledge should be acquired by way of proofs and evidence. Some considered research and reflection to be the correct methods. Some believed that from the teachings of the Qur'an and Tradition obligatory knowledge should be sought. The Sufis added their personal experiences to all these three methods.

In the first section an effort is made to determine the sources from which the Sufi concept of obligatory knowledge originates. It has been found that the source is a Tradition recorded in the *Sunan* of Ibn Majah, and that for practical reasons some orthodox Sufis of the medieval times have sought to specify the knowledge which was unspecifically mentioned in that Tradition to be obligatory upon every Muslim. In the second section is given an account of al-Makki's view as well as the views of eleven other scholars or groups of scholars on obligatory knowledge. The account given there is purely descriptive, having no critical examination or evaluation of them whatsoever. It seems proper to undertake, in the present section, a somewhat impartial evaluation of these views—impartial in the sense of having no undue sympathy for, or prejudice against, them.

The views deserving an evaluation first are those which were held by scholars other than al-Makki, for these views were prior to his own theory and exerted an influence, however small, upon it.

Some of these views held by esotericists (*ahl al-batin*) and gnostics (*ahl al-ma'rifah*) are: by the obligatory knowledge the Prophet meant knowledge of the state between man and God, afflictions of the outward self, the devil and his guiles, details of passing thoughts and so on. These views have not been accepted by al-Makki as fully correct, although he speaks of them as "good and possible" (*hasan wa muhtamal*). It seems that anyone familiar with the nature of prophetic teaching will find it obvious that the Prophet did not make acquisition of knowledge of these mystical things obligatory upon every Muslim. This point may be made clear by elucidating the nature of Prophetic teaching: All teachings of the Prophet may be subsumed under two broad categories: general and special. The latter was taught to some, not all, companions (*sahabah*) when they sought guidance about certain matters related to the higher level of faith (*iman*) and action (*'amal*) appropriate to the higher level of paradise. These matters are very subtle and difficult in nature and, therefore, comprehensible and appreciable only by men of superior intelligence and serious interest. Examples of such men from among the Companions are: 'Ali ibn Abi Talib, Abu Hurayrah, Hudhayfah ibn al-Yaman, and Abu Dharr al-Ghifari. Hudhayfah privately received from the Prophet knowledge about many subtle matters and was called *"sahib al-sirr"* (possessor of secret). "One of such matters is the hidden signs of hypocrisy (*nifaq*) in addition to its obvious signs made known publicly to all Companions.

The general teachings of the Prophet, on the other hand, were addressed to all people of his community (*ummah*), including the less intelligent multitude. The nature of these teachings consists in simplicity, clarity and easy comprehensibility in respect of exposition as well as subject-matter, so that they are comprehensible to all sane, adult human beings. If any general teaching is not of this nature but ascribed to the Prophet, then doubt may be entertained about its genuineness. There are such subtle and difficult matters as are beyond the intelligence of most people, and so the Prophet prohibited them from making efforts to understand these. Examples of such matters are: the inmost of the soul (*sirr al-ruh*) and the inmost nature of predestination (*sirr al-qadar*). Now, since simplicity, clarity and comprehensibility are generally recognized to form the nature or mark of Prophetic teachings of the general type, one can safely assert that the Prophet did not make it obligatory upon every Muslim to acquire knowledge of such mystical issues as the relationship between man and God, afflictions of self, details of passing thoughts, etc., for these subtle, complicated, inward matters are incomprehensible to general people, whereas the knowledge which he made obligatory must be sought by such people as well. If these matters are considered in light of the criteria of simplicity, clarity and intelligibility, it becomes apparent that it is highly unlikely that knowledge of them is meant in the Tradition on obligatory knowledge which is of general type. Thus the interpretation (*ta'vil*) of this Tradition which the esotericists and the gnostics made in order to hold the views that knowledge of the state, etc., is what was meant by the Prophet is not correct.

As for the scholars who do not interpret Traditions but accept their outward meaning (*ahl al-zahir*), their views were: by the obligatory knowledge the Prophet meant knowledge of sales and purchase, marriage and divorces, principle of Divine commands and prohibitions and so on. These things are clear and understandable to general people; yet al-Makki's rejection of these views seems justifiable on the ground that these things are not binding upon every Muslim, whereas knowledge of a thing becomes binding upon him if the thing itself is equally binding.

Coming to al-Makki's own theory we find that its sole concern is with the question of "what" obligatory knowledge, and that the question of "how" is totally omitted. It assumes that knowledge itself, a mental process, is neither good, nor bad, nor obligatory, etc., but that it becomes good, bad or obligatory according to the goodness, badness or obligatoriness of the object known. This assumption seems to be correct and is later incorporated in the theory of al-

Ghazali. In the light of this assumption both al-Makki and al-Ghazali have sought to determine the obligatory form of knowledge. The core of al-Makki's argument in found to be this: since it is the obligatory knowledge, of which the Prophet spoke, its object must be something obligatory; since the things obligatory upon every Muslim are only five actions, it is the knowledge of performance of only these five which must be regarded as obligatory. This argument is also logically valid, and hence its main elements, too, are incorporated in al-Ghazali's theory. However, al-Makki's statement that only the five actions are binding upon every Muslim is not fully correct, for al-Ghazali subsequently shows that there are other obligatory actions, seeking knowledge of which is also obligatory upon every Muslim.

The question of "how" (*kayfiyah*) has different aspects, two of which are most important. One of them concerns the methods of acquisition of obligatory knowledge, and the other deals with the manner in which its acquisition becomes obligatory, i.e., the acquisition becomes obligatory at once or gradually. These aspects have totally been omitted in al-Makki's own theory, but are, later on, discussed in detail by al-Ghazali. The extent of obligatory knowledge which is to be acquired about an action is also not mentioned by al-Makki; it is later specified by al-Ghazali. Thus al-Makki's theory, though correct in essential elements, suffers from omissions and inaccuracies.

Despite its shortcomings al-Makki's theory is important inasmuch as it is the first correct, though incomplete, answer to the question concerning the form of knowledge stated obligatory in a Tradition. These shortcomings have later been removed by a greater thinker, al-Ghazali, and consequently a better and complete theory of obligatory knowledge has evolved. Most Muslims have accepted it as fully correct, but some intellectuals have put forward different theories of their own.

(Revised and edited; originally appeared in Islamic Culture, and a miscellany).

10

The Sufi Concept of Knowledge and its Implications for the Life

MIR VALIUDDIN

> To know Him in all His attributes and the way these manifest themselves in the infinity of things and in the untold conditions and states of spiritual existence...lies the primary end of knowledge.

The first revealed verse, "Read! In the name of thy Lord who createth", with its categorical injunction to read lays an undeniable emphasis on that aptitude of man which the Creator has endowed him with as pre-eminently human. The *raison d'etre* of man, the `why' of his being cannot be but to understand and learn and, with this purpose in view, Divine Wisdom has equipped man with senses for observation and reason for deduction. The object of knowledge can only be primarily the world within and the world without and ultimately the Creator of all that is within and without. The knowledge of God presupposes appreciation of the signs that speak from within the order of nature. The Qur'an beholds in the knowledge of God alone the end of life. What more can bring peace and tranquility to man and be a life-giving solace to him in his hours of travail and moments of despair than the realization of God and the constant awareness of His all-pervading presence. As Rumi says:

Ye ! Everybody, tell me who is better then He
With whom, even from a moment, can I be happy?
Seek I neither happiness nor Kingship,
Seek I from Thee—Thyself?

The primary end of knowledge, then, is the gnosis of God; in other words, to know Him in all His attributes and the way they manifest themselves in the infinity of things and in the untold conditions and states of spiritual existence. If guided by the light of the Qur'anic injunction, reason subordinates itself to revelation and reflects back on the world, every leaf waxes eloquent in praise of God and every particle of existence becomes and irrefutable witness of His unity and the world at large grows into a reflection of His beauty. For him who has eyes to see, says the famous Persian poet and mystic, Shaikh Muslih al-Din Sa'di, the world indeed mirrors His beauty. When faith awakens to a world resplendent with divine beauty, the mind glows with His love and is suffused with His awe and knows a delight all its own, a bliss truly divine. "His remembrance eliminates sorrow," says Rumi:

> *O God! In thy remembrance my*
> *soul goes into ecstasy,*
> *In thy remembrance it hath beholden me*
> *of grief.*
> *The delights of the world are trodden under*
> *my feet,*
> *In thy remembrance such is the delight that*
> *I feel.*

When the knowledge of God is attained to the full and realized in all its significance and import, we are directed to know what actions, beliefs and states of mind conform to Divine approval and what run counter to His will. The Qur'an has explained at length what God approves and what He does not approve to detailing its views on faith, unity, sincerity, constancy, remembrance and absorption in God and His realization, and has not minced words on the crooked ways in which man invariably falls when he resorts to *shirk*, (i.e., joins others in divinity and worship of God), hypocrisy, innovations, apostasy, ignorance and absorption in the creation. The Qur'an has further stated at length the characteristics of the "men of the Right Hand" and "the men of the Left Hand." None but God bestows good and evil, knowledge that is guidance and knowledge that leads man astray, and it is none but He "who enables us to distinguish the good from the evil" "its enlightenment as to its wrong and its right."

It is He who inspires into us piety and through him also misdeeds first sink into our hearts.

No wonder that they who are blessed with knowledge in all its truth and purity act accordingly, in full conformity with the divine approval, and eschew everything that runs counter to the dispensations of His will. 'Let Thy will be done' is their motto. When their efforts are crowned with success they rise from the august place of 'the men of the Right Hand' to the rank of the chosen few who enjoy 'His company, the *muqarrabun*, and seek their ever lasting abode in Him. They live in and move with and have their being in God; to speak with St. Paul in the Sufi way, as a poet says:

I desire to live longing for Thee alone,
Be dust and be underneath Thy feet;
Broken and perplexed, of all the worlds, I quest
for Thee alone,
I wish and desire to live and die for Thee and for Thee
alone.

The above are the ends of knowledge as determined by the Qur'an. Imam Ahmad has quoted Ma'ruf for the saying that true knowledge is the fear of God. "The fear of the Lord is the beginning of wisdom"[1] declares also the Bible in unmistakable terms. The basis of knowledge is the fear that drives us to God. The love and the fear of God brings God nearer. Indeed it is the knowledge that kindles and fans enthusiasm and yearning in the soul and this can come about only by the knowledge of divine Attribues and Names. Next, in the order of value, is the knowledge that imparts the imperatives and injunctions that have been ordained by His will and words and the deeds that please Him. The *Sunna* or tradition calls this knowledge alone valuable or useful in the best sense of the words. The increase in and growth of such knowledge is prayed for. "Lord, let the knowledge that thou hast taught me bring me good and let me grow in knowledge and impart me knowledge from which I can derive benefit." Another tradition calls for 'useful' knowledge and seeks protection from knowledge that brings no good. "Lord, I ask of Thee knowledge that brings good and seek Thy protection from knowledge that is in vain."

He who has been graced with this knowledge has found as its fruits a God-fearing heart, a contented soul, and his prayers seldom come to nought but receive the gift of being heard of. His heart is now too big for the world, says Shaikh Akbar:

The mind big enough for God cannot be
Narrowed for the world: Did you get me, Listener?

His heart has a breadth that surpasses the expanse of the universe and indeed he holds all that the world has to offer in light steem.

Let us reflect for a while on the fruits borne by the knowledge that alone can bring us in conformity with the station assiged to us by God. The soul becomes God-fearing, the mind become content and prayer assumes a quality which ordinarily it may not have. In result, we are awarded necessarily the following:

i. A God-fearing Soul

When knowledge sinks into the heart, the heart becomes 'broken' and awed. Over-powered by Divine Majesty it regards itself as nought and feels humble in love and reverence. Inspired with love and filled with fear, knowledge grows in full and culminates in a surrender and resignation without any reserve or restraint. The famous lines of Sa'di speak of this condition:

In the country of the two Balks a pious man I came across:
Said I! Train to cleanse me of my ignorance;
Said he! Be patient Ye like the dust,
Or, bury all that thou hath learnt into dust.

The fruit of knowledge is fear of God and fear of God is given only to the chosen few who have knowledge. Ibn Mas'ud says:

Knowledge which breeds fear of God is enough,
For arrogance (and conceit) towards God ignorance is enough.

But knowledge cannot be confused with unsystematic tit-bits of it, however rich and extensive they may be. One may cram one's head with such tit-bits and stray anecdotes without even touching the fringe of knowledge. "The man who fears God is the man of knowledge and the learned one, and he who disobeys God is the ignoramus." Rudolf Otto, with his concept of *mysterium tremendum*, appears to have an inkling of the significance of the fear of God in the development of religious consciousness.

When we know what constitutes knowledge and who a man of knowledge truly is, we cannot freely accord the dignity of a scholar to one and sundry. Imam Sha'bi was wont to say to the scholars of his day: "You are no men of knowledge but intellectual dandies. You take delight in intellectual discussions and this delight is what you aim at and to this goal you dedicate yourselves." The man of knowledge indeed acts for God, in God and with God. In other words, the man of knowledge endowed as he is with God's knowledge, filled as he is with God's fear, acts for God's sake and the end of all his endeavours is the approval and the love of God and God alone is the object of his love and desire. It is a pleasure to observe that even Kierkegaard, the father of modern Existentialism, strikes the note when he exclaims: "What is man without Thee! What is all his knowledge, even if it be rich in detail, but a fragment only, when he knows Thee not. What is his endeavour and striving, even if the world as a whole be its object, but incomplete and partial, when he knows Thee not, who is One and All."[2] And a poet sings:

Do away with the sorrows of the world, it's better.
Forget everything except Thy remembrance, it's better.
The eye that is not illumined by Thy light,
Tear it and throw away into dust, it's better.

ii. A contented Soul

The contented soul is the necessary outcome of a God-fearing disposition. When man humbles himself before God, the soul becomes reconciled with God and saves itself from the 'other'. He is now independent of all that is, and realize that as there exists nothing higher than God, we cannot aim and strive higher. He now attains all!

He reaches the august height of greatness and to him alone are addressed the words:

You alone are exalted: God is with you.

Even when man has attained all that he aims at, he remains dissatisfied: his invetrate desire and appetite says 'encore'. But when he has attained God, he comes to know Him; the world loses all its worth and becomes the object of his unreserved contempt. An ancient tradition of the Jews says:

"Son of Adam, ask Me and Thou shalt find me, and when Thou hast found Me Thou hast found all, and when Thou hast Me thou hast lost all. I should be more in your love than aught else." And a poet overpowered by divine fervour exclaims:

There is a recompense for all that you lose
But when you lose God there is no recompense.

Rumi expresses the same thing in his mellifluous language:

He who loves God more than himself,
Finds he the panacea of all his ills.
When he succeeds in being face to face with God's love,
He grows cool towards the world and its holdings glamorous.

With this attachment to and knowledge of God he becomes indifferent to the world and the ways of the world please him not. He seeks not worldly gain or honour. Fame he despises and riches the esteems lightly. He yearns not for a privileged place among his contemporaries. In the words of Imam Hasan, "He goes the way of piety and restraint in the world, inclines to the Next; has an insight in religion and becomes a devoted votary of the Lord." He envies not the great and laughs not at those who stand low. With the growth of his knowledge, the fear of God gains in strength and humility too grows apace. He lives for God and dies for God alone; he lives not for riches and wealth and dies not in sorrow and fear.

Now we may listen to what Jalal al-Din Rumi says in his characteristic vein:

He who follows the Everlasting Way of God's Commands,
To him life and death amount to the same.
For God and not for treasure he lives,
He dies for God and not in sorrow and fear.
His faith has His approval as its object.
He relishes not the Houris, fruits and the brooks.
Infidelity he avoids for God,
And not from fear of Hell.
He is happy as he has His approval
And God's will appears to him pleasing as sweetmeat.

iii. His Prayers are Accorded

When the heart is infused with prayer and is resplendent with His love and is satiated with the world, the finds delight in His remembrance, enjoyment in prayer and joy in the fulfilment of his duties. "Ask and it shall be given, knock and it shall be opened," says the Lord. His prayers are answered. A *hadith qudsi* promises: "When my votary approaches Me with his supererogatory works, I draw his near. Now he hears by Me, he sees by Me, he touches by Me, and by Me does he walk. If he asks of Me I give him, if he seeks refuge I grant him and if he prays I accord his prayers." When man has found God, his prayers are answered and he comes under complete divine protection. In these words had the Prophet given his testament to Ibn 'Abbas: "Boy, bear god constantly in your mind (i.e., do what is commanded and avoid what is not allowed and reconcile yourself with your destiny) and God with bear you in mind and protect you: Always have God in view (with the realization of His knowledge and with incessant awareness of His presence), remember Him so and you will find Him before you. (i.e., He will protect you against the ills of this world and the next). Remember Him in hours of tranquillity and peace and God will remember you in moments of distress and hardship (i.e., He will accord your prayers and remove your hardship)."

Says Rumi:

Life without Friends is life's agony.
Oblivion of God is being dead while alive.
Life and death are both pleasant with God.
Without God even the nectar of life is poison and fire.

We now see clearly how closely knit with life is the Sufi concept of knowledge. The great Christian Father of the Church, St. Augustine, had no doubts about the vanity of learning that alienated man from God and ended in scholastic trifles. "Behold, is not all this smoke and wind? Was there nothing else too on which I could exercise my wit and tongue."[3] The Sufi with his concept of knowledge aims at the transformation of man and delivers him from the vanity of words and deeds. When knowledge truly useful and valuable has accorded us the gains of a God-fearing soul, contented mind and the prayers have been graced with the virtue of acceptability, we become fully absorbs in God. Dead to the world we live and move with God. All that is other than God is left out and God is realized and found world of creation and engage ourselves with God; we leave the known and occupy ourselves with the knower. Behold where this knowledge leads to and the fruits that it bears! Let us then pray in all humility for "the knowledge that brings good and seek His protection from knowledge that yields no gain, from a heart that fears not, from an ego that remains unsatiated and from prayers that are made in vain."

REFERENCES

1. The Proverbs, 1:7.
2. Sorren Keirkegaard, Religion der Yat, p. 141.
3. St. Augustine, Confessions, p. 22.

(Revised and edited; originally published in Studies in Islam, July 1965)

11

Sufi Studies: Problems and Issues

E.A. POLIAKOVA

Describes the various patterns of studying the different tariqahs. What is required today is scholars from pass from abstractions to concrete problems and compare research of sufi works of individual writers and epochs.

The study of Sufi dogma was always considered to be of importance as Sufism had for ages a great influence on many Muslim countries. But such a study is difficult as Sufism is characterized by different interpretations. This fact makes it complicated to define various trends without knowledge of sufi treatises.

The first step of scholars, apart from a study of individual authors and works, had been to compile at least a general code of elements, common to the majority of interpretations. Such essays are presented, for instance, in works by E.A. Bertels and A. Schimmel. The former states: "Different trends of sufism are characterized by an extreme variety and single sufism had never existed. That is why, trying to mark out principles, more or less common to all trends, we inevitably approach great abstraction, which only approximately reflects the real state of things."[1]

One problem is the necessity of researching discrepancy between Sufi theory and Sufi poetry. It is generally known that from the earliest period Sufi poetry and theory existed simultaneously presenting specific rendering of various Sufi dogmata. In some research works on Sufism, the fact of the dependence of Sufi poets on Sufi theory is mentioned. Thus, A.J. Arberry touching upon one of the poems by

Sana'i (d. 525/1130 or 536/1141) states that this poem should be considered as an attempt to set to verses the ideas narrated in prose by such Arabic authors as Abu Nasr al-Sarraj al-Tusi, (d. 378/988), Abu al-Qasim al-Qushayri (d. 465/1072) and 'Abd Allah al-Ansari (d. 481/1088).[2]

Another rule which is marked by scholars is the influence of Sufi poets on the development of Sufi theory. For instance, E.H. Palmer declared that lyric poets had been theorists of Sufism.[3] He is certainly right. It is common knowledge that Jalal al-Din Rumi (604-672/1207-1273) was a founder of the Mawlawi order and had made a significant contribution to the development of the corresponding trend of Sufism though he had not been the author of any theoretical treatises.[4] In connection with such statements in generalized works, aimed at narration of the fundamental principles of Sufism, poetry is used equally with theoretical treatises.[5]

Beside natural community of ideas in Sufi theory and its poetical interpretations, scholars took notice of principal differences between them. For example, E.A. Bertels had marked a functional discrepancy between Sufi theory and poetry, as poems were intended to influence feeling of readers or listeners.[6] Besides, it was easier to express complicated Sufi dogmata through poetry. E.A. Bertels wrote bout one of the poems by Baba Kuhi: "This poem gives a vivid and lively picture of that very *hal* which theorists tried in vain to describe."[7]In addition, according to Bertels, poetry helped to conceal some extreme views, considered by Muslim clearly to be blasphemous, behind vague terms.[8] But this idea had been expressed in general outline. Now it is necessary to reveal some rules of such differences. To demonstrate the significance of this comparative analysis, I shall give some concrete examples.

Quite often the same terms being used in theory/prose and in poetry symbolized different and even opposite notions. Such a discrepancy can be found in one and the same treatise, in which rendering of theory is interfused with poems by the same author—tradition which had become almost compulsory. Poems were included in the majority of medieval prosaic works of various genres. For instance, in chronicles they usually played an important ideological part. While trying to introduce emotional colouring into their narration by means of verse, historians sometimes expressed in them their attitude to the events they described. Sharaf al-Din 'Ali Yazdi (d. A.D. 1454), the author of the history of Timur, *Zafarnamah*, having declared the official appreciation of Timur's activity, expressed in his verses, included into the chronicle, such a grief in connection with destruction of cities and countries that in fact in some cases he opposed the version presented in the prosaic text.[9]

I shall try to prove this idea using examples from the *Tamhidat*, a treatise by 'Ayn al-Qudat al-Hamadani (executed in 525/1130 or 533/1138-39), which is especially rich with versified insertions. The widespread Sufi term "idolatry" (*but-parasti*) is used in this treatise in two meanings. At its beginning, in the prosaic part the author declares the observance of traditional Muslim ceremonies to be idolatry, which should be rejected.[10] Many authoritative Sufi authors before and after 'Ayn al-Qudat al-Hamadani used this analogy, having a clear understanding of the difference between Muslim monotheism and pagan ideas. But this allegory had been so canonized by the time of 'Ayn al-Qudat that it became a Sufi term. Later, in the course of narration the author uses the term "idolatry" again in an allegorical sense, but in the case, being used in a versified insertion, it has a different meaning. In accordance with traditions of Sufi poetry the Beloved (that is God) was usually compared with an idol and correspondingly ecstatic love for God and striving for Him were called idolatry, while the *murid*, who had taken the path of spiritual perfection, was termed an idolater. So the author, following this tradition of Sufi poetry, called himself and those similar to him idolaters and profanes.[11] A number of poems, included into the treatise, are devoted to this idea.[12] Thus "idolatry" as a term of Sufi theory symbolized the thing that should be rejected decisively according to 'Ayn al-Qudat and the majority of other theorists. As for Sufi poetry, the same term, used by the same author, refers to the aim of recommended striving. It cannot be understood as a mere contradiction and should be classified as a literary method, characteristic of the medieval period when authors combined in one and the same work different genres, following their canons.

But the demonstrated transformation of terms does not exhaust the differences between Sufi poetry and theory. It is extremely important, from my point of view, to pay attention to the difference in accents. For instance, it is well-known that the leading theme of Sufi poetry is the love for God and presentation of corresponding emotions. As to theoretical treatises, love for God not only changes its meaning, having a number of shades not peculiar to the poetry, but also loses its central position. The significance of this discrepancy is especially vivid in the work by 'Abd Allah Ansari, which is known by the title *Manazil al-Sa'irin* (*Pseudo-Manazil*).[13]

In the cases where 'Abd Allah with more or less consistency touches upon theory, the notion "love" is used as a synonym for term "gnosis" (*ma'rifah*) and sometimes "intellect" (*'aql*). Ansari distinguishes none of them either in quality or in the order of following the path of spiritual perfection. Thus, in one case, when he narrates a story, attributed to Ibrahim b. Ad'ham, Ansari expresses the idea that a seeker of the Truth (*Haqq*) having tasted the wine of love for God, taken from the hands of the eternal cup-bearer, finds himself in a state of senselessness and of special clairvoyance.[14] It means that the love for God precedes the knowledge of the Truth and helps it. In the other case, giving an expressive description of the love for god and of the reciprocal love of the Creator for His creatures, Ansari considers this notion to be the ultimate, the achievement of which should be preceded by the gnosis (*ma'rifah*) and knowledge (*'ilm*), that requires primarily an understanding of the concealed secrets of the Qur'an.[15] So, having researched the work, known under the title *Manazil al-Sa'irin*, one can draw the conclusion that on the theoretical level Ansari is inclined to consider the "gnosis" (*ma'rifah*) and the "love" (*'ishq, muhabbah, mahr*) to be the main and compulsory stages of the path to God (*tariqah*). The similarity of the two notions is strengthened by the fact that Ansari declares inadmissibility of the knowledge of the material world and also rejects the love for all perishable things. So a lover of the Truth is usually opposed by a lover of the material world. The latter is compared with a puppet.[16]

On the other hand, the versified parts of the same treatise are marked with the traditional tendency to understand the love for God as Absolute Being, the only true way to the divine substance: "The being of that one, who has mounted the runner of the love, will reach the Omnipresent One."[17] Love is compared with fire, able to burn everything, with the boundless ocean and with an incurable disease. Such a way of narration, close or analogous to the Sufi poetry, removes accents and changes the idea of the final aim of love. Ansari uses the allegory widespread in Sufi poems: the lover of the Truth (that is of God) is compared with a moth flying to a burning candle. He says, "...learn from a moth to be a lover. It performs ritual walking round the tent of the candle. When it approaches the candle, it cannot bear this closeness and goes back. Then again it feels a passionate desire to come nearer to the candle until it becomes senseless and gives itself up to the candle. Its wings burn out and it falls down. The candle says with the tongue of ecstasy: 'Oh, poor thing, you do not realize what is your position and what is ours! Why do you love us despite the fact that we burn the affectionate friend.' The moth says: 'What am I burning out for? Not to go out of your arms anywhere and to look at you.'"[18]

Thus, when the narration is transferred from the level of theory into the sphere of poetic allegories and extremes, Ansari declares the possibility of union of a creature with God at least on the verge of life and death. To soften the impudence of this statement and make it acceptable to the orthodox Islam, Ansari attributes to the Prophet Muhammad the following saying in the spirit of this Sufi conception: "I am the first sincere lover who has achieved union with the beloved."[19] More than that, even the prophet is compared with a butterfly burning on the candle of love for God: "Oh, Ansari, Muhammad had been thrown like a butterfly to the candle of magnificence, of unity of being and he had made his being a victim of a tongue of flame of love, of the candle of magnificence, of unity."[20]

But Ansari can hardly be considered a follower of the extreme pantheistic trend of Sufism. In the theoretical parts of his treatise, he completely rejects the possibility of such union (*wasl*). Moreover, he considers it impossible even for a pious man to be in a direct contact with God even after his death. Describing the path of a pious man's soul towards God, Ansari states that even in the valley of judgement a pious man will appear before supreme angels, while God will send him only an honorary garment, the mythical horse Buraq and His blessing.[21] It is stated that God's greeting will also be sent.[22]

Thus, Ansari demonstrates in his treatise an intermediate position between the extreme and the moderate trends of Sufism and uses for this purpose the junction of two genres. They are: Sufi theory or separate sayings of theoretic character and their poetic interpretation, which allows greater licence and change of meaning and position of some terms. For instance, in poetical or versified parts the opposition of "intellect" (*'aql*) "love" (*'ishq*) is considerably hyperbolized.

As it has been demonstrated above, in prosaic theoretical parts, Ansari, in a number of variants, recognizes that functions of love and knowledge are identical. The "intellect" is classified as one of the means of achieving gnosis (*ma'rifah*), but an imperfect means, which is not capable by itself of ensuring true knowledge. In this respect, according to Ansari's theory, "intellect" is inferior to "love" in perspicacity. But in his version of the legend of Yusuf and Zulaykha, Ansari proves that "love" too can make mistakes.[23] But this correlation of the two terms turns into opposition in the versified parts of the treatise.[24] There the "intellect" is connected with the knowledge of the material world and affection for it, while "love" is presented as the greatest renunciation of earthly blessings showing the contempt for the benefit. Thus, in the corresponding chapter "intellect" is mentioned as a "means of getting wealth," as a "totality of the populated world."[25] At the same place "love" is referred to as "a butterfly, that has lost its senses because of intoxication" after a "drink of self-annihilation," who is not a "slave of thoughts."[26] The narration is in the form of an argument of "love" with "intellect." Love states that intellect's task is to be a messenger who brings messages "from the Lord to love," according to the order that runs as follows: "You remain embarrassed and cannot distinguish the head from the legs. When you are in the city of heart, there is discord there out of the hand of enmity or in the country of breast there is confusion because of spite. Who can demonstrate his courage and snatch the sword out of the enemy's hands? In the stronghold of the body there would be a reasonable *amir*. Love is that very sovereign who is obeyed because it has such qualities. That is why it is the *amir* of the country of heart."[27]

Using similar poetic interpretations, Ansari repeatedly expresses the idea of complete unity of the "lover" (i.e. *murid*) and the "Beloved" (i.e., the Divine Substance): "When the lover looks at himself, he sees his Beloved and when he looks at his beloved, he sees himself."[28]

At the same time, the frequent use of the allegory of a butterfly and a candle Ansari to the idea of physical self-annihilation of the "lover" for the sake of eternal union with the "Beloved".[29] In confirmation of his words Ansari mentions the opinion of Abu Bakr Shibli (d. 334/946), that the lover, having achieved union with the object of his desires, immediately loses the attainment and suffers from the separation, that makes him wish non-existence for himself.[30]

Though Ansari tries to connect his conception of enmity between "intellect" and "love" with some of his cosmological views,[31] such fragments are also of expressive character and cannot be considered as a theory.

Thus in the treatise, known as *Manazil al-Sa'irin*, Ansari's theory is completely based on rejection of the pantheistic joining of a human being with the Creator. He considers it impossible even to see somehow the divine substance. The same idea is expressed by Ansari in his other work *Maqamat-i Ma'nawi*.[32] This treatise exhibits nowhere the author's versified interpretations and presents consistent rendering of the theory of spiritual perfection. Accordingly, the idea of any union of a *murid* with God is completely avoided there. Even the idea of closeness it God and approaching Him is permitted only in connection with the Prophet Muhammad, who, according to Qur'an, approached God at the distance of "two bows" during his ascension.[33] As to the notion "union," it is interpreted allegorically. First of all, Ansari declares that it cannot be understood by the intellect. Love is nowhere mentioned in connection with the stage (*maqam*), which is preceded by the annihilation (*fana'*) of one's existence and by the achievement of the eternal subsistence with the Truth (*baqa*).[34] Ansari declares the necessity of the *murid's* complete estrangement from all worldly troubles and considers it to be a kind of his ascension to the summit of union (*wasl*), which is divided into three degrees. At the first one, the human being achieves purity of thought and gets rid of sins. At the second one, he achieves "the contemplation with his own eyes" (*mushahidah*), that means rejection of any rationalism, when the *murid* avoids taking into account reasons and evidence. The third degree is named "the joining of existence" and means transition to the Truth (*Haqq*). In this case, the author does not give any more details as this degree, according to his opinion, cannot be realized by the human intellect.[35] This part is concluded by stating that the idea of joining is expressed in the Qur'an: "Verily we belong to Allah and we are to come back to Him."[36]

The given examples make it clear that in rendering his theory of *tariqah* Ansari superficially uses the terminology that corresponds to the pantheistic trend, while in its essence his theory presents the moderate trend of Sufism, which does not permit union of the mortal greature with God. Ansari does not try to make things clear. His aim is to unite in his works the two opposite trends of Sufism. But in fact he has not united them, they simply coexist in his treatises in prosaic and versified parts. From my point of view the ideological position of an author determines the means he uses. Representatives of the extreme trend of Sufism usually prefer poetry. It is characteristic that Ansari's contemporary 'Ali al-Hujwiri (d.c. 465/1072), a follower of the moderate trend, does not use verses in his treatise *Kashf al-Mahjab*.

It seems to me that the following two conclusions may be drawn on the basis of the above-mentioned observations:

(1) There is a difference of principle between Sufi theory and poetry. In this paper I have marked only the discrepancy between prosaic and versified parts of separate treatises, when verses should be considered as a part of the author's conception. It proves, to my mind, that the difference between Sufi theory and completely versified works by

Sufi poets should be still greater and must therefore be taken into account by scholars.

(2) Various combinations of prosaic and versified texts are determined by views of Sufi authors and cannot be explained simply as their passion for poetry.

Another significant problem of the present stage of Sufi studies is the necessity of research work on separate dogmata. In this paper I shall touch upon the Sufi path of spiritual perfection, which is usually named *tariqah*.

Almost every researcher of Sufism has presented some data on the point in his works. We may now have some idea of the great variety of different *tariqahs* followed by Sufis. For instance, M. Smith presents the variety of *tariqah*, taken from the works by Abu Talib al-Makki (d. 386/996).[37] This path of spiritual perfection is rather simple and consists of about twenty stages or stations (*maqams*). A.J. Arberry takes as a principle the *tariqah* of al-Qushayri and composes the scheme consisting of stages or stations (*maqams*), that is of gradually ascending degrees of spiritual perfection being achieved as a result of the Sufi's own efforts, and of states (*hals*), granted by God.[38] But the forty-five degrees, mentioned by him, are left undivided between *maqams* and *hals*.[39] A.J. Arberry also mentions al-Ghazali's *tariqah*, consisting of ten main stages (*maqams*) and ten intermediate ones without the category of *hal*.[40] I.P. Petrushevskiy mentions a concise variety of Abu Hamid al-Ghazali's (d. 505/1111) *tariqah*.[40a]

The division of *tariqah* into stations or stages (*maqams*) and states (*hals*) is clearly explained by E.A. Bertels who describes in detail seven *maqams* and nine *hals*.[41] A. Schimmel begins with enumeration of stages of *tariqahs*, introduced by Dhu al-Nim Misri (d. 245/859) Yahya ibn Mu'adh (d. 258/877) and Sahl al-Tustari (d. 283/896) Then she follows the same principle and mentions the most frequently used *maqams* and *hals* in various *tariqahs*.[42] Though A. Schimmel gives a much more detailed description and uses a good number of sources, she mainly represents the system similar to that of Bertels.

The most complicated system of *tariqah* is given by K. Kazanskiy with reference to Ibn 'Arabi. (d. 638/1240). It comprises 19 stations (*manzils*) and 360 stages (*maqams*). While traversing the path the traveller (*salik*) is successively seized by seven states (*hals*).[43] So, having studied a great number of research works on Sufism we can get only a general idea of the main stages of the path of spiritual perfection as well as of some individual interpretations of this notion by separate theorists. Some scholars tried to create a comprehensive kind of *tariqah* for Sufism in general on the basis of various *tariqahs*. They single out the most frequent stages and states and join them together. But such systems are obviously the result of the scholars' imagination and have never existed in Sufi practice. Other scholars, having avoided this generalization, prefer to choose an individual *tariqah* and declare that it is the most characteristic one for Sufism. As a result, we can hardly find two scholars with one and the same point of view concerning the *tariqah*. Their common feature is the fact that they pay no attention to individual, ideological and temporal peculiarities of systems of the *tariqah*, introduced by various theorists.

Thus the task of Sufi studies at present is to reveal particular features of each system probing the distinct trends among them. In this respect it is necessary to decide which indications of the *tariqah* must be considered to be fundamental.

First of all, it should be mentioned that the number of stages or stations (*maqams, manzils*) is not a matter of principle. Sufi preachers themselves did not attach importance to this point. For instance, Abu Bakr Muhammad al-Kalabadhi (d. 380/990) considered it possible to form one system of the *tariqah* on the basis of joining schemes of more than thirty authors. He mentioned that he had excluded some intermediate stages.[44]

Undoubtedly fundamental is the division of the *tariqah* into stages, reached by the traveller according to his own efforts and will, and states, granted solely by God and not depending on the Sufi's desire. Such a division cannot be understood as the system of spiritual perfection got complicated in the course of time. For example, in the 10th century al-Makki advocated the *tariqah* that had not been divided into *maqams* and *hals*,[45] while his contemporary al-Kalabadhi, a representative of the group of theologians, introduced the path that consisted of seventeen *maqams* and fourteen *hals*.[46] In the 13th century, simultaneously with the extremely complicated *tariqah* attributed to Ibn 'Arabi, there existed the most simple scheme without any category of *hals*, which has been extracted by Palmer from the works of 'Aziz ibn Muhammad al-Nasafi (d. 662/1263).[47] I feel that this division of the *tariqah* into *maqams* and *hals* might have occurred as a result of attempts to permit some freedom of choice for the human being alongside the theory of predestination. Accordingly, taking into account the existence of different degrees of freedom of will in various *tariqahs* may help scholars to classify them from this point of view.

Now, it is necessary to decide in which of the two varieties of *tariqahs* (with *hals* or without them) the degree of freedom of will is greater. It is rather difficult to answer this question. If the above-mentioned definition of the term *maqam* is taken into account, all the varieties of *tariqahs* without the category of *hal* should be understood as an act of will. But the analysis of concrete material gives quite a different idea. For example, the system of the *tariqah*, taken as the basis by Palmer from the works of al-nasafi, does not include *hals*.

But Palmer's explanation of the second stage of this path proves that the achievement of this *maqam* is not at all connected with an effort of will: "When in answer to his prayers to the Divine influence or attraction he has developed his inclination into love of God, he is said to have reached the stage called Ishak, Love."[48]

It is clear, that this variant of the Sufi path does not require an act of will on the part of the human being. Even the feeling of love for God appears according to the Divine will. It is characteristic that the love for God is frequently presented in a number of *tariqahs* as *hal*.[49] The inconsistency in understanding the term *maqam* by Sufi theorists does not allow scholars to rely completely on this division of the Path in solving the problem of the degree of freedom of will in *tariqahs*.

In researching the *tariqah* from this point of view the *maqam* of *tawakkul* (trust in God alone) is of special interest. Almost all experts of Sufism marked this notion and had given a detailed analysis either in a general way or in interpretations by various authors.[50] But it had been viewed only in respect of its meaning and its correlation with the same term in Islam in general. I suppose, it is necessary to reveal how the presence of the stage *tawakkul* in a *tariqah* influences the level of freedom of will permitted in it. It should be mentioned that this stage led to the blatant declaration of inactivity in Sufism that had frightened many of the authorities, such as al-Ghazali.[51] But the stage itself had been understood as a significant effort of will. E.A. bertels marks within the bounds of the *maqam* a number of stages, beginning with the exclusion of all kinds of troubles about the future upto complete rejection of efforts of will.[52] It corresponds to the system of *tariqah* presented by E.A. Bertels and to the widespread understanding of the term *maqam*. It is important to pay attention to the fact that the presence of the *maqam* of *tawakkul* in a *tariqah* does not mean, as a rule, that the freedom of will is still limited. The variety of the *tariqah* introduced by 'abd al-Qadir Gilani (d. 561/ 1166), the founder of the Sufi order Qadiriyah, is of special interest in this respect. Its main feature is the absence of a detailed clear-cut scheme, as a result of great importance attributed in this *tariqah* to relying of traveller (*salik*) on God's will (*tawakkul*). But Gilani had not included the *maqam* of *tawakkul* into his Path. It is the highest possible limitation of the sphere of human activity that makes it almost impossible to define all the stages which God would like to grant to his slave, whole-heartedly devoted to His will, like a baby in the arms of its wet-nurse.[53]

Thus, according to Gilani the particle of will available for the human being should be directed exclusively to the boundless obedience to Allah's will.[54] It can be achieved mainly by means of zealous observation of the *Shari'ah* laws, studying of the Muslim Holy Writ and suppressing carnal passions. Finally, the *murid* becomes crushed, that is, he loses all worldly desires.[55] This very moment is defined by Gilani as *fana* or annihilation of the *murid* in the Truth.[56] Only after that the human being is bestowed with God's love and gets from Him the sacred knowledge: "God the Almighty and Supreme, pours out the streams of His love in the heart of His slave and kindles in him the happiness of self-knowledge."[57]

So, while in the above-mentioned varieties of the *tariqahs* the stage (*maqam*) or the state (*hal*) *fana'* was usually placed at the end of the Path, in Gilani's *tariqah* the state of *fana'* is supposed to be at the very beginning being preceded only by two stages (*maqams*): patience (*sabr*) and satisfaction (*rida*).[58] From my point of view, it is the characteristic features of Gilani's *tariqah* that makes it an embodiment of the highest restraining of human will and of a traveller's estrangement from the material world.

My aim then is to demonstrate, using as an example Gilani's *tariqah*, correlation between the extreme limitation of human freedom of will advocated by him and the design of his Path intended for the realization of this idea in practice. It may be supposed in this respect that the presence of the *maqam tawakkul* (relying on God's will) is not at all indicative of reducing efforts of will in the *tariqah*. Rather on the contrary, the degree of relying on God is limited in this case within the bounds of the concrete stage.

Certainly my submissions cannot be considered to be final. But the aim of this paper is to prove the necessity of such research work which can lead scholars to more complete defining of ideological trends in Sufism.

In conclusion, I would like to draw attention to the significance of researching the already revealed trends. For instance, in research works two main trends have been defined and described. They are: the moderate Sufism, which rejects possibility of union of the material world with the Divine substance; and the extreme Sufism, based on pantheism. At the present stage of Sufi studies it would be useful to initiate a comparative analysis of these trends and their branches. I.P. Petrushevskiy has compared the two outstanding representatives of both the trends—Ghazali and Ibn 'Arabi—and has maintained that the moderate Sufism of Ghazali was characterized with an assumption of some freedom of human will, while the extreme trend completely rejected it.[59] If such a comparison is made in some other respect it would be important to study an intermediate stage between these two extremes. I have already mentioned the presence of moderate conceptions in prosaic parts of Ansari's treatises and also the extreme ones in versified fragments. It means that this famous theorist assumed the extreme pantheistic unity of the human being and god as a poetic licence but he did not consider it possible to advocate the same idea in the theoretic aspect. At the same time he does not disprove it either.

Thus, to my mind, it is possible to state that between the moderate and the extreme Sufi trends there is an intermediate position. But more important is to take into account the fact this trend was not fading away. On the contrary, there were adherents of it who tried to give theoretical grounds for the contradiction mentioned in the treatises by Ansari. One of his followers, Abu Bakr Najm al-Din al-Razi (d. 654/1256), known by his pen-name Najm al-Din al-Dayah,[60] cites frequently some parts from *Manazil al-Sa'irin* in his treatises *Mirsad al-'Ibad*. To develop Ansari's views, he had added a special chapter under the title "The Achievement of the Almighty God without Joining and without Parting with Him."[61] Al-Razi, completely excluding poetical expressiveness, declares that from one point of view the joining of a creature with God can be considered possible because in the process of the creation the rays from God had touched the particle of the human spirit (*ruh*) before it was placed into the human body. But from the other point of view the author thinks that this interpretation allows consideration that the joining does not take place, as the particle of the spirit communicated only with the Divine attributes or qualities, that is with God's rays, coming from His radiance or with sparks, flying off it.[62]

The limits of the paper do not allow an analysis of this trend, particularly its development, in detail. My aim is only to express the idea of the sign.

REFERENCES

1. E. A. Bertels, Sufism in sufiyskaia (Moscow, 1965) pp. 35-36
2. A. J. Arberry, Sufism: An account of the mystics of Islam (Lomdon, 1950). pp. 106-107.

3. E.H. Palmer, Oriental mysticism (London, 1938) p.x.
4. I.P. Petrushevskiy, Islam v Irane (Leningrad, 1966) pp. 338-39.
5. A. Schimmel, Mystical dimensions of Islam (The University of North Carolina Press, 1976) pp. 13048.
6. E A Bertels., p. 60.
7. Ibid., p. 61.
8. Ibid.
9. O. Murodov and E A Poliakova, Transformation mifologicheskih i legendarnih obrazov v tadjiksko-persidisk ih hronikah, 11-15v.v. dushabe, 1985.
10. 'Ayn al-Qudat al-Hamadani, al-Tamhidat, MS. Institute of Oriental Studies of the Academy of Sciences of the Uz. SSR (IOSAS Uz. SSR) no. 9852, fol. 7b; no. 9881, fol. 8a.
11. Ibid., MS. IOSAS Uz. SSR, no. 9852, fol.97a; MS. no 9881, fol. 108a.
12. Ibid., MS. no. 9852,fol. 97a, 102a; MS. no. 9881, fol. 108a, 112b.
13. V. Zjukovsriy, "Pesni Geratskogo strata," in the collection of articles Vostochniye zameiki (St. Petersburg, 1859); E A Bertels, pp. 67-72; ibn `Ata 'Allah, The Book of Wisdom; Khwajah `Abd Allah Ansari, Intimate conversations (New York, Ramsey, Toronto, 1978), p.174.
14. 'Abd Allah Ansari, Manazil al-Sa'irin (Pseudo - Manazil, MS. IOSAS, UZ, SSR, no. 497, fol 138a-139a.
15. Ibid. fol. 162b, 163a.
16. Ibid. fol. 137a.
17. Ibid. fol. 68a.
18. Ibid., fol.136b; MS. no. 1484, fol.325a.
19. Ibid., MS. no. 497, fol. 257a.
20. Ibid., MS. no. 497, fol. 270a: MS. no. 1484, fol. 369b.
21. Ibiid., MS. no. 497, fol. 235-236a.
22. Ibid., fol. 236a.
23. Ibid., MS. no. 497, fol. 163-167a; MS. no. 1484, fol. 334b-346a.
24. The antithesis intellect-love(`aql-`ishq) is mentioned by E A Bertels, p. 310.
25. Ms. no. 497, fol. 85a.
26. Ibid., fol. 84b.
27. Ibid., fol. 85b, MS. no. 1484, fol. 310ab.
28. Ibid., Ms. no. 497, fol. 87a.
29. Ibid., fol. 93a.

30. Ibid., fol. 93b.
31. Ibid., fol. 181ab; MS. no. 1484, fol. 340b-341a.
32. This treatise is written in Arabic and devoted toa detailed description of all the stages of the tariqah introduced by Ansari.
33. Khwajah~Abd Allah Ansari, Maqamat-i-Ma`nawi, vol, iv, p. 65; al-Quran, LIII: 9.

34. ibid., p.67.

35. Ibid., pp.68-71.
36. Ibid., p.72 (al-Quran, II:151-156).
37. M .Smith, Readings from the Mystics of Islam (London, 1950), pp. 3-4
38. Arberry, p.75.
39. Ibid., p. 75-79.
40. Ibid., p. 82.

40a. I P Petrushevskiy, p. 331.

41. Bertels, pp. 36-38.
42. Schimmel, pp. 98-148.
43. K. Kazanskly, Missitsism v Islame (Samarkand, 1906) p. 141.
44. Al-Kalabadhi, Kitab al-Ta`arruf li Maahhab al-Tasawwuf, MS. IOSAS Uz, SSr, no. 3154/v, fol. 144b.
45. Smith, pp. 3-4.
46. Kalabadhi, MS. no. 3154/v, fol.144b-156a.
47. Cf. Kazanskiy, p. 141; Palmer, pp. 66-67.
48. Palmer, p. 66.
49. Bertels, p. 38.
50. V. Benedikt Reiner, Die Lehre vom tawakkul in der alteren Sufik (Berlin, 1968).
51. Petrushevskiy, p. 333
52. Bertels, p. 37.
53. Gilani, Futuh al-Ghayb, MS. IOSAS, Uz.SSR, no. 2632, fol. 6b.
54. Ibid., fol. 25b.
55. Ibid., fol. 12a.
56. Ibid., fol. 109a.
57. Ibid.
58. Ibid., fol. 81b.
59. Petrushevskiy, pp. 36-37.

60. V A Zjukovskiy, Chelovek i poznaniye u persidskih mistikov (St. Perburg, 1895); Schimmel, p. 257.
61. Abu Bakr al-Razi, Mirsad al-`lbad, Ms. IOSAS Uz.SSR, no. 569, fol. 108a.
62. Ibid., fol. 108a-109a; MS. no. 570, fol. 126a-127b.

(Revised and edited; originally appeared in Islamic Culture, vol. LXI: no. 3, 1987.

12

Cleaning of the Heart: The Sufi Approach

MIR VALIUDDIN

Deals with the Heart (or qalb), i.e., the spirit of a human being, and describes what will purify it from the worldly desires.

Cleaning of the heart' is removing from it the love of the world and effacing from it mundane sorrows and worry over futile things. The word 'heart' (*qalb*) has a dual meaning. In one sense it is a mass of pineshaped flesh, filled with blood, which has been placed on the left side of the chest, which has a cavity inside and is considered to be the source of the spirit. We are not concerned with this heart. In the other sense, it is a receptacle of God's Grace and is spiritual in substance. This spiritual substance is the essence of man. It alone has perception, knowledge and gnosis (*ma'rifa*). It is the heart which is admonished, reprimanded and punished. It has the same relation with the pine-shaped piece of flesh as an accident has with the body, as an attribute is related to the substance attributed, and a spatial object to the space which it occupies and an instrument to the man who uses it. It is this heart which has been interpreted as God's Throne and this alone must be cleansed in *suluk* or Devotion to God.

For cleaning the heart, the Sufi Shaikhs insist on keeping in view the approved practice ordained by God. They hold that in the infinite wisdom of the All-Wise, the more a man is involved in worldly affairs and is hand-in-glove with material things, the more is he involved in troubles and vexations; the more he keeps himself busy in pampering his body and the more he indulges in keeping up appearances, the more his mental state deteriorates his spiritual faculties decay, the purity and effulgence of his heart lose their vigour, and impurity and darkness increase. That is the reason why self-mortification and austerity are the conditions of *suluk*, and abstaining from every object except God is one of the essentials of *tariqa*.

An ignoramus unaware of own reality regards his own flesh and blood as his essence, forgetting the simplicity and abstract nature of his heart and keeping himself busy in feeding his body and fulfilling the vain desires of self according to the dictates of his animal nature. He is bent on satisfying senusous desires and wastes life which, in reality, is the place where provision for the Hereafter is to be made. He runs in the quest of the unsubstantial world, and entirely forgets the 'Place of Return'. The outcome, naturally, is that by obeying the demands of the self, he is eventually destroyed by it. The self by its domination kills him. In regard to such ignoramuses it has been said:

> Ye tempted one another and hesitated and doubted and vain desires beguiled you. The ordinance of Allah came to pass; the Deceiver deceived you concerning Allah.

Some interpret "Ye tempted one another" as lust and sensuous pleasures. "Hesitated," i.e., from repentence. "Doubted" until "ordinance of Allah," i.e., the ordinance of death came to pass, and "the Deceiver deceived you" in respect of God. That is why the Prophet expressed surprise at the man who, though he believes in the Everlasting Home, still strives for the House of Deception:

> It is most surprising that a man should vouch for the Everlasting Home and yet endeavour and exert himself in pursuit of the House of Deception.

Cleaning of the heart is impossible unless love of the world is dispelled from it. The world in itself is not despicable, for it is the "Farm, or, corn-field of the Hereafter" and a means of attaining it. Love of the world and attachment to it is despicable. This is the meaning of the Prophet's saying:

Love of the world is at the root of all sins (al-Baihaqi).

The world is capable of allowing a man to rise to the loftiest spiritual plane, or, of plunging him into the deepest depths of degradation. The man who uses the world as a means of securing the abiding joys of the life Hereafter and does not concentrate merely on the fleeting pleasures of this life, and bears in mind the Divine threat contained in the words which the Unbelievers will hear:

> You received your good things in the life of the world and you look your pleasures out of them.

and acts on the injunction, "Spend out of what we have provided," is outwardly an inhabitant of the world, but, inwardly, he is passing the days of his life in the "Exalted Assembly". He is alive for God and not for carnal pleasures. The world proves for him a mighty help-mate in guiding him on the right path and he has been praised thus by the Prophet:

> How good is the wealth of a righteous man. (al-Baihaqi)

If the heart is void of the love of the world and severs its ties with it if it derives pleasure in contemplation of God, then the man in possession of such a heart can call himself poor in the same way as Solomon, who, though he possessed a vast Kingdom, called himself poor. The explanation of this point by Rumi is as follows:

What is the world? To be forgetful of God;
It is not merchandise and silver, weighing
scales and woman.
Since he dispelled from his heart the desire for
wealth and possessions,
On that account Solomon did not call himself
(by any name) but poor.
Whoever was profited by beholding God,
Regarded this world as dead and lifeless.
Both this world and its people are good for
nothing;

Both are alike in infidelity.
Light appears like fire and fire like light.
Otherwise, the world could not have been
regarded as a place of deception.

Again,

O, Son! burst thy chains and be free;
How long wilt thou be a bondsman of silver
and gold?
The world's life is not a day or two, but an hour;
Whosoever renounced it lived in comfort.
Listen, the meaning of renunciation is comfort,
After renouncing it, drink of the cup of ever-
lastingness.

Consequently, al-Ghazali says:

> The man who forsakes the world as a show of generosity, or in the quest of the Hereafter, cannot be called a recluse. According to the saints, even to abandon the world for the sake of the Hereafter is weak abstinence. Truly, a gnostic is he who does not care for the Hereafter, as he does not care for the world, and nothing except God has value in his eyes. He has no other object in life except God; this is 'the abstinence of the gnostics'. It is likely that such a gnostic does not eschew wealth and worldly possessions. On the other hand, he acquires them and spends them duly and also gives them to the deserving. For instance, Hadrat 'Umar had the control of the nascent but mighty Islamic State, but his heart was void of it. Like 'Aisha, the gnostic would spend a hundred thousand drachmas in a single day and would not but mutton worth a penny for personal use. It is possible that a gnostic may be in possession of hundreds of thousands of drachmas, and yet may be a recruse, and another man may not have a penny and they may not be a recluse. The reason is that the gnostic neither regards the world

as his friend nor as his enemy. The man who considers somebody as his enemy, of course, busies himself with him just like the man who regards him as his friend. He would reach perfection when his heart becomes independent of everything except God. 'Abdallah ibn Mubarak was addressed by somebody as a recluse. He said, "'Umar ibn 'abd al-'Aziz is a recluse, who is in possession of, and has control over, untold wealth and yet he is a recluse. I possess nothing, so how can I rightly be called a recluse?"

Abstinence means forsaking the thing which will keep thee busy by drawing thee away from God.

Renouncing the world means emptying the heart of the love of the world. If this is not done, no king of austerity can be beneficial. In his book *Thamarat al-hayat,* Shaikh Burhan al-Din illustrates the meaning of the above statement by the following example. Suppose of rat fell accidentally into a well and died; the water would emit a foul smell. If somebody wants to cleanse the water of the well, he should, first of all, find out the dead rat and draw out a few bucketsful of water and throw them away. The water will then be purified. Even if a large quantity of water is drawn out, without taking out the body of the rotting rat from the well, the well will still be unclean and the stench will also be there. Similarly, no amount of self-modification will be of avail if one has the love of the world in one's heart.[1] The cherished object of the heart is usually its Deity (*ma'bud*). For this very reason, it has been said: "What ever is dear to thee is thy Lord" and "Thou art the slave of the thing which thou desirest." Unless the diverse impressions, which are the effects of the love of the world are effaced from the heart, its cleaning is not possible.

How canst thy heart receive the Divine Grace
Unless thou hast cleaned the page (of thy heart) of scattered impressions?

The companions of the Prophet, inspite of their good and virtuous deeds, always remembered Death, the destroyer of all pleasures of the world. They always kept in view the reward appointed by God for the obedient and the punishment for the disobedient and thus the longing for the fleeting pleasures of the world was dispelled from their hearts. They read the *Qur'an*, reflected on it and listened to the sermons which softens the heart.

Reflection on the verses of the *Qur'an*, revealing the real nature of the world, is useful for cleansing of the heart. Here I may mention a few of them.

The Almighty God has termed the comforts of this world's life as 'short' (*qalil*) and has described the Hereafter as 'best' (*khair*) for the righteous. What a pity if these 'short' and scanty comforts of the world were to come in the way of attaining the infinite good, and these spurious and adventitious comforts, having no real content, close the door of the reality which is eternal and everlasting.

> Say: Short is the enjoyment of this world; the Hereafter is the best for those who do right. Never will ye be dealt with unjustly in the very least.

The life of the world has been regarded as 'play and amusement' and the Hereafter as an asset. The former is the object of the slaves of passion and lust, and the latter that of the devotees of God. One is evil and the other is absolute good.

> What is the life of this world but play and amusement? But best is the home in the Hereafter for those who are righteous. Will you not understand?

The comforts of this world's life which have been spoken of as 'short' of 'scanty' and indulgence in which has been regarded as 'play and amusement' are nothing but love of women and offspring, love of hoards of gold and silver, gaudy conveyances, well-tilled farms, quadrupeds and cattle.

> Fair in the eyes of men in the love of things they covet, women and children, hoards of gold and silver, horses branded (for blood excellence); and (wealth of) cattle and well-tilled land.

> Such are the possessions of the world's life; but nearness to God is the best of the goals (to aim at).

Forsaking lusts is (as it were) houri, and
renouncing home, house of Paradise;
For the men of heart the houris and places in
Heaven are something different.

Again,

Enlightened people are not pleased with the
wealth of the world,
So long as the candle is crowned with a flame,
it goes on weeping (melting).

Those who forget God, being engrossed in the pursuit of lusts and pleasures, will be forgotten on the Day of Judgment in the same way as they have today forgotten the Day of Resurrection, and are oblivious of the Divine Presence.

> Such as took their religion to be mere play and amusement and were deceived by the life of the world, that day shall We forget them as they forgot the meeting of this Day of theirs and as they were wont to reject our signs.

Really, it is surprising that man, despite knowing the everlastingness of the Hereafter, should concentrate on attaining only the scanty comforts of the worlds and would not care for the immense good of the Hereafter; and even after knowing the 'mirage', he should be engrossed in its spectacle.

> Ye cling heavily to the earth? Do ye prefer the life of this world to the Hereafter. But little is the comfort of this life, as compared with the Hereafter.

I saw the fountain of this existence which is called
the world;
It did not contain even so much water with which

the hands could be washed.

The *Qur'an* has described the life of the world in a simile. It is this: The life of the world is, as it were, the rain sent down from the sky; by its mingling with earth arose the produce of the earth. When the earth was embellished by this water and verdure, and people thought that this earth came into their possession, suddenly came and command of the Creator of the earth, by night or by day, and it destroyed all the decoration in such a way as if not a single blade of grass had sprouted. Such indeed is the life of man, however lovely and beautiful it might appear; and foolish people being enamoured of its glamour, forget and reality. But its fertility and excellence are transitory and will, before long, be effaced by decay and annihilation.

In this garden where Spring and Autumn
came together
Time holds a chalice in its hand and bears a coffin on its shoulder.

The *Qur'an* says:

> The likeness of the life of the Present is as the rain which we send down from the skies; by its mingling with earth arises the produce of the earth, which provides food for men and animals: it grows till the earth is clad with its golden ornaments, and is decked out (in beauty); the people to whom is belongs think they have all power of disposal over it; then comes our command, by night or by day, and we make it like a harvest clean mown, as if it had not flourished only the day before! Thus do we explain the signs in detail for those who reflect.

It would be pitiable if, even after knowing the nature of the worldly life, we are pleased with it, and, deceived by the spectacle of this mirage, are deprived of the boons of the Hereafter.

What is world? For us it is like a bubble.
Or, is it the upper storey of smoke, or like a
mirage?

The heart of the man who does not regard it
as such
Always burns with anxiety like a rissole.

Says the *Qur'an*:

> (The worldly) rejoice in the life of this world; but the life of the world is but little comfort in the Hereafter.

This world is the corn-field of the Hereafter; whatever is sown here is reaped there. Whoever is firm in faith while living in this dustbin (world), will be awarded with peace and bliss and 'ataraxia' in the Hereafter, and he who remains empty-handed in this old caravanserai (as regards faith and action) will be worried and painstricken in the Hereafter.

Become pure so that thou mayst be counted
among the believers,
Live thus that thou mayst become thus,

The *Qur'an* says:

> God will establish in strength those who believe, with the world that stands firm, in the world; but God will leave to go stray, those who do wring: God doeth what he willeth.

Even the Prophet is forbidden to cast a longing glance at worldly possessions and to covet them. How dare others behold the amorous and prosperous world and long for it. This world is an ephemeral spring-time by which our trial and test is intended.

My advice to you is only this:
Beware! as you are a child and the world has
a variety of shows.

> Now strain not the eyes in longing for the things we have given for enjoyment to pairs of them, being the splendour of the life of the world through which we test them: but the provision of thy Lord is better and more enduring.

Whatever is in our possession today is the provision of this worldly life, and due to our ignorance we are enamoured of its form and colour. Owing to our forgetfulness, we are loath to appreciate what is in possession of God and is better and more enduring. This is our understanding, at which we should weep; and this is our endeavour at which we should shed tears:

> *O heart, how long wilt thou be deceived by*
> *this and that in this prison?*
> *Come out once from this dark path that thou mayst*
> *see the world.*

> The (material) things which ye are given are but the comforts of this life and the glitter thereof; but that which is with God is better and more enduring; will ye not then be wise?

Those who forget the Hereafter lament the passing away of the world, and when they look at a millionaire they wish that they might have been endowed with the same wealth and grandeur. However, the wise, who are desirous of the Hereafter, fix their gaze on the reward of the Hereafter and in comparison with it, regard the world and all that is in it as a mere trifle.

> Said those whose aim is the life of this world: "Oh that we had the like of what Qarun had! For he was truly the lord of a mighty good fortune!" But those who had been granted (true) knowledge said: "Alas! the reward of God (in the Hereafter) is best, for those who believe and work righteousness; but this none will attain save those who steadfastly persevere (in good).

The life of the world has been spoken of as play and amusement at various places in the *Qur'an*, and those who prefer it to the life in the Hereafter have been reprimanded in many a verse. This shows clearly that the world is a child's play and every thoughtful man should make provision for the Hereafter.

> What is the life of this world but amusement and play? But, verily, the Home in the Hereafter is life indeed if they but knew.

Again:

> The life of this world is but play and amusement; and if ye believe and guard against evil, He grant you recompense.

Thou canst buy the Hereafter in lieu of the
world:
O, dear! of course thou shouldst bargain thus,
or else thou wilt regret!

The *Qur'an* had given another example of the life of the world and has described its nature. It says that this life is play and amusement; it consists in pomp, mutual boasting and rivalry in multiplying riches and children, that is, man in the early years of his life busies himself in play, then in show, make-up and fashion craze, and, finally, in winning popularity and fame. When death approaches, the thought of possessions and offspring worries him. He desires that after he is no more, his home should remain intact, and his children should live comfortably. But, all this equipment, pomp and glory is decadent and mortal. It is like the charm of a farm which is transitory; it withers and men and animals crush it to bits; not a trace of its freshness and beauty remains. The same may be said of the life of the world, its paraphernalia, pomp and ornament. It is really "the goods and chattels of deception"—a mirage! Man deceived by its fleeting glamour is forgetful of his end! After death these things prove of no avail, there is something else which helps him in the Hereafter—that something is faith and good deeds. Whosoever took them with him own the goods pleasure of his Master and dire punishment awaits him who went empty-handed without providing himself with good acts, and saddled with the load of unbelief and sin. He who, in spite of being a believer, would fall short of good deeds, will be pardoned and released after punishment.

Know ye(all) that the life of this world is but play and amusement, pomp and mutual boasting and rivalry (in) multiplying of riches and children. Here is simile: How the rain and growth which it brings forth delight the farmers; soon the growth withers; thou wilt see it grow yellow; then it becomes dry and crumbles away. But in the

Hereafter is a penalty severe (for the devotees of wrong) and forgiveness of God and his good pleasure (for the devotees of God). And what is the life of the world but goods and chattels of deception.

At one place the *Qur'an* complains that man in theory and practice gives preference to the life and luxury of the world over the Hereafter, notwithstanding that the world is of short duration and unsubstantial, and the Hereafter is far better and real:

> Nay (behold) ye prefer the life of the world; but the Hereafter is better and more enduring. And this is the books of earliest (revelations), the Books of Abraham and Moses.

The above verses would show that the beliefs that the Hereafter is better and everlasting is handed down from the times of Abraham and Moses, and in all ages and among all people the world was not preferred to the Hereafter. It appears also that the faith in the existence and reality of this Everlasting Home was in all ages the unanimous belief held by all the prophets and revealed in all the sacred books.

The above verses of the *Qur'an* dwell upon the fleeting existence in this world and the everlastingness of the Hereafter, and proclaim that so long as the heart is not cleansed of the love for the treasures of the world and love of pleasures, one cannot take even one step forward on the path to God.

> *Shed tears and like the devotee let the dust subside,*
> *So long as we are wrapped in the dust we cannot*
> *see the face of the moon.*

Like the *Qur'an*, the authentic Traditions also lay emphasis on the subject. Some of them are mentioned below.

The Prophet of Islam said:

> By God, the world, when compared to the Hereafter, is not even so much as when one of you dips his finger in a sea, and then observes what he has obtained by dipping it.

It means that the Hereafter is, as it were, a sea and the world, compared with it, a drop of water.

On another occasion he remarked:

> These riches are luscious and sweet. Whosoever acquires them rightly and spends them in the name of God will find them a good helpmate, And if a person acquires them unlawfully, he would be like the person who, though he eats well, yet can never satisfy his hunger, and the riches will give evidence against him in the Day of Judgment.

The above tradition has been narrated by Hakim ibn Hizam.

He says:

> I begged of the Prophet of Islam. He gave me; I begged again; he gave me again. I begged of him a third time; he obliged me even then and said, "O Hakim! the money and the things which I gave you are good and most welcome; they are blessed when they are accepted without greed, not so when a person takes them avariciously; such as person would be like the man who eats but his appetite is never satisfied. The upper hand that gives is better than the lower hand that receives.

Hakim said: "I swear by the Supreme Being who has sent you as a true Apostle, after taking this from you, I shall not accept anything from anybody, till I leave this world." (*Bukhari* and *Muslim*)

Accordingly, he stood firm by his resolve and did not accept anything from anybody till he died. How truly has someone said:

> *There is a courage in independence which is*
> *known to the generous,*
> *By rejecting things, we bestow them, as it*
> *were, on others.*

'Aisha narrates that the Prophet said:

> The world is the above of him who has no home, and is the property of him who possesses nothing. He alone hoards for it who has no reason. (*Ahmad* and *Baihaqi*)

In a long Tradition narrated by 'Umar ibn 'Auf, the Prophet is reported to have said:

> I swear by God that I am not afraid of your poverty, but I fear that the world will spread out and open for you, as it so expanded for the peoples before you, and you will compete among yourselves in attaining it, as people had done before you and it will destroy you as it had destroy you as it had destroyed people before you. (*Bukhari* and *Muslim*).

There is another tradition which conveys the same sense, and which is narrated by Abu Sa'id al-Khudri:

> What after me I fear most for you is the expansion, the charm, attraction, richness and embellishment of the world. (*Bukhari* and *Muslim*)

The history of Islam bears out that this fear of the Prophet came true. When, after this rule of the first four Caliphs, Islam won many more victories, the Muslims fell a prey to the charm and glamour of the world, and few were the persons who were saved from this tribulation.

It is easy to drink wine and remain sober:
But indeed thou art a he-man, if thou gainest wealth
and is not intoxicated.

Another tradition narrated by Abu Sa'id al-Khudri is as follows:

> The world is sweet and pleasant, and God will make you His deputy in it, and will keep an eye on what you do. So steer clear of the world and avoid women. (*Muslim*)

How aptly has Baha' al-Din Amili said:

If thou lookest at every fresh flower which is the
Jewel of this garden,
It is a flower: if thou pickest it, it is a thorn.
Behold the candle from a distance, do not go near it,
For though it appears aslight, yet it is fire.

And again:

> This world is a stage which will pass away. The Hereafter is a stage to come. Each of them has sons; if it be possible for you do not become the sons of the world. Act, because you are in a place where acts are needed and there is no reckoning, and tomorrow you will be in the Hereafter where acts are not needed. (*al-Baihaqi*)

The above tradition has also been narrated by Bukhari as handed down by Hadrat 'Ali. There, instead of occur the words which have the same meaning.

The Prophet is reported to have said the following also about the world:

> The world and all that is in it is accursed except the remembrance of God and its corollaries (e.g., performance of duties, abstinence from things prohibited, and things necessary for God's remembrance, e.g., mosques, religious literature, religious schools) and the learned and the student.

For understanding this tradition, it is necessary to bear in mind that in remembrance of God and things which help His remembrance all good deeds are included and only love of the evil world is denounced, for it enamours a man and prevents him from the love of god and emboldens him to do prohibited acts.

These traditions clearly show that the purpose of sending the apostles is to turn man away from love for the evil world and draw his attention to the Hereafter. I have quoted above a few verses of the *Qur'an* and some traditions of the Prophet to show the same. Lastly, I quote also a few sayings of the saints of the *Tariqa*. Fudail b. 'Iyad has said:

> I have pondered on this verse for a long time: That which is on earth we have made but as a glittering show for the earth, in order that we may test them—as to which of them are best in conduct. Verily, what is on earth we shall make but as dust and dry soil (without growth or berbage).

In this connexion, one day Ibn 'Umar inquired of the Prophet of Islam about the people whose conduct was best. He said:

> Those who are wise, whose abstinence from things prohibited is greater and who are readier to obey the commands of God.

The meaning of the holy verse on which Fudail b. 'Iyad was wont to meditate is that the people, who are taken in by the glamour of the world, should know that its pomp and splendour will not last long. However, they may amass the goods the chattels of the world, and turn the earth into a garden by material resources, still, they would not attain eternal bliss and salvation, so long as they lack Divine guidance and spiritual wealth. They alone achieve success who, to gain the good pleasure of their Lord, sacrifice every fleeting mortal joy, and in no circumstances are afraid of traversing the right path, neither do their steps falter on intimidation by the magnates of the world.

The *Shaikhs* of the *Tariqa* have compared the world to a shadow. It is a fact that a moving shadow appears stationary, that is, though it is really moving yet apparently it looks as if it is stationary. Its movement is not perceived by the outward eye, but is discovered only by the inward eye. Once people were talking of the world with Hasan of Basra. He remarked:

> *The world is like a dream or a passing shadow—*
> *A wise man is not deceived by such a thing.*

Imam Hasan would often recite the following couplet:

O devotees of the pleasures of the world! See
they are not everlasting:
It is folly to be deceived by a passing shadow.

The story goes that an ascetic saw the world in his dream in the form of a virgin. He was surprised and said, "How is it possible for thee to remain a virgin with this beauty and adornment and in spite of having thousands of husbands?" The world replied: "Shall I tell the truth to thee: the fact is that really no potent man paid any attention to me and hundreds of impotent persons rushed towards that is the reason why I have maintained my virginity." A poet has rendered this story in the following couplets:

A recluse reflecting fell asleep,
He saw the world in the form of a Virgin.
Said the recluse, "How has thou with this beauty
and excellence
Preserved thy virginity, whereas thou hast
innumerable husbands?"
The world said, "I tell the truth to thee,
He who was really a man did not like me,
And he alone loved me who was impotent,
That is why I have maintained my virginity.

Finally, the dialogue between 'Umar Khayyam and Reason is interesting and throws light on some of the truth discussed in this treatise:

Yesterday, I was conversing with Reason,
Some truths were revealed to my heart.
Said I to it, "O thou who art the
storehouse of Wisdom!
I want to ask a few questions of thee.
What is this life of the world?"

It said: "It is either a dream or some fancies."
I said, "Tell me what is gained by it?"
It said, "Headache and a few misfortunes."
I said, "When is this self subjugated?"
It said, "When its ears are boxed a few times."
I said, "What the cruel people are?"
It said, "They are the wolves, dogs and
jackals."
I said, "What are these discussions of the
people of the world?"
It said, "It is the stuff and nonsense."
I said, "In what work are the worldly people
engaged?"
It said, "In amassing riches and wealth."
I said, "What is matrimony?"
It said, "The luxury of an hour and
grief of a few years."
I said, "To what can the world be compared?"
It said, "It is like an old woman who has
adorned herself."
I said, "What thinkest thou about the sayings
of Khayyam?"
It said, "It is advice which is apt in some condi-
tions for some people."

For cleaning the heart it is necessary to reflect on the truths mentioned above. What is stated above is a lesson on renunciation of the world taught by the eminent *sufis*. They have aptly drawn out attention to the advice of the Almighty God:

> Verily, the promise of God is true: let not then this present life deceive you, nor let the Chief Deceiver deceive you about God.

Do not seek the world so that there may remain

> *for thee only religion:*
> *If thou seekest the world thou shalt get neither*
> *this nor that.*

The man who makes his goal the world and its paraphernalia, becomes the instrument of the guiles of Satan, and spends his whole time in attaining the pleasures of the 'soul depraved', is a blind ignoramus, unaware of the world, and it is regarding persons like him that the *Qur'an* has said:

> They known but the outer (things) in the life of this world; but of the End of things they are needless.

The truth is that God has not created this world without a purpose and meaning:

> Our Lord: nor for naught has thou created all this...

This colossal workshop of the universe is not useless, having no purpose. Surely the series of these wonderful and wise arrangements must have been based on some grand purpose and that is the Hereafter, which is really the final outcome of the present life of the world.

All this vast universe, the heavens and earth, have been created only for man, and placed under his control, as the *Qur'an* proclaims:

> And He has subjected to you, as from Him, all that is in the Heavens and on earth.

It is evident that if man does not use the things of this universe, and, fleeing from them, inhabits forests and mountains, the very purpose of the Creation of the world will be defeated. This is the reason why Islam does not preach monasticism. It has been prohibited by the *Qur'an*:

> But the monasticism, which they invented for themselves, we did not prescribe for them.

It is also clear that though the world has been created for man, yet man has not been created for the world, to be captivated by it and lost. On the contrary, he is created for some noble purpose. This noble purpose is presented by the *Qur'an* in the following words:

> I created the jinn and humankind only that they might worship Me.
>
> And the same thing has been expressed in a tradition thus:
>
> The world has been created created for you and you are created for the Hereafter.

So, according to the *Qur'an*, giving up the world, fleeing from it, or choosing monasticism, is totally unwarranted. On the other hand, the world is meant for man and man is meant for God and the Hereafter. This means that man must use the world according to the Commandments and good pleasure of God, so that he may attain salvation in the Hereafter, for which he is created. In brief, the task of a Muslim is neither to become a hermit, nor a lover of the world. He is a man of the world but never a devotee of the world.

In the light of this discussion, the meaning of "the cleansing of the heart" may not be determined. Man should subject all his desires, passions, powers, control over the things of the world, to the command, pleasure and love of God. For the cleansing of the heart, it is not allowed that man should renounce the world, and sever all ties with it; neither it is allowed that, on principle, he should give up matrimony and forsake wife and children; it is also not allowed that he should destroy or abrogate all his physical and mental faculties. On the contrary, the method of cleansing the heart is that he should subjugate all his physical and mental faculties to the guidance of God Almighty, that is, he should use the things of the world to the extent of, and according to, the method commanded by God, and make use of his faculties and powers also according to His Commands. In other words, even with the ties of wife and children, engaged in earning means of livelihood by employment, trade and industry, he should not transgress the limits prescribed by God in respect of them and their accomplishment should be for God's good pleasure only, and nothing be sought and loved except God.

The teachings of the *Qur'an* create neither defeatism nor quietism. It prevents one from worldliness on the one hand, and from mosasticism on the other. On the one hand, it stops us from indulging in vain things, and, on the other, prohibits us from going to extremes in worship. Ibn Mas'ud narrates that the Prophet of Islam said:

> The Extremists are dead, the extremists are dead, the extremists are dead.
>
> On another occasion, he appropriately said:
>
> The Commandments of religion are easy, and he who goes to extremes in religion is defeated by it. Stick fast to the right path, choose the *via media*, be happy at the glad tidings brought by me and seek assistance by praying early in the day, at the end of the day and late at night (*Bukhdri*)

Another tradition is as follows:

> Hold fast to the right path, choose the middle course between extremes, pray early in the day, at the end of the day, and late at night. Take the middle path, you will achieve your object.

In the above tradition, to travel in the early or last hours of the day (*rauha*) or late in night (*dulja*) are metaphors. They mean that one should seek assistance of God by praying to Him at the time of one's rest and leisure and while one's mind is unoccupied, so that one may derive pleasure from prayer and may not feel tired, and reach one's destination as a wise traveller travels at the aforesaid times and allows himself and his mount rest at other hours and reaches his journey's end without trouble and difficulty.

By his saying that "religion is easy" the Prophet had made it clear that the commandments of the *shari'a*, which God has commanded us to follow, are easy and based on convenience. By the observation, "Whosoever fights against religion will be defeated by it" he means that the person who is hard upon his self by performing unnecessary penances, as the hermits do, will eventually be unable to accomplish them and, defeated, will have to give them up.

To explain this *via media* it has been said:

> The Lord has a claim on thee, thy self has a claim on thee and thy wife has a claim on thee. Pay the dues to everyone who has a claim on thee.

By the claim or right of the self is meant the means of assistance for worship of God. There is necessarily a difference between the 'claim of the self' and 'pleasure of the self'. They are antithetical to each other. To pay what is due to the self is to perform what has been ordered, and following lust is prohibited. It is necessary to keep this difference in view in the cleansing of the heart, otherwise a man falling a prey to lust may imagine that he is only paying the dues of the self and will be lost.

The purpose of opposing the imperious self and lust is to come in agreement with the Will of God as has been said by the prophet:

> Until one's desire becomes obedient to what I have brought (one does not become a true believer).

If the self agrees with the Will of God without effort, and lust becomes subject to *shari'a*, it is, then, perfect. 'Umar ibn 'Abd al-'Aziz has said: "If lust agrees with the Will of God, this state resembles honey and butter which mix well together." For example, if the parents direct a boy to eat sweets and forbid him to eat bread, the eating of the sweets and deriving pleasure from it is more beneficial for him than eating the bread and forsaking the pleasure of eating it. It is customary with the *Shadhiliya* Shaikhs that they guide and train a disciple in a manner consistent with his convenience. They do not try to pull him immediately out of the state in which he is found, nor do they ask him to perform hard penances. They suggest to him such *sufi* practices as are compatible with his temperament and disposition. Thus, by degrees and with case and convenience they take him to the destination. These great Shaikhs say that whosoever's path towards God is according to his taste and aptitude, the attainment of the proximity of God, too, is easy for him. The more he is remote from his natural bent, the slower will be his journey to God, and slower will be the attainment of the Proximity of God. consequently, Shaikh Ibn 'Ata Sikandari would say:

> Choose only such *dhikrs* attaining the love of God as are according to your natural aptitude.

He said this, keeping in view the Prophet's warning: "He will be defeated by religion who opposes it." In view of this, Shaikh Abu'l-Hasan Shadhill, who is the imam of the *Shadhiliya* Order, has said: "Shaikh is he who guides you in a manner consistent with your comfort" and this saying is in pursuance of the Prophet's remark, "Religion is easy" and also of the tradition: "Be lenient, do not be severe." He would say also:

> He, who guided you towards the world, played a traitor to you, and he, who insisted that you should practise unnecessary austerity and self-mortification, caused you grief and trouble, and he who showed you the paath to God, was really well-wisher and adviser.

Undoubtedly, a spiritual guide is a person who is gifted with the miraculous power of smashing by his will-power the shackles of the self, makes effective changes in the selves of the worldlings who consider Reality as 'play and amusement' and narrows the world of self, until the earth, despite its vastness, is straitened for them, and they realize that there is no refuge from God. As the *Qur'an* says:

> The earth seemed constrained to them, for all its spaciousness and their (very) souls seemed straitened to them—and they perceived that there is no fleeing from God and no refuge but to Himself.

The earth, due to the gloom of those who deny love,
Requires cleaning and washing, where is Noah?

All men endowed with inward sight concede that penance and austerity is beneficial only under the instructions of a perfect Shaikh. The way of Providence seems to be that purification from moral impurities and attainment of earnestness and humility in prayers and worship in not secured unless the path to God is traversed under the guidance of a perfect Shaikh, who is conversant with psychological treatment, and is in the know of spiritual matters by his learning, taste and experience. If a votary of lust and passion studies and learns by heart books on ethics, it cannot be considered that he has no need of training by the Shaikh as it cannot be considered that a patient suffering from some physical ailment can treat himself by reading books on Medicine. Accordingly, Sha'rani writes in *Anwar-i qudsiya*:

> The Adepts who know the way leading to the Presence of God agree that the guidance of the Shaikh is necessary for traversing the path to God, so that such weaknesses and failings may be eradicated from human nature that hinder man from attaining the Presence of God; that his prayers might be corrected and earnestness and humility may be developed in worship. It is true, beyond a doubt, that the treatment of inward maladies is obligatory, because the verses of the *Qur'an* and the traditions of the Prophet are replete with the directives that these inward maladies must, at all costs, he cured. Therefore, if the instructions of a perfect Shaikh are not followed to cleanse the heart, purity the self, and to get rid of abominable qualities, it would necessarily mean disobedience of God and the Prophet's behests. If a man endeavours to root them out by his personal efforts, without the aid of the Shaikh, he may never succeed. His case would be just like that of the man who, though he memorizes books on medicine yet can neither prescribe the right medicine for a disease, nor can diagnose the disease and treat it according to the particular condition of the patient. It has always been the way of God that the living are benefited by the living and one light is enkindled by another. "*No change wilt thou find in the practice (approved) of God.*"

That is the reason why it has been said:

> Keep company with God. If it is not in your power to keep company with God, then choose the company of him who lives

in the company of God, until you, too, may reach the company of God the Almighty.

The same thing was explained by Rumi by an example thus:

Nothing came into existence by itself;
No iron did become a sword by itself;
The Maulawi could never become Maula-i Rum
Until he became the slave of Shams-i
Tabriz.

And Khwajah Naqshband had advised:

O son! it is not possible in the path of love
To traverse the path without the aid of a guide.

It is necessary, therefore that the mirror of the heart should be placed before a perfect man whose heart is alive, and has been blessed with the observation of God. Then only whatever is there on the mirror of the heart of the perfect man is reflected on the mirror of our hearts; the way of receiving spiritual benefit is widened and we cry out:

For years we wandered around the world
to achieve our object.
The Friend was in the house and we had been
roaming around the world.

After the cleansing of the heart only, we come to know that God is nowhere but in our hearts; we are oblivious of Him; He is present every moment and we are forgetful of Him.

The pod of musk thou seekest is in thy patched
cloak only,
Thou didst not smell its scent due to thy
ill-luck.

It is said that in his loving discourse with God, David said to God, "O Almighty God! where should I seek thee?" Said God, "Seek me in the hearts which (cured of pride and vanity and freed from carnal pleasures) are broken for Me alone."

> *The trace of the thing thou desirest to find,*
> *Is with thee only; thou seekest it at other*
> *places.*

When the heart is veiled by sins and is full with the presence of things other than God, the fountain of *aqua vitae* is filled with earth and is dried up:

> *The spring out of which Khidr drank the*
> *water of life*
> *Is in your possession, but is filled with earth.*

Men blessed with inward sight have regarded the remembrance (*dhikr*) of God as the most effective method for the cleansing of the heart. The object of all worship is remembrance of God, and regular and constant remembrance alone creates love of God and the heart is emptied of the love of the world. Real Islam is implicit belief in the article of faith, "There is no other object worthy of worship except Allah," and this is nothing but the remembrance of God; all other forms of worship emphasize this remembrance only. What is the spirit of prayer? This very remembrance! Renewing the same with awe and reverence! The object of 'fasting' is to smash sensuality, for when the heart is purged of its filth it is filled with the remembrance of God. The object of 'pilgrimage' to Mecca (*hajj*) is the remembrance of the Master of the House, and the longing to meet Him. Renouncing the love of world and eschewing sensuality is for the sake of acquiring leisure for the aforesaid remembrance only. The goal of Command and prohibition also is *dhikr* or remembrance. The outcome of *dhikr* is that the heart is emptied of the love of all things, and severed from all, is inclined towards God alone, and according to the demand "Devote thyself to Him whole-heartedly" is overflown by the love of God, so much so that it has no room for anything else; the link of love with everything else is cut off and there remains no object of love, except God.

When the Devotee, after receiving instructions on *dhikr* from his Guide, busies himself wholeheartedly with it (of course, after the performance of the obligatory prayers) and limits himself to and indulges in *dhikr* alone, night and day, and even every moment, or, hour; regards all other things as a tribulation; is relieved from the fears and sorrows of the world, and in every state is concerned with this *dhikr* alone, then the veils are lifted off his heart. These veils are the result of the reflection of phenomenal forms. He who is engaged in the remembrance of God negates the contingent forms of the world, by the unsheathed sword of *la ilah*, negates all stray thoughts, and by *illa'llah* beholds the existence of the Enternal Being of God alone, considering Him to be his Ultimate Goal. He negates whatever he has a liking for, and regards it as false, and instead establishes the love of god by affirmation, until gradually the heart becomes void of its beloved things completely and the essence of unity of God (*tauhid*) is firmly rooted in the heart. His inward eye is opened; now, for him, there does not remain any contradiction between reason and Unity, and at this time the reality of *dhikr* and the substance of heart become one. This state has been interpreted as "trans-substantiation of heart" by Shaikh Shahab al-Din Suharwardi. No thought other than that of god remains in the heart. He who is engaged in remembrance of God, masters *dhikr*, the *dhikr* overwhelms him and the heart is released from all else. According to the famous tradition:

> My earth and My heaven contain Me not, but the heart of My faithful servant containeth Me.

Beauty and grandeur is revealed to the heart, and the reality of "Everything that exists will perish except His own self" is manifested. And in the words of Baba Kuhi of Shiraz he cries out:

> *In the market, in the cloister—only God I saw*
> *In the valley and on the mountain—only God I saw*
> *Him I have seen beside me oft in tribulation;*

In favour and in fortune—only God I saw.
In prayer and fasting, in praise and contemplation,
In the religion of the Prophet—only God I saw.
Neither soul nor body, accident nor substance,
Qualities nor causes—only God I saw.
I opened mine eyes and by the light of His face around me
In all the eye discovered—only God I saw.
Myself with mine own eyes I saw most closely,
But when I looked into nothingness, I vanished,
And lo, I was the All living—Only God I saw.[2]

This is cleansing of the heart and its end. The *sufis* call this state 'annihilation' or 'passing away' and regard it as the end of the journey to God.

There is no admittance for anyone till
he becomes naught
Into the audience-chamber of (Divine) Majesty.
What is the means of ascension to Heaven,
this not-being?
Not-being is the creed and religion of the
lovers of God.

In respect of this purified heart the author of *Ruh al-arwah* has described the Almighty God's address in the following words:

> God talked of Lord-ship to the bodies, and to the hearts talked of love. Said He, O bodies! I am God, and O hearts! I am Friend. O bodies! Undergo pain and trouble, because Lordship demands that you should serve and worship Me, and O hearts! be joyous! O bodies! Enjoy the blessings secured from austerities, and O hearts! Enjoy the beatific vision. O bodies! Do not give up obeying Me. O hearts! Do not obey without My remembrance. O bodies! Suffer pain, and O hearts! Secure the treasure.[3]

REFERENCES

1. Quoted from Jawahir-i Ghaibi by Saiyid Muzaffar Ali Shah, p. 357. Lucknow, 1887.
2. Quoted from Nicholson's Mystics of Islam, p. 59. It is the translation of a part of a Persian ode by the dervish-poet, Baba Kuhl of Shiraz, who died in 1050 C.E.
3. Quoted from Shama'il-i atqiya, p. 263, by Shaikh Rukn al-Din Kashani of Khuldabad, Hyderabad, 1347 A.H.

(Revised and edited; originally appeared in Studies in Islam, January 1970).

13

Problems of Translating Sufi Texts from Indo-Persian to American English

BRUCE B. LAWRENCE

Translating the foreign language text into one's own language is a task bound to be very tough and highly demanding job. Examines lyrical passages and presents the principle problems encountered and strategies for further research.

Translation is either an outrageous act of extraordinary hubris, or an everyday transaction indispensable to human existence. According to theorists, it is both, though the quotidian quality of translation is more often stressed.The literary critic George Steiner once declared that "(all) human communication, inside or between languages, equals translation."[1] Yet speech and writing are not equivalent means of communication. While speech implies the preunderstanding of thought, writing requires the further refinement of speech into units of commonly held discourse. Translation, even literary translation, resembles speech more than writing: it offers metaphors of what we do every day, consciously but also unconsciously, in the privacy of our homes as well as in the fully gaze of public attention.

Translation requires resources, and the resource requirements vary from context to context. As difficult as it may be to forge and maintain a viable idiom within a single cultural field mapped by different languages, it is still more difficult to translate unrelated languages from disparate cultures, e.g., Chinese to German, Arabic to French or Urdu to English.[2] The most difficult chore of all, however, is to bridge, or try to bridge, disparate cultural traditions through a written translation that moves from one hybrid language to another.

Let me explain what I mean by hybrid language. Americans speak a hybrid language. Though labelled English, it is actually American English, not only because Americans have a different vocabulary, but also because there is a different tonality to language on the western than the eastern side of the Atlantic Ocean. American English is derived from Britain but it is not a replica of the original. Nor is the language with which I work much of my professional life related, except as a simulacrum, to what Middle Easterners call Persian. There is a common body of literature, a parallel grammar, overlapping vocabulary, but a different pronunciation as also a divergent sensibility between Persian and Indo-Persian. The latter developed on the Indian subcontinent, from the 13th to the 19th century. Both Amir Khusraw and 'Abdul Qadir Bedil were Indo-Persian poets, and yet they differed as much from one another as did Anee Bradstreet, a 17th century American poetess, from Adrienne Rich, a contemporary lyricist. The differences may seem slight to outsiders, i.e., to those who are unfamiliar with either American or Indo-Persian poetry but for those who rhyme words or else listen to others who do, the differences are at once apparent and striking.

How then can one bridge the linguistic space between Indo-Persian and American English? or once straddling that space, how can one then try to bridge the still wider distance between the two cultures within which Indo-Persian and American English serve as vehicles of communication? Indo-Persian stands at an ambivalent mid-point in Islamic civilization. Beyond the classical but prior to the modern, it is middle or medieval but without a stable point of original or canonical authority. It becomes an evolved linguistic/literary convention. It embodies Islamic loyalty, it projects Islamic piety but it also reflects an India-specific notion of fluid boundaries, the metaphysical correlate to a society at once highly structured on class lines yet tolerant of spiritual athleticism, the attainment of spiritual boons by the common as well as the elite. Indo-Persian literature could and did pose a challenge to all Muslims, from those in power to those with no power.

Late 20th-century America, on the other hand, is characterized by a diversity that admits of enormous class fluidity but very little spiritual innovation or adventuresome-ness. Those who stand out as spiritual are frequently alien outcasts, such as the Reverent Jim Jones of Jonestown fame, or the flamboyantly disingenuous, such as Jim Bakker, founder of Heritage USA and the PTL (Praise the Lord) Club but now a convicted embezzler. In the United States true spirituality never challenges the incumbents of either the Republican or Democratic Party, despite the furore about the Moral Majority a decade ago and the fuss about the Robertson Presidential campaign in 1988. Late 20th century America is securely, almost smugly secular, and if any spiritual contestant does emerge to the front ranks, that individual will not survive the scorching review of the national press, operating not merely as a torchlight for freedom but also in defence of its own thoroughly commercial and complexly pluralist interests.[3]

From the Persian that is not quite Persian to an English that is less than its mother tongue, from a controlling religious culture to a culture beyond the control of religion, how does not translate? And if that task is not sufficiently daunting, how does one add a further variable, the variable of translating from poetry to poetry rather than from prose to prose?

Professor Hamid Algar, in rendering the 13th century Sufi manual *Mirsad al-'Ibad (min al-Mabda' ila'l Ma'ad)* into English, called attention to the obstacles he faced. The stylistic qualities of the original, he noted, "addressed themselves to an esthetic and spiritual sensibility different from that of the modern world." Through his own translation Professor Algar offered his reader(s) an invitation to transpose oneself to the realm of an archaic sensibility. He strived to become "not merely the translator of Daya (i.e., Najm al-Din Razi Daya, author of *Mirsad al-'Ibad*) into English but also, in some measure, his interpreter to a new audience."[4]

Refreshing as is Algar's candour about the difficulties of translating middle Persian into modern English, even he refrains from trying to provide more than a workmanlike rendition of Daya's frequent verses into English equivalents. When an expert of Algar's stature hesitates to render poetry into poetry, all should pause. It may be an impossible undertaking.

Warned but still hopeful, I have taken up this challenge. Before sharing with you some of my own efforts at rendering Indo-Persian verse into American English, let me background my labour. Almost ten years ago, at the request of the editor for a series called Classics of Western Spirituality,[5] I began translating the foremost Indo-Persian *malfuzat, Fawa'id al-Fu'ad* (hereafter abbreviated as FF). FF is the recording of conversations with Shaykh Nizam al-Din Awliya (d. 725/1325), made by his poet-disciple, Amir Hasan Sijzi. Five years later, thanks in part to a sabbatical in India, where I was able to enjoy the company and partake of the wisdom of Syed Vahiduddin, I had nearly completed the prose portions of FF. All that remained was some poetry. Since a contemporary Indian Muslim scholar, Ziya ul-Hasan Faruqi, had earlier begun an English translation,[6] I felt confident that I could benefit from his renditions in shaping my own.

My confidence was shaken, however, when I chanced upon a wide ranging paper by the Chinese American linguist Eugene Eoyang. In his paper Professor Eoyang delineates three levels of translation: surrogate, contingent and co-eval.[7] At the first level the work of translation stands as its own literary achievement, with no appreciable reference to any other work. It presupposes monolingual readers, readers knowing only the language into which the translation is being made. The translation becomes a replacement of surrogate for the original. By contrast, the second or contingent level of translation always privileges the original, appealing to a potentially bilingual audience. It is effective if it makes the translated text accessible to a student of that text. Finally, there is the co-eval translation. To quote Professor Eoyang, "If a translation is to be considered a correlate to the original, to co-exist with it, neither as its replacement for those who do not read the original, nor as an aid for those who wish to approach the original, but *as a possible rival* (and in the event of the disappearance of the original, its replacement), then its audience is equivalently bilingual, its readers a more cosmopolitan polyglot tribunal. We may call these co-eval translations."[8]

There are problems, of course, associated with each level of translation. The surrogate invites pseudo configurations of the original; often they stress what is romantic or exotic. The effect is to encourage what the French call *distanciation*, a term given a certain currency in American English by the philosopher Paul Ricoeur.[9] The alienness or otherness of the original is glaringly maintained, even accentuated. The contingent, on the other hand, appeals to two, widely variant groups—beginning language students and natives who want to see what foreigners make of their legacy. Neither group is very large, and their literary tastes are minimal. Moreover, contingent translations offer the illusion of compatibility without suggesting any way of communicating what has been heard or understood to monolingual others. Only co-eval translations have the potential to succeed as cross-cultural windows, opening out simultaneously in two directions. Superseding contingent translations, they can also supplant the need for surrogate translations, for among the three levels they alone would attain a literary fidelity engaging both groups of native speakers.

As attractive as the ideal of co-eval translation appears to be, it would seem to be unattainable in the case of poetry. Not only are there semantic disparities between the translation and the original, not only are rhyme and meter elusive, but also there is what Valery once posited as the absolute criterion of excellence for poetry: "the prolonged hesitation between sound and meaning."[10] Few are the persons gifted as powers in their own right who can harness their art to the raw data of another artist from another culture. One such person is Naomi Lazard, twentieth-century American poet who has rendered selections from Faiz Ahmed Faiz's verse into English. Lazard worked with Faiz for nearly a decade, in order "to bring his full-throated voice into English." She discovered in herself "an infinite patience for translations, the same patience I have for writing my own poems. I have learned that it doesn't matter how long it takes, how many transformations a poet must be brought through, until the English version works in the same way that a poem I have written myself works. It must be faithful to the meaning Faiz has given it. It must move in his own spirit, with the same feeling and tone. It must have the same music, the same direction, and, above all, *it must mean the same thing in English that it means in Urdu.*"[11]

I have stressed that last line because it sets such a high standard of cross-cultural communication that it would defy the ambitions of all but the most gifted and dedicated poet. If this was what co-eval translation required, then I had to admit my own limitations: by myself I could not coax from Shaykh Nizam al-Din's Indo-Persian verses anything like equivalents in American English. Until spring 1989, I resigned myself to the more modest task of producing surrogate renditions of the FF original. I felt that such poems, though they did not prolong the distance between sound and meaning, would at least satisfy those monolinguist Americans who might read the Paulist Press series, just as the contingent translations of FF offered by Professor Faruqi provided grist for English reading Indian Muslims who could comprehend the Persian original.

Yet I remained unhappy with the results. The English words cloyed the mind as well as the tongue. They seemed too flat and pedestrian. Uninspiring and insipid, they mimicked instead of memorializing the great Shaykh who once remarked that "while lying is a sin, a lie conveyed in verse is not a sin."[12] My dilemma persisted till summer 1989, when I attended a conference in Heidelberg on pre-modern South Asian Islam. There I met Professor Christopher Shackle of the School of Oriental and African Studies, London. Professor Shackle had read some of my earlier translations of FF.[13] A skilled translator of Punjabi verse, he was convinced that beyond the surrogate or contingent renditions of poetry in the FF, co-eval translations were possible. He read through all my prior efforts and then crafted a full forty pages of his own efforts. By October 1989 I had received them (along with a cover letter thanking me for getting him "into that magic world again, after too long on the periphery." It is, of course, he not I who deserves thanks). I worked through Professor Shackle's translations. In some cases I agreed with him, in others I came up with further possibilities of my own. At each point I benefited from the generous gift of critical imagination which marked Professor Shackle's labour and made possible our unusual collegial exchange.

Integral to this exchange has been a common and constant wrestling with technical issues: what English meanings of Persian words best suit the text? what rhymes or metres in English seem appropriate to capture a sense of the original Persian? Closely linked to such technical issues are hermeneutical questions: how does one communicate cross-culturally the pathos or the *elan* of verses that are not explicated but simply offered in the original text? how can one register for late 20th century American readers the power of verses that in 13th century North India had the potential to literally kill their listeners?[14] In Professor Algar's words, how does not coax the modern post-Christian American reader to transpose herself or himself into the realm of an archaic sensibility? For me the key move is to conjoin hermeneutical strategies with technical options, and to allow the former to guide the latter. In many of the later translations that I've made from FF, due to Professor Shackle's inspiration and assistance, it is interpretive hunches that inform technical choices, especially when the context suggests that an American accent might unlock and yet enfold the oddity of the Indo-Persian original.

To illustrate the results of this protracted, often frustrating process, I have selected a few cases that thematically cohere on a single point, the beauty of cruelty of the Beloved, I begin with verses that come from classical Persian poetry, from Sa'di and Sana'i, before giving examples from Indo-Persian authors.

Often, beauty and cruelty are but janus-like expressions of the same divine countenance. It is a mystery not easily wrestled into words, and so it is through verse rather than prose that one often finds the most sensitive registers of the seeming paradox that to be cruel is beautiful and vice versa. A necessary correlate of this same theme is the exclusivity of love: before either beauty or cruelty can be experienced, there has to be the intention of seeking the Beloved, and when that intention is lacking then to speak of love is more hypocrisy as the famed bard of Shiraz, Shaykh Sa'di, once said using the protracted *ramal* metre:

Ba-zaban-e har ki juz man be-ravad hadis-e 'ishaqat
cu mu'amala na-darad sukhan ashna na-bashad

(F)[15] People, other then me, who talk of your love
Fail to arouse the passioned response,
As they know not
What genuine love is.

(L 1) On no other tongue but mine
Can there come a report of your love
Those who have not relation to You,
How can their speech have any foundation?

(S) When others than myself tell of their love for you.
Because they're not involved, their words do not ring true.
(or) They lack experience to make their words ring true.

(L2) Who else but I can try to talk of loving You?
Since others have no basis, their words do not ring true.

This couplet is quoted approvingly by Shaykh Nizam al-Din in FF (Book Two, Assembly 26). It is the sole quotation from Sa'di in FF. Its evocative appeal to experience seems better rendered by a couplet than by a quatrain, as Professor Faruqi and I (initially) attempted to render it. Nor does the absence of terminal rhyme in the original Persian preclude its introduction into the translation. Both moves are suggested by Professor Shackle, and I have followed his lead. Though neither strategy seems justified on logical grounds, the mood conveyed by the resultant translations seems right. I differed from Professor Shackle, and also from the Persian original, by turning the initial verse into a rhetorical question. In American English the affirmation of the second verse has a stronger ring as answer to question rather than main clause following subordinate clause:

The task of love has many perils. Talking about the Beloved, even with a firm basis, remains a risky proposition. In the convention of both Persian and Indo-Persian poetry, the beauty of the Beloved can only be alluded to, it can never be exposed. Once exposed, the agent of exposure, that is, the Sufi adept, puts himself at risk. The penalty for such bravado may be nothing less than physical death. It is a point made by Hakim Sana'i in short verses composed in the explosive *khafif* metre.

besh ma-nam jamal-e jan afroz
cun numudi bar-o sipand bi-soz
an jamal-e to cist masti-ye to
van sipand-e to cist hasti-ye to

(F) Do no exhibit your bewitching beauty before any body;
If it is made to glitter, go and burn seeds of *sipand.*
What is, after all, your bewildering beauty except
your own bewilderment (arising out of the contemplation of God)?
And what is that *sipand* but your own existence?

(L1) Show me not that soul scorching beauty.
But if it appears, go burn the wild rue.
What's that beauty of yours?
The cause of drunkenness.
And that wild rue of Yours?
The basis of existence.

(S) Show less your loveliness, which burns my soul right through.
Once shown, though, on these flames cast well for luck wild-rue.
What is your loveliness? Your insobriety!
What is then your wild-rue? Your true reality!

(L2) Display not that beauty which burns men's souls right through.
Once displayed, though, go cast upon those flames wild rue.
For what's that beauty of yours but your drunkenness?
And what's that wild rue but your very existence?![16]

Even when one opts to make a surrogate rendition of these

verses, as does Professor Faruqi (F), they retain the aspects of a defiantly difficult poem, one that requires, before all else, a cultural understanding of wild rue. The seeds of wild rue, when burned, were thought to ward off the evil eye. Without such a prophylactic, it was thought, the evil eye would afflict those endowed with the marks of beauty.[17] But who is the agent at once beautiful and burning seeds to protect his beauty? Professor Faruqi opts for a human beauty, Professor Shackle the transcendent Beauty. In the first two stanzas, the loveliness alluded to may be divine. But men, especially saintly men, can mirror the divine, and even reflect His beauty. In such instances, for the individuals' protection, seeds of *sipand* must be cast on fire. But the divine beauty, having been displayed, may resist, or become immune to, prophylaxis. It can cause loss of control. It can cause the saint to become so out of control that he appears to be drunk. To ward off ill effects of such loss of control, not just wild rue, but the person who displays divine beauty, must himself burn, i.e., he must be physically destroyed or expire.

Perhaps one should not even venture the co-eval rendition of such an intricate poem, yet so crucial is it to Shaykh Nizam al-Din's message in this FF narrative that to miss it is to miss the major point he is trying to communicate. For Shaykh Nizam al-Din the verse refers not to any saint but to the saint who cannot refrain from displaying God's beauty. He divulges the image of the Artist in his soul by performing miracles. The miracles succeed. Other benefit. They are duly impressed with the saint's sanctity. But despite his sanctity, the saint is doomed to death: like the wild-rue thrown on fire, he sacrifice his physical body to produce a salutary smoke, for his burning then becomes a warning to later saints, saints who, like him might be tempted to display their own divinely given beauty.

The true sense of this poem can only be communicated, or at least hinted at, by restoring it to its original context. Here is the full passage of FF within which it occurs. It constitutes the epitome of an entire assembly, the assembly recorded in Book One as Assembly 29, which took place on Monday the 20th of Shawwal, A.H. 708 (11 April, A.D. 1309). It reads as follows:

I obtained the benefit of kissing the master's feet. He started to tell a story about Shaykh 'Uthman Khairabadi—may God have mercy upon him. From his blessed lips came the pronouncement: "Shaykh 'Uthman was a very saintly person. He also wrote a commentary on the Qur'an." He then went on to note that the Shaykh resided in Ghazin, where he used to prepare a vegetable stew of turnips, beets and such things: after putting all the ingredients in a pot, he would boil them. The resulting stew was very tasty.

Afterward, in explaining divine favour, the master recited the following verse:

God upon the shepherd puts a prophet's crown.

How else could shepherds as prophets gain renown?

He was referring here to the Prophet Moses—peace he upon him—and his relationship with Khizr. And then he began to expound upon the spiritual states of Shaykh 'Uthman. "If someone came and gave him a counterfeit *diram* in order to buy some of his stew he would take it: even though he knew it to be counterfeit, he would say nothing to the buyer. And if someone gave him a *diram* which was good currency, he would also take it and give the person stew. Hence people assumed that Shaykh 'Uthman did not know the difference between counterfeit and good money. Many used to come and give him false currency. He would accept it as good money and give then food. At the time of his death, Shaykh 'Uthman looked skyward and prayed: "O God, you know better than anyone that people gave me false currency and I accepted it as good. I have not taken offence at what they did. If there has come to you from me false devotion, then in Your mercy please do not take offence at what I have done."

The master told one further anecdote about Shaykh 'Uthman Khairabadi. Once a dervish who was the master of his spiritual state (*sahib-e hal*) came to Shaykh 'Uthman and asked for some food from his cauldron. Shaykh 'Uthman dipped his ladle into the pot, and when he pulled it out, there were only pearls! Exclaimed the dervish: "What can I do with this?" Shaykh 'Uthman put the ladle back into the pot, and this time he scooped out gold! "These are but pebbles and gravel," groused the dervish. "Pull out something that I can eat!" A third time Shaykh 'Uthman dipped his ladle into the pot and scooped out the same vegetable stew that he had been boiling. Observing Shaykh 'Uthman's self-disclosure of his spiritual state, the dervish declared, "You must no longer stay here (i.e., in the world). Within a few days Shaykh 'Uthman—may God have mercy upon him— expired and left this world."

"When a dervish discloses something of such magnitude," observed the master, may God remember him with favour, "it is not suitable for him to remain in the world, as Hakim Sana'i has said:

> Display not that beauty which burns men's souls right through.
> Once displayed, through, go cast upon those flames wild rue.
> For what's that beauty of your but your drunkenness?
> And what's that wild rue but your very existence?!"

After that the master explained:

It is because saints disclose the divine secret due to their drunkenness that they are called 'exponents of intoxication' (*sukr*), in contrast to the prophets, who are called 'exponents of sobriety' (*sahw*). Sana'i not only alluded to their drunkenness; he also implied that when one discloses the divine secret, one should not delay leaving the world. Hence he said:

> For what's that beauty of yours but your drunkenness?
> And what's that wild rue but your very existence?!

"Disclosing divine secrets and performing miracles (*karamat*)," concluded the master, "are actually a hindrance in the Path. For true devotees the real task is to be firm in the pursuit of love." And praise be to God for that (counsel)!

FF abounds with other examples illustrating the pathos of the human engagement with transcendent Beauty. Less linguistically dense than the above verses from Sana'i, they are no less taxing to communicate with the evocative tone of the original Persian. All rest on the conceit of being able to express through the ear that which cannot be experienced by the eye. Among Indo-Persian poets who've tried to encapsulate this theme, perhaps non has exceeded Qadi Hamid al-Din Nagawri, a 13th-century Suhrawardi saint much esteemed by the Chisti standard-bearers.[18] It is the following quatrain from Qadi Hamid al-Din that transfixed Shaykh Nizam al-Din as also other Sufi masters:

An 'aql kuja ki dar kalam-e to rasad
Van ruh kuja ki dar jalal-e to rasad
Giram ki to parda bar firifti zi jamal
An dida kuja ki dar jamal-e to rasad

(L1) Where is the intellect to perceive Your perfection?
Where is the soul soul to attain Your majesty?
I want you to remove the veil from the face of beauty.
But where are the eyes to behold your beauty?

(S) What mind can truly grasp Your perfectness?
What soul can truly feel your awesomeness?
Your loveliness, I know, You have unveiled:
What eye, though, can behold your loveliness?

(L2) Where's the mind grasp Your sovereignty?
Where's the soul to mirror Your majesty?
Beauty's face, I know, Your could unveil
But where are eyes to behold *Your* beauty?

At first, I wanted to change the rhyme scheme to 2-3-4 but Professor Shackle's effort convinced me to try again with the 1-2-4 rhyme scheme of the original poem. As in the preceding poem from Sana'i,

I differ with Professor Shackle principally in the word choice of beauty rather than loveliness to render *jamal*. Either could fit but there is more of an edge to -ty than -ness for a final rhyme in American English, or at least there seems to be to my ear. It is for each reader of the Indo-Persian and then our attempted translations to make the preferred choice for herself or himself.[19]

In both Persian and Indo-Persian Sufi poetry a theme which complements the extraordinary, yet unattainable, beauty of the divine Beloved is the affirmation of death. Death is affirmed but not as a natural process; rather it is affirmed as a necessary and welcome sequal to unqualified love. The primary exemplar of love to the point of physical death is Mansur al-Hallaj. A literal martyr to love, who lost his limbs before being beheaded, burned and his ashes tosses on the Tigris, his memory is hallowed by all those Sufis who symbolically also commit themselves to losing selfhood on the path of love.

The Indo-Persian difference from classical Persian verses on the same theme may be seen by comparing verses that reflect the Hallajian pattern of unstinting love. Consider the following two verses that come from Shaykh Najm al-Din Daya's depiction of Hallaj in *Mirsad al-'Ibad*:

Bar atesh-e to besozam
Gar sukhtan-e manat besazad
Gufti ke bibaz jan cun mardan
'ashiq che konad ke jan nabazad

Professor Algar translates this poem as follows:

Let me burn on the love's fire
If for me to burn pleases thee.
Thou said, "Lose thy life in manly style";
What is a lover to do, except lose his life?[20]

The sense of commitment in these verses is balanced by a delayed acquiesence to the Beloved. The bold acknowledgement of the Beloved's demand is followed by a rhetorical question rather than a blanket submission: *'ashiq che konad ke jan nabazad?* But the final verse of this same narrative on Hallaj in *Mirsad al-'Ibad* removes all doubt about the sacrifice required on behalf of love:

> *'ishq amad o shud chukhunam andar raq o pusht*
> *Ta kard mara tahi o pur kard az dost*
> *Ajza-ye wojud-e man hame dost girift*
> *Name ast az man bar man o baqi hame ust.*

Again Algar's renedition captures the above in blank verse:

> Love came and like blood ran through my flesh and veins
> Emptied me, then filled me with the Friend.
> The Friend took from me every part of my being,
> Of me, a name remained to me; the rest in all HE.

In this final verse, love is all consuming and transforming yet the concrete sense of being killed by the Beloved remains attenuated, as is the sense of constant renewal through love. Indo-Persian Sufis preferred the image of physical death through the sword to extinction on flames, and in the poetry they selected, as in the poetry they wrote, the dagger as well as the sword loom large. Consider the following verse. Like most of the above, it comes from Persian rather than Indo-Persian, being credited to the little known Khorasanian mystic Shaykh Ahmad Jam (d. 1141). The verse, like the name of Ahmad Jam, was celebrated in the subcontinent chiefly among the Chishtiya brotherhood:

> *Kushtagan-e khanjar-e taslim-ra*
> *har zaman as ghaib jane digar ast.*

(L1) Those who are slain by the dagger of submission
Each moment from the Unseen receive a new life.

(S) On all the victims of submission's knife
Each moment comes from the Unseen bestows new life.

(L2) To those killed by the knife of submission
Each moment comes from the Unseen new life.

or (L3) All those by the knife of submission killed
Each moment from God with new life are filled.

The verse requires familiarity with the Sufi antonyms of *fana* (annihilation) and *baqa* (permanence). Within that referential field, *fana* is tantamount to loss of self, surrender to the Beloved, who is the Transcendent Creator, who is God. Total surrender equals self-effacement or death; hence those who submit are slain by the dagger of submission. But they do not die, for in each moment that they die, beyond death they experience *baqa* persistence or permanence. It is a permanence vouchsafed by the same one who demands death and it is a permanence continuously renewed. *Each* moment from the Beyond or the Unseen or God the slain receives a new soul, which is to say, new life in Him. The pivotal image that empowers this verse in the dagger or knife of submission. It is pivotal because its agent is ambiguous: is it God, or is it the submission to Him, that produces death? To the extent that the act of submission induced a response it is unimportant who or what the agent of death is, but the beauty of the couplet is its ability to play on the ambiguity as also the dyad of *fana/baqa* and thereby inspire would-be Sufi adepts. In this sense, it resembles the famous couplet from Sana'i, to be found in the both *Mirsad al-'Ibad* and also in *Maktubat-i Sadi* of Maneri:

Sufiyan dar dami do 'id konand
'ankabutan magus qadid konand.

Again, Algar's rendition of this couplet in blank verse is worth noting:

The Sufis celebrate two festivals in one breath,
Just as the spiders make salted meat out of flies.

The image is awkward, at least to our ears, but the point rests on the speed with which the Sufis experience *fana* and *baqa*. They are simultaneously self-effaced and restored by their total devotion, their surrender to the divine Beloved, to the Transcendent, to God. It is the dynamism of this process that Sana'i captured, just as did Ahmad Jam in the less obscure couplet quoted above.

Apart from juggling cross-cultural meanings in vastly different contexts, how does one render such a line into American English? It is in order to sharpen the focus of the original for an American audience that I have followed Professor Shackel in providing rhyme where there was no rhyme. Indeed, I have exceeded Professor Shackle's initiative by doubling the rhyme, rhyming not only two verbs at the end but also two nouns in the middle of this highly charged couplet. In two other aspects Professor Shackle's approach has improved my own earlier efforts: (1) the linking of the first to the second line and (2) the generalizing of *baqa* from a life to life.

Even more graphic, at once more poignant and more lyrical, that the couplet of Shaykh Ahamd Jam on death is the following anonymous verse, extant, as far as I know, only through its citation by Shaykh Nizam al-Din in FF:

dari sar-e ma vagarna dur az bar-e ma
ma dost kushim o to nadari sar-e ma.

(L1) Take heed of me,
Else begone from me.
Though I kill my friends,
Still you heed me not.

(S) Take heed of me, or else Begone I say.
My friends I kill, but no heed you will pay.

(L2) Take heed of me, or else Begone I say.
Though my friends I kill, still no heed you'll pay.

Numerous are the critics who have commented on fondness of Persian poets for word or phoneme repetitions, but in this short verse it is carried to extremes: *dar-sar-gar-bar* in line one are followed by *dar-sar* in line two. The message is all the more powerful because the voice speaking from Beyond is understood to be the Divine Beloved. Rather than the passive voice of the submissive lover, which dominates Persian poetry, here we have the active voice of the jealous lover. It echoes the evocation of love's mystery provided by Shaykh Ahmad Ghazzali in his *Sawanih*. "Jealousy (*ghayrat*), when it shines, is a ruthless sword. . . This is because jealously belongs to the supreme domain of love's justice (*`adl*), and love's justice does not want equality, and the state of a rival or a peer. It wants nothing but commingling with love and attachment to it—even at the expense of doing injustice to the lover."[21]

How then can one recapture the power of this unusual imagery? Moreover, *ma* is accented twice in each line, each time in a stress position. Initially I rendered *ma* as me (rather than us/we), with a nod to be (in begone), while Professor Shackle expanded the rhyme to include the terminal say/pay rhyme. In L 2, I retained his suggestion and added a further kill/still, in order to stress the thematic point of this intricate rhyme: the Friend/God kills His friends, yet they remain unaware that He requires death or *fana* (as the prelude to larger life or *baqa*). Without a sense of the cultural idiom being invoked, the reader might misread this verse as an instance of divine sadism. For those in the Indo-Persian Sufi tradition, however, it becomes a further, exquisite reminder of the high demands that Love makes on the would-be lover.

When so much is at stake, even the selection of a single word becomes crucial, especially when the poet is striving to communicate the flavour of that longed for death! Usually one does not find either a poet or a mystic reflecting on the difficulty of choosing particular words Shaykh Nizam al-Din, the master whose presence animates FF, makes but one such disclosure. It occurs at the point when the Shaykh alludes to the intensity of desiring God which he experienced in a dream. He had been speaking about the taste which is evoked in Sufis through *sama'* (or musical assemblies). "It resembles a fire set ablaze," he observed, and them he goes on to remark: "Once something appeared to me in a dream, and I uttered this verse:"

(L1) "O Friend you have slain me with the *hand* of anticipation"!

And again, I repeated in my dream:

> "O Friend, you have slain me with the *wound* of anticipation"!
>
> But when I woke up, I remembered that the correct form of the verse went like this:
>
> "O Friend, you have slain me with the *sword* of anticipation!"

(S) You have slain me, my friend, with the hand of this waiting.

wound
sword

This marks one of the few instances where I did not modify my prior translation in response to Professor Shackle's suggested rendition. In this case, the Persian in very direct:

Ai dost ba-dast-e intizaram kushti
ba-zakhm-e
ba-tegh-e

Not only is the friend so invoked clearly the divine Beloved, but the invocation must come in the initial position, with a capital, if one is to capture the immediacy of Shaykh Nizam al-Din's dream. He is, after all, addressing God about his innermost spiritual state: like the earlier verse that had literally killed his grand-*pir*, the master of his master, this verse connotes the deadliness of the game of Love when played at the advanced level of Sufi Shaykhs. For Nizam al-Din, unlike Qutb al-Din, the point of death is not submission (*taslims*) but expectancy or waiting (*intizar*). To non-Sufis that may sound like a quibbling, minor distinction but to a Sufi it suggests the subtlety with which Nizam al-Din is at once conjoined to, and separated from, his predecessor: Qutb al-Din literally expired during *sama*, while Nizam al-Din found that its fire propelled him towards the metaphysical goal of his quest without requiring his immediate physical extinction. Killed by anticipation, he nonetheless lived, but he lived for others rather than for himself.

Still, it was important to note in the above verse that the instrument of killing was the *sword* not the *hand*, which would be too anthropomorphic, and not the *wound*, which would be too bodily. The right word to convey the Shaykh's innermost spiritual condition is *sword*, for it alone accents both the Friend's intervention and the instruments of psychological extinction.

It is perhaps fitting to end all this talk of killing and dying with a short couplet from FF, where not only did I differ from Shackle but I differed from myself, that is to say, I could not decide which of two translations fits the sense of the original Indo-Persian:

O sukhan az kushtan-e man mikunad
man ba-hamin khush ki sukhan mikunad.

(L1) Though He speaks of killing me,
That *He* speaks is thrilling to me.

(S) When He Speaks, I know he says He'll kill me —
That he speaks is still enough to thrill me.

(L2) When He speaks, He declares that He will kill me.
Yet that it is He who speaks cannot but thrill me.

Perhaps it is to be expected that after having poured over texts and contexts, meanings and interpretations for so long, I would at last find myself unable to choose between options. For whatever reason, I do find myself in a quandary over the above couplet. Even though both L1 and L2 convey the sense of the Indo-Persian original, they have different metres. L2, like so many others, is a response to S. While it does remove the undesirable *bold lettering* on *He*, it still requires a longer metre than L1, which seems to diminish the immediacy of the pungent imagery. Most days I still prefer L1, although I encourage the reader to opt for either S or L2 or, better still, to construct a fourth option, such as:

(L3) Though He says He'll kill me,
That He says it thrills me.

Conclusion

The brief examination of lyrical passages from FF has provided the pretext for looking at the larger problem of translation. Let me summarize some of the principal problems encountered and at the same time suggest strategies for further research.

1. While ther are no fixed criteria for effective translations, the technique used must reflect both the receptor language and the source language. When syntactic and grammatical features vary widely between the languages involved, the perils of translation increase, and they increase exponentially when the source and receptor audience are further separated by time as well as cultural expectations. If a translator must cope with both cross-cultural and diachronic difference, the likelihood of co-eval translation is markedly reduced.

2. From Indo-Persian to American English involved engagement with two hybrid languages at contrasting moments in their respective cultural histories. The development of American English is at most two hundred years old, while Indo-Persian flourished for over six hundred years. Yet American English continues to function for an extant community while Indo-Persian, shunted into anterior texts, has become, like Latin, a dead language. The temporal symmetry of the two languages must inform the translator's labour.

3. Poetic translations from Indo-Persian to American English are not easily sorted out into categories of surrogate, dependent and co-eval. Surrogate is preferable to dependent it one wants to convey the flavour of the original to American readers. Co-eval, on the other hand, entails a series of decisions about metre and rhyme that vary from translator to translator.

4. Co-eval translation of poetry, to succeed, requires nothing less than as inner ear that functions in two registers with comparable facility. It entails maximum labour with minimal visible result. Yet when co-eval poems are inserted into prose texts and the translator manages to mesh the former with the latter, the poems work like a series of incandescent mirrors, refracting in the receptor as well as in the source language that inner glow of authorial imagination which

no other literary form can capture. At least that is the goal.

The reader must linger over the language of each translated poem, judging the results one by one. When less than fiery flashes appear, he or she must experiment with his or her own imagination. Surrender to prose must be a tactic of last resort, for as Tolstoy once observed, "mysticism without poetry is superstition, while poetry without mysticism is prose!"

REFERENCES

1. George Steiner, After Babel: Aspects of language and translation (London, Oxford Univ., Press, 1975), p. 47.
2. See note 12, below, for an example of translation from Urdu into English.
3. On the complex relationship of the press to religios values, actors, and institutions, see my book Defenders of God: The fundamentalist revolt against the modern age (London, I B Tauris, 1990).
4. Hamid Algar, tr., The path of God's bondsmen from origin to return: A sufi compendium by Najm al-Din Razi, known as Daya, UNESCO Persian Heritage Series no. 35 (Delmar, Carvan Books, 1982), p. 21.
5. For another translation on Indo-Muslim spirituality, see Paul Jackson, tr., Shrafuddin Maneri, The hundered letters (new York, Paulist Press, 1980), with my foreword.
6. Refer, Ziya ul-Hasan Faruqi, tr., Fawa'id-ul-Fu'ad of Khwajah Hasan Dehlawi, Islam and the Modern Age, a series of article in its issues from vol 11 to 16 (1980-1985).
7. Eugen Eoyang, "Translation as excommunication: Notes toward an intraworldly poetics", (Indian University, 30 May 1983). Though this deals with Chinese to English, such obstacles are in all translations that attempt to cross seemingly unbridgable cultural and temporal divides. Hence its relevance here.
8. Ibid., p. 51, the added stress is mine.
9. Riccoeur's terminological assault on cultural subjectivity is discussed in John B Thompson's Studies in the theory of ideology(Berkeley, University of California Press, 1984), pp. 188-264.
10. Josue Harari, Textual strategies (Ithace, Cornell Univ. Press), p. 372; quoting Roman Jakobson, Elements de linguistique generale (Paris, Minuit, 1963), p. 233.
11. Naomi Lazard, tr., The true subject: Selected poems of Faiz Ahmed Faiz

(Princeton, Princeton Univ. Press, 1988), p. xii.

12. Fawaid al-Fu'ad, Book V, Assembly 23, the end. In response to a question from Amir Hasan, Shaykh Nizam al-Din quotes this remarks from an anonymous work he had read. He quotes it approvingly and, on imagines, with a smile at the religious scholars who would be ofended by such an impios suggestion.
13. See my book, Notes from a distant flute: The extant literature of pre-Mughal Indian sufism (Tehran, Imperial Iranian Academy of Philosophy, 1978), pp. 28-29.
14. Shaykh Nizam al-Din's grand-pir, that is master of the master, Shaykh Qutb al-Din Bakhtiyar Kaki, was one of those who had died listening to a verse that he could apply except an invitation to join his Beloved at once. The story of his death is recounted at length in Fawa'id al-Fu'ad, Book IV, Assembly 20.
15. In the excerpts here included, F connotes Faruqi, L1 = Lawrence, first try; (S) = Shackle; (L2) = Lawrence, second try.
16. The poem from Sana`i appealed not only to shaykh Nizam al-Din but alos to Shaykh Sharaf al-Din b. Yahya Maneri. For a varient translation, see Jackson's work, p. 180.
17. As above, Father Paul Jackson did translate another sufi classic, Maktubat-i Sadi of Shaykh Sharaf al-Din Maneri, (Populist Press). In the letter titled "Mystical knowledge of the transcendent Creator" (Ma'rif-e Bari - Letter 45), Maneri tries to illustrate why God's beauty is at once desirable yet unattainable. In this connection he quotes the above verses, which Father Jackson renders as follows:

    Before us is the dazzling beauty of the city

    When you have observed it, go! Burn some wild rue!

    What is that beauty before you? It is your intoxication!

    And what is that wild rue? It is your being!

    The first line reads jamal-e shehr afroz instead of jamal-e jan afroz. While both versions are technically possible, the FF variant seems preferable because of the inernalization of the struggle between containing and disclosing beauty that it evokes. Like the Faruqi rendition of FF, the last two lines here also have both a human subject and an external referent.
18. On this extraordinary lyricist combining juridicial skills with mystical sensibilities, see my article, " The Lawa'ih of Qadi Hamid ad-din Nagauri", Indo-Iranica 20 (1975) 34-53.
19. Father Jackson also encountered this verse in the above letter from Maneri. His translation aptures the spirit of the original in blank verse without metre:

Where is the intellect that can attain to your perfection?
Where is the spirit which can aspire to Your majesty?
We want You to raise the beauty-concealing veil,
But hwere is the eye that can see Your beauty?

20. The poem epitomizes the paean to Hallaj's passion that concludes Part Three, Chapter Twenty of Daya's masterpiece. See Algar, p. 330.
21. Nasrollah Pourjavady, tr. Ahmad Ghazzali's Sawanih (London, Routledge, 1986), p. 17.

(Revised and edited; originally published in Islamic Culture April-July 1990).

14

Unusual Sufi Utterances: Problems of Interpretations

WALTER J. EISENBEIS

Sets certain issues and oreintation from which this significance can be highlighted; lists the comments with considerations; illustrates how the acquistion of deeply rooted viewpoints occurs. Aims to see the conceptual framework working in this context, under which perceptions of the sufis are also considered, perceptions which are important in their unusual utterances.

The idea of unusual utterances seem to contrast starkly with the Sufis' acknowledged debt to religion. These utterances have been explained by the concept of intoxication. This, however, may have been an accretion merely to pacify the theologians, implying that with this one exception, the Sufis are good Muslims and accept Islamic concepts and practices. The statements, however, remain and each statement of this type creates a certain turbulence which needs to be stilled.

The issue appears to be one of dogma and the intellectual acceptance of certain premises in contrast to the mystics' "experiential" understanding of religion. Once must bear in mind the opposition of the theologians towards Sufis, and the fact that Sufis have been executed for their words. It is noteworthy that in the case of Hallaj, the Sufis did not condemn him for what he said, but the fact that he said it. In essence, these incidents seem to point towards a distinction between doctrine and dogma and one's relationship with God.

In Islam this question emerged in the concept of there being both an internal and an external aspect to the Qur'an. This necessarily raises the question of what this means and, subsequently, the significance of this distinction in reference to ritual, belief and practice. Images and concepts in religious traditions (including the mystical tradition) are initially based on experiences and illuminations. These later become condensed into doctrine and dogma and even though they can be accepted, until the individual has a similar verifying experience, they are not "real."

> .....we need to have constantly in mind that our outward practices have no meaning or any proper role in religion which is not derived, directly or indirectly, from religious experience.[1]

A religious community usually divides into two major camps, which may be variously labelled: externalist, internalist; theologian, mystic; Ulama', Sufis; followers, seekers. The Sufis have their own dogmas and traditions, which tend to assume the same role as the "official" position and its supporters. It is in reference to this situation that these Sufi statements become crucial and pointed.

> ....credit is given to formal notions for what only properly belongs to them in the service of something else, namely live experience of God. In this way the dogmas become themselves the ultimate terms of religion and are allowed to attract to themselves the glory and splendour they should be transmitting. Being first degraded to barriers and absorbers of energy they become counterfeits, false gods or idols reverenced, with all their appurtenances, in a properly religious way *on their own account.*[2]

Those religious experiences which gave a religious tradition its unique flavour become idolized and their directive purpose, i.e. their pointing towards truth and God, is lost. Furthermore, this change leads to a hierarchy of "caretakers" of the faith with inevitable results: the religion becomes interpreted by an elite class of people. All becomes mediated by them instead of being directly between an individual and God.

> There is nothing accidental about this difference between a church and its Founder. As soon as absolute truth is supposed to be contained in the saying of a certain man, there is a body of experts to interpret his sayings, and these experts infallibly acquire power, since they hold the key to truth. Like any other privileged caste, they use their power for their own advantage.[3]

It is the same in reference to Sufism. In the 4th/10th and 5th/11th centuries a change occurred in Sufism wherein the *shaikh/pir* became the undisputed authority and the disciples were expected to obey him at all costs.

> .....whereas in the 3rd/9th century Junayd of Baghdad taught that a seeker should behave, vis-a-vis God, as a puppet, it was not (4th/10th century) said that he should be in the hands of his preceptor as 'a dead body in the hands of its washer.'[4]

This drastically changed the focus of Sufism. It, in fact, becomes parallel to the inter-relationships between theologians, doctrines, traditions and the religious community in general. The only difference is the scale. Gibb's comment about what Sufism is compared with theology delineates a difference in emphasis :

> Sufism was an attitude rather than a doctrine. Its personal, imaginative and experiential character meant that, in contrast to theology, it could not remain one and the same thing, finding expression at all times and in all places in the same formulas. On the contrary, it was bound to differ even from individual to individual, and to express the widest variety of reactions to stimuli of widely differing kinds.[5]

The latter part of Gibb's comment accentuates personal experience, which, as noted above, is the basis of religious validation and the source of those practices which are subsequently defined as "orthodox."

With the change in Sufism that brought the spiritual guide into new prominence and ultimately institutionalised Sufism with its particularised approaches, a new issue emerged.

Not only, then, did the later institutional Sufism reintroduce that intermediary authority [the guide] between God and man which early Sufism had protested against and repudiated, but reintroduced it on a lower level. For now both worship and authority were no longer concentrated on a universally and rationally intelligible object.[6]

A system of this kind [guide/disciple] constitutes an open invitation to the ordinary man to attach himself to persons rather than to doctrines and ideas.[7]

Due to the desire of the mass mentality for guarantees, and the existence of Sufi organisations, a dangerous tendency to saint-worship appeared. This led to the Shaikh becoming extremely important.

In the long run it undermined the structure of Sufi ethics, both through its excessive assertion of spiritual authority, rationalised by a doctrine of secret knowledge possessed and transmitted only by the *pir,* and through the spiritual presumption which it fostered in the *pir* himself.[8]

This issue of "spiritual presumption" has bedevilled Sufism right down to the present day. Furthermore, these conditions within Sufism, even though they became well-established, do contrast sharply with the Qur'an.

....He said : Unless my Lord guide me, I shall surely be among those who go astray, (Quran, VI:77).

....Nor have ye, besides God, anyone to protect or help.(Quran, XLII: 31).

R.A. Nicholson observes :

It may be dangerous to worship God by one's own inner light, but it is far more deadly to seek him by the inner light of another. Vicarious holiness has no compensation.[9]

The Sufis themselves have raised the same points and their

unusual sayings seem to refer to these. Bayazid (Abu Yazid) Bistami says:

> Nothing is better for man than to be without aught, having no asceticism, no theory, no practice. When he is without all, he is with all.[10]

Abu'l-Khayr, another sufi says:

> "Even this Sufism is polytheism (*shirk*)." "Why, O Shaykh?" They asked. He answered, "Because Sufism consists in guarding the soul from what is other than God; and there is nothing other than God."[11]

Both of these statements are stunning in their clarity. The impact on Islam and Sufism, not to mention the individual, is devastating. They undercut the generally accepted foundational concepts of both religion and Sufism with the result that one has to face the question of their meaning.

> Abu'l-Khayr is the author of another statement with similar content:
>
> And never will true Musulman appear
> Till faith and infidelity are one.[12]

To clarify these points it is necessary to see them in relationship with the points noted above on institutionalised religion. It would be incorrect to interpret these remarks to mean there is no value in religion. What is important is the attitude or intention of a person towards various aspects of religious tradition. These are the very aspects of a religion which may usurp the place of God in the mind and practice of an individual. These are "other than God", and hence, polytheism. These practices, traditions, beliefs and dogmas of religion are both secondary and useless without the primary religious experience from which they are derived. It is this type of misunderstanding against which these utterances are directed.

This problem was early recongised in Sufism, although in a

slightly different context. Rabi'a al-'Adwiya said: "Yes, Sufyan (al-Thawri) would be a (good) man, if he did not love the Traditions", and she also used to say, "The seductive power of the Traditions is stronger than the enticement of property and children" (i.e. the study of Traditions distracted him from the life with God even more than worldly possessions would have done), and she said once, "If only Sufyan did not love this world, that is to say the gathering of people round him for (discourses on) the Traditions, what a good thing it would be."[13]

Since the realisation of Divinity must be experienced in a direct encounter, all of the dogma, ritual, theology, 'Ulama', shaikhs and traditions may become obstacles to that goal. Exploring for the unknown from within the known is impossible. Every person is shaped by his upbringing and by the time one is out of infancy he is already imprisoned by his culture. This makes him unable even to conceive of certain possibilities. Religious instruction, as a part of his culture, can also confine vision. Consequently, everyone is buried under hundreds of cultural ideas and values which he has been trained to accept and which he has accepted because he had no choice. These are restricting and debilitating. They keep one from truth as a first-hand encounter, only allowing one to see through another's vision and authority, which was also arrived at in the same manner. One "sees" through a hundred thousand veils and it is this problem to which the Sufi quotations refer. Abu'l-Khayr, for example, was referring to this, in part, when he defined Sufism as "guarding the soul from what is other than God" and then negating it with "there is nothing other than God."

The issue crystallizes around the dynamics and dangers of a systematic approach, of which these "intoxicated" sayings are critical. However, as mentioned above, the term "intoxication" seems to be more utilitarian than explanatory. It excuses and prevents these people from being executed, thereby nominally keeping them in the system. "intoxication" implies that the person has been overwhelmed by God and that it is really God speaking. If this is the case, then these utterances become even more significant, not less. These sayings, however much they seem to attack tradition and a traditional approach, come from people who have become accepted as authorities, thereby making it more complex and paradoxical.

Since a tradition, consisting of values, beliefs and behaviour, invariably shapes a person's mind and conditions him, the individual is constantly selecting. This is "good" and that is "bad", or, this is "correct, proper and acceptable" while that is "false, improper and unacceptable." Now, since the individual is doing this, his information becomes biased, selected on the basis of predetermined norms and values. This can lead to a distorted and self-confirming viewpoint which keeps one remote from reality and oneself. Everything is censored and as a result one never knows who one is because one is forever trying to be what one's tradition or culture prescribes.

The Sufis appear in unusual statements of the type illustrated to have had a vision of this and realised its significance. All culture encapsulates and prevents one from seeing the truth; it keeps one cut off. The real seer does not do this. He sees both the role of tradition and its limitations. Any system, such as a culture, prevents freedom of the mind, which is crucially necessary. It is only the vast panorama of life and thought, when viewed in all its aspects, without barriers, in which one is personally engaged, that allows deep religious consciousness. Hence these statements which are critical of the stylization and the formalism of religion. The Sufi does not approve of a restrictive, blind approach because the very stresses and strains, the intense interplay and contradictions of life stimulate the mind to resolve and understand them. Gradually, or suddenly in some cases, the person sees. He is able to follow the intricacies. He does not withdraw himself from daily life, but sees through it, and this can only occur when he is "without aught, having no asceticism, no theory, no practice." In fact, he is not seeking and the world and his self recede from him.

In the light of this, these Sufi comments on the gnostic are condensed summation :

A gnostic is not one who rejects all Paths other than his own, thereby contemplating only his "travel" and "examination." The genuine traveller surely travels along all the "roads."[14]...

All, good and evil, parts of the dervish be,
And who so is not so, no dervish is he.[15]

Dervishhood in all its meanings is a metaphorical poverty, and amidst all its subordinate aspects there is a transcendent principle. The Divine mysteries come and go over the dervish, so that his affairs are freed from the bonds of acquisition (*kasb*), his actions are no more attributed to himself. Then he is the way, not the wayfarer, i.e., the dervish is a place over which something is passing, not a wayfarer following his own will. Accordingly, *he neither draws anything to himself nor puts anything away from himself:* all that leaves any traces on him belongs to the essence.[16]

It is in this latter sense, when the currents and eddies of life flow through an individual, that he transcends these daily fluctuations and perceives a deeper and more enduring foundation. This does not mean that he is insensitive, but highly sensitive, so that "He has become an image of his community, mankind, and the rest of the world."[17] This can occur only if there is total acceptance. If there is no total acceptance then segments will be left out and the mind is closed, or not fully in contact, fragmented. One might say there is no *tauhid.*

Unfortunately, it is not possible to tell another person what these possibilities are. One reason is that the person may get intellectually involved, or trust in them too much, thereby recreating the situation from which he needs to escape. This is self-defeating. It has to be undergone, the path must be traversed, and for every person it is necessarily different in particulars. As far as guidance and literature is concerned, Ibn 'Arabi's comment is pertinent:

Gnostics cannot impart their feelings to other men; they can only indicate them symbolically to those who have begun to experience the life.[18]

REFERRENCES

1. H D Lewis, Our experience of God (London, George Allen and Unwin, 1959), p. 188.
2. Ibid., p. 162 (emphasis added).
3. Bertrand Russell, Why I am not a Christian (London, Unwin Books, 1975), p. 28.
4. Fazlur Rahman, Islam (New York, Holt, Rinehart & Winston, 1966), p. 137.
5. H A R Gibb, "The structure of religious thought in Islam: IV Sufism" Muslim World, 38 (1948) p. 281.
6. Ibid., p. 287. "...rationally intelligible object" is an unfortunate choice of words as the implication is impossible to fulfil in reference to God.
7. Ibid., p. 286f. Attachment to either a person, doctrine or idea is a lesser possibility. One is supposed to be attached to God alone. See comment by Bistami in the following lines.
8. Ibid., p. 286.
9. R A Nicholson, The mystics of Islam (London, Routledge, 1966), p. 90.
10. R A Nicholson, " A Historical enquiry concerning the origin and development of Sufism," Journal of the Royal Asiatic Society, 1906, p. 327.
11. R A Nicholson, Studies in Islamic mysticism (New Delhi, Idara Adabiyat-i-Dehli,1976, reprint), p. 49f.
12. R A Nicholson, The mystics of Islam, p. 146.
13. Margaret Smith, Rabi`a the mystic and her fellow saints in Islam (Amsterdam, Philo Press, 1974, reprint), p. 16.
14. Edward Jabra Jurji, " Illumination in Islamic mysticism," trans., of al - Shadhili's Qawanin Hikam al-Ishraq (Princeton, Princeton Univ., Press, 1938), p. 66.
15. Rumi, Discourses of Rumi, trans. R A Nicholson (London, John Murary, 1961), p. 88.
16. Hujwairi, Kashf al-Mahjub, trans. R A Nicholson, (London, Luzac, 1959), p. 28f. (emphasis added)
17. A Reza Arasteh, "Psychology of the Sufi way to individuation" in L F Rushbrook Williams, Sufi studies: East and west (Octagon Press, 1973), p. 109.
18. R A Nicholson, The mystics of Islam, p. 103.

Revised and edited; originally published in Islamic Culture April 1984.

Bibliography

Margaret Smith, Rabia the Mystic. — Kazi Publications, Incorporated, 01/1996. 212 p. ISBN 1-56744-475-X Trade Cloth. : $19.95.

A. G. Farhadi, Abdullah Ansari of Herat (1006-1089 C.E.) : An Early Sufi Master. — Humanities Press International, Incorporated, 04/1995. 228 p. — (Curzon Sufi Ser. ; No. 1) ISBN 0-7007-0313-6 Trade Paper. : $18.50.

Herbert W. Mason, Al-Hallaj. — Humanities Press International, Incorporated, 04/1995. 228 p. — (Curzon Sufi Ser. ; No. 2) ISBN 0-7007-0311-X Trade Paper. : $18.50.

Hamid Dabashi, Ayn al-Qudat al-Hamadhani : An Intellectual Portrait. — Humanities Press International, Incorporated, 08/1995. 220 p. — (Sufi Ser. ; No. 6), ISBN 0-7007-0360-8 Trade Paper.: $19.95.

Leonard Lewisohn, Beyond Faith & Infidelity : The Sufi Poetry & Teachings of Mahmud Shabistari. — Humanities Press International, Incorporated, 07/1995. 220 p. — (Sufi Ser. ; No. 5) ISBN 0-7007-0343-8 Trade Paper. : $19.95.

Hazrat Pir The Fragrance Of Sufism., 03/01/1995. ISBN 0819197947 Trade Paper. : $14.50 Ingram — UNIA.

Titus Burckhardt, Introduction To Sufism., 07/01/1995. ISBN 1855384582 Trade Paper. : $12.00 Ingram — HRSF.

J. T. De Bruijn, Persian Sufi Poetry : An Introduction to the Mystical Use of Classical Persian Poems. — Humanities Press International, Incorporated, 04/1995. 228 p. — (Curzon Sufi Ser.; No. 1) ISBN 0-7007-0312-8 Trade Paper. : $18.50.

Nahid Angha, Principles of Sufism. — Jain Publishing Company,

01/1995. 144 p. ISBN 0-87573-061-2 Trade Paper. : $12.00.

Rumi, Rending the Veil : Literal & Poetic Translations of Rumi— Hohm Press, 01/1995. 280 p. ISBN 0-934252-46-7 Trade Cloth.: $27.95.

Carl W. Ernst, Ruzbihan Baqli : Mysticism & the Rhetoric of Sainthood in Persian Sufism. — Humanities Press International, Incorporated, 05/1995. 210 p. — (Sufi Ser. ; No. 4) ISBN 0-7007-0342-X Trade Paper. : $19.95.

Regula Burckhardt Quershi, Sufi Music Of India And Pakistan; Sound, Context, Meaning In Qawwali., 05/01/1995. ISBN 0226700925 Trade Paper. : $18.95 Ingram — UNCH.

Llewellyn, Vaughan-Lee Edited by Traveling the Path of Love : Sayings of Sufi Masters. — Golden Sufi Center, 04/1995. 200 p. ISBN 0-9634574-2-X Trade Paper. : $12.00.

Mohammad A. Jamnia, Under the Sufi's Cloak : Stories of Abu Sa'id & His Mystical Teachings. — Writer's, Incorporated, 04/ 1995. 144 p., ISBN 0-9627854-6-6 Trade Paper. : $10.00.

H. Wiberforce-Clarke Edited by An Account of Sufi Mysticism : With a Glossary of Their Symbolic Terms. — Holmes Publishing Group, 06/1994. ISBN 1-55818-300-0 Trade Paper. : $5.95.

Toshihiko Izutsu, Celestial Journey: Far Eastern Ways of Thinking: Comparative Studies in Buddhist, Taoist, & Confucian Philosophy. — White Cloud Press, 03/1994. 200 p. ISBN 1-883991-04-8 Trade Paper. : $16.00. ISBN 1-883991-08-0 Trade Paper. : $16.00 Ingram.

Leonard Lewisohn, Edited by Classical Persian Sufisu-from Its Origins to Rumi. — KhaniQahi Nimatullahi Publications, 1994. 708 p.: ill. ISBN 0-933546-50-5 Trade Cloth. : $49.95. ISBN 0-933546-51-3 Trade Paper. : $29.95.

Idries Shah, The Commanding Self. — Institute for the Study of Human Knowledge, 06/1994. 380 p. ISBN 0-86304-066-7 Trade Cloth. : $27.00.

Louis Massignon, Essay on the Origins of the Technical Language of Islamic Mysticism. — University of Notre Dame Press, 08/1994. ISBN 0-268-00928-7 Cloth Text. : $34.95.

Llewellyn Vaughan-Lee, In the Company of Friends : Dreamwork Within a Sufi Group. — Golden Sufi Center, 12/1994. ISBN 0-9634574-1-1 Trade Paper. : $12.00.

Javad Nurbakhsh, Masters of the Path : A History of the Masters of the Nimatullahi Sufi Order. — KhaniQahi Nimatullahi Publications, 1994. 132 p. : ill. ISBN 0-933546-03-3 Trade Paper. : $9.95.

Sufi George, Mind Blow : Understanding Consciousness. — Sufi George Books, 06/1994. 72 p. ISBN 1-885570-00-7 Trade Paper. : $5.95.

Sufi George, Mind Blow : Understanding Consciousness. — Sufi George Books, 06/1994. 68 p. ISBN 1-885570-01-5 Trade Paper. : $5.95.

Knut S. Vikov, Sufi & Scholar on the Desert Edge : The Heritage of Muhammad b. Ali al-Sanusi. — Northwestern University Press, 11/1994. (Islam & Society in Africa Ser.) ISBN 0-8101-1226-4 Trade Cloth. : $54.95.

Sufi George, Sufi George's Coloring Book of Consciousness Management Study Aids. — Sufi George Books, 07/1994. 78 p., ISBN 1-885570-03-1 Trade Paper. : $14.95.

Martin Lings, A Sufi Saint of the Twentieth Century : Shaikh Ahmad, Al-Alawi. — Atrium Publishers Group, 01/1994. 242 p. ISBN 0-946621-50-0 Trade Paper. : $15.95.

Javad Nurbakhsh, Sufi Symbolism : Inspirations, Revelations, Lights, Charismatic Powers, Spiritual States & Stations, Praise & Condemnation. — KhaniQahi Nimatullahi Publications, 1994. 167 p. ISBN 0-933546-53-X Trade Cloth. : $25.00.

Marietta T. Stepanyants, Sufi Wisdom. — State University of New York Press, 07/1994. 132 p. — (SUNY Series in Islam), ISBN 0-7914-1795-6 Cloth Text. : $44.50. ISBN 0-7914-1796-4 Paper Text.: $14.95.

Lynn Wilcox, Sufism & Psychology. — Kazi Publications, Incorporated, 11/1994. 256 p. ISBN 0-614-01622-3 Trade Paper. : $14.95.

Mojdeh Bayat, Tales from the Land of the Sufis. — Shambhala Publications, Incorporated, 04/1994. 192 p., ISBN 0-87773-955-2 Trade Paper. : $12.00.

M. R. Muhaiyaddeen, To Die Before Death : The Sufi Way of Life.—Fellowship Press, 04/1994. 300 p., ISBN 0-914390-37-6 Cloth Text. : $20.00. ISBN 0-914390-39-2 Trade Paper. : $12.00.

Victoria R. Holbrook, The Unreadable Shores of Love : Turkish Modernity & Mystic Romance. — University of Texas Press, 05/1994. 256 p. ISBN 0-292-73080-2 Cloth Text. : $37.50.

Omar Khayaam, The Authentic Rubaiyyat of Sufi Poet Omar Khayaam. — Institute for the Diffusion of Sufi Ideas (I D S I), 03/1993. 100 p. ISBN 0-9636083-0-4 Cloth Text.

Llewellyn Vaughan-Lee, Bond with the Beloved : The Relationship of the Lover & Beloved on the Sufi Path. — Patch Publishing, 05/1993. 160 p. ISBN 0-9634576-8-3 Trade Paper. : $12.00.

Llewellyn Vaughan-Lee, The Bond with the Beloved : The Relationship of the Lover & the Beloved on the Sufi Path. — Golden Sufi Center, 05/1993. 160 p. ISBN 0-9634574-0-3 Trade Paper. : $12.00.

Irina Tweedie, The Chasm of Fire : A Woman's Experience of Liberation Through the Teachings of a Sufi Master. — Element Books, Incorporated, 04/1993. 208 p. ISBN 1-85230-040-X Trade Paper.: $15.95.

Maria Jaoudi, Christian & Islamic Spirituality. — Paulist Press, 11/1993. 112 p. ISBN 0-8091-3426-8 Trade Paper. : $7.95.

Ananda, Comparative Study of Religion : A Sufi & a Sanatani (Ramakrishna). — South Asia Books, 1993. ISBN 81-202-0373-9 Trade Cloth. : $22.00.

Farid Ud-Din Attar, The Conference of the Birds : A Sufi Fable. — Shambhala Publications, Incorporated, 04/1993. 160 p. : ill.

ISBN 0-87773-031-8 Trade Paper. : $11.00.

Shadia S. Fahim, Doris Lessing : Sufi Equilibrium & the Form of the Novel.— Saint Martin's Press, Incorporated, 11/1993. ISBN 0-312-10293-3 Trade Cloth. :

M. R. Muhaiyaddeen, Gems of Wisdom : Beyond Mind & Desire. — Fellowship Press, 03/1993. 80 p. — (Gems of Wisdom Ser.) ISBN 0-914390-36-8 Trade Paper. : $5.00.

Julian Baldick, Imaginary Muslims : The Uwaysi Mystics of Central Asia.— New York University Press, 04/1993. 300 p. ISBN 0-8147-1206-1 Trade Cloth. : $50.00.

Arthur J. Arberry, An Introduction to the History of Sufism. — Apt Books, Incorporated, 04/1993. ISBN 0-86311-257-9 Cloth Text. : $8.95.

Osho, Just Like That : Talks on Sufism. — Osho Chidvilas, 02/1993. 455 p. — (Sufi Ser.) ISBN 3-89338-113-9 Trade Cloth. : $24.95.

Reshad Feild, Last Barrier : A Sufi Journey. — Element Books, Incorporated, 04/1993. ISBN 1-85230-196-1 Trade Paper. : $15.95.

Leonard Lewisohn, The Legacy Of Mediaeval Persian Sufism., 00/01/1993. ISBN 0933546467 Trade Paper. : $29.95 Ingram—KHAN.

Albrech Hofheinz Annotations by. The Letters of Ahmad Ibn Idris.— Northwestern University Press, 06/1993. (Islam & Society in Africa Ser.) ISBN 0-8101-1070-9 Trade Cloth. : $49.95.

Henry Corbin, Man of Light in Iranian Sufism. — REP ed. — Omega Publications, Incorporated, 08/1993. 174 p. ISBN 0-930872-48-7 Trade Paper. : $12.00.

Ibrahim M. Abu-Rabi, Introduction by The Mystical Teachings of al-Shadhili: Including His Life, Prayers, Letters, & Followers: A Translation from the Arabic of Ibn Al-Sabbagh's Durrat Al-Asrar Wa Tuhfat Al-Abrar. — State University of New York Press, 10/1993. 274 p. — (SUNY Series in Islam),

ISBN 0-7914-1613-5 Trade Cloth. : $59.50.

Shems Friedlander Ninety-Nine Names of Allah : The Beautiful Names. — Harper San Francisco, 10/1993. ISBN 0-06-063034-5 Trade Paper. : $10.00.

Grace M. Smith, Poetry of Yunus Emre, a Turkish Sufi Poet. — University of California Press, 08/1993. (Publications in Modern Philology ; Vol. 127) ISBN 0-520-09781-5 Trade Paper. : $16.00.

Al-Qushayri, Principles of Sufism. — Mizan Press, 01/1993. 366 p. ISBN 0-933782-21-7 Cloth Text.: $25.95. ISBN 0-933782-20-9 Paper Text. : $14.95.

Avideh Shashaani, Promised Paradise : Agha Jan-Sufism's Secret Divulged. — University Press of America, 12/1993. 130 p. ISBN 0-8191-9254-6 Library Binding. : $34.50.

Javad Nurbakhsh, Psychology of Sufism. — Aries Press, 08/1993. ISBN 0-933646-49-6 Trade Cloth.: $22.95.

Javad Nurbakhsh, The Psychology of Sufism. — KhaniQahi Nimatullahi Publications, 09/1993. ISBN 0-933546-49-1 Trade Cloth. : $22.95.

Muhammad A. Salam, The Reality of the Path. — Pacific Research Publications, 12/1993. 54 p.

Wheeler Thackston, Signs of the Unseen : Discourses of Rumi. — Threshold Books, 11/1993. ISBN 0-939660-34-2 Trade Paper. : $15.00.

Darshan Singh, Streams of Nectar : Lives, Poetry & Teachings of Saints & Mystics. — S. K. Publications, 09/1993. 423 p. : ill. ISBN 0-918224-25-X Trade Cloth. : $20.00.

Javad Nurbakhsh, Sufi Symbolism, Vol 6 : Spiritual Titles & Epithets the Nurbakhsh Encyclopedia of Sufi Terminology.— KhaniQahi Nimatullahi Publications, 06/1993. ISBN 0-933546-48-3 Trade Cloth.: $25.00.

Javad Nurbakhsh, Sufi Symbolism : Contemplative Disciplines, Teophanies & Visions, Family Relationships, Servants of God, Names of Sufi Orders. — KhaniQahi Nimatullahi

Publications, 1993. 208 p. ISBN 0-933546-52-1 Trade Cloth.: $30.00.

Idries Shah, Tales of the Dervishes : Teaching-Stories of the Sufi Masters over the Past Thousand Years. — Viking Penguin, 10/1993. 224 p. ISBN 0-14-019358-8 Trade Paper. : $10.00.

M. R. Muhaiyaddeen, Treasures of the Heart : Sufi Stories for Young Children.— Fellowship Press, 1993. 110 p. : ill. ISBN 0-914390-33-3 Trade Cloth. : $10.00.

Bahram Elahi, The Way of Light : The Path of Nur Ali Elahi. — Element Books, Incorporated, 03/1993. ISBN 1-85230-381-6 Trade Paper. : $15.95.

Muzaffer O. Al-Jerrahi, Adornment of Hearts. — Pir Publications, Incorporated, 03/1992. 145 p. ISBN 1-879708-01-9 Trade Paper. : $9.95.

Llewellyn Vaughan-Lee, The Call & the Echo : Sufi Dreamwork & the Psychology of the Beloved. — Threshold Books, 05/1992. ISBN 0-939660-43-1 Trade Paper. : $13.00.

Raymond Lifchez, Edited by The Dervish Lodge : Architecture, Art, & Sufism in Ottoman Turkey. — University of California Press, 1992. (Comparative Studies on Muslim Societies ; No. 10) ISBN 0-520-07060-7 Trade Cloth. : $50.00.

Carl W. Ernst, Eternal Garden : Mysticism, History, & Politics at a South Asian Sufi Center. — State University of New York Press, 01/1992. 381 p. : ill. — (Muslim Spirituality in South Asia Ser.) ISBN 0-7914-0883-3 Trade Cloth. : $59.50. ISBN 0-7914-0884-1 Trade Paper. : $19.95.

William C. Chittick, Faith & Practice of Islam : Three Thirteenth-Century Sufi Texts. — State University of New York Press, 11/1992. 322 p. — (SUNY Series in Islam) ISBN 0-7914-1367-5 Trade Cloth. : $59.50. ISBN 0-7914-1368-3 Trade Paper. : $19.95.

Shahrokh Meskoob, Iranian Nationality & the Persian Language : Roles of Government, Religion, & Sufism in Persian Prose Writing.—Mage Publishers, Incorporated, 10/1992. 175 p. ISBN 0-934211-21-3 Trade Cloth. : $29.95.

Javad Nurbakhsh, Jesus in the Eyes of the Sufis. — KhaniQahi Nimatullahi Publications, 08/1992. ISBN 0-933546-21-1 Trade Paper. : $8.95.

Leonard Lewisohn Edited by The Legacy of Medieval Persian Sufism. — Khani Qahi Nimatullahi Publications, 1992. 450 p.: ill. ISBN 0-685-59457-2 Trade Cloth. : $44.95. ISBN 0-933546-47-5 Trade Paper. : $29.95.

Kabir E. Helminski, Living Presence : The Sufi Way to Mindfulness & the Unfolding of the Essential Self. — Jeremy P. Tarcher Incorporated, 07/1992. 180 p. ISBN 0-87477-699-6 Trade Cloth. : $11.95.

Ali S. Karrar, The Sufi Brotherhoods in the Sudan. — Northwestern University Press, 11/1992. 300 p. — (Islam & Society in Africa Ser.) ISBN 0-8101-1045-8 Trade Cloth. : $39.95.

Sarah F. Ansari, Sufi Saints & State Power : The Pirs of Sind, 1843-1947. — Cambridge University Press, 01/1992. 208 p. : ill. — (Cambridge Asian Studies Ser. ; No. 50) ISBN 0-521-40530-0 Trade Cloth. : $54.95.

S. A. Abidi, Sufism in India. — South Asia Books, 1992. ISBN 81-224-0418-9 Trade Cloth. : $19.00.

John Grant, Travels in the Unknown East. — Institute for the Study of Human Knowledge, 12/1992. 198 p. ISBN 0-86394-971-1 Trade Cloth. : $27.00.

Muhyiddin Ibn 'Arabi, What the Seeker Needs : Essays & Glossary on Surfism. — Threshold Books, 05/1992. 150 p.ISBN 0-939660-41-5 Trade Paper. : $10.00.

Shems Friedlander, When You Hear Hoofbeats Think of a Zebra. — Mazda Publishers, 04/1992. 176 p. ISBN 0-939214-06-7 Trade Paper. : $6.95.

Shems Friedlander, The Whirling Dervishes : Being an Account of the Sufi Order Known As the Mevlevis & Its Founder the Poet & Mystic Mevlana Jalalu'ddin Rumi. — State University of New York Press, 1992. 160 p. — (SUNY Series in Islam) ISBN 0-7914-1155-9 Trade Cloth. : $49.50. ISBN 0-7914-1156-7 Trade Paper. : $16.95.

Muhtar Holland , Translated by The Works of Shaikh Abd al-Qadir al-Jilani Series.—Al-Baz Publishing, Incorporated, 12/1992. ISBN 1-882216-04-0 Trade Paper. : $57.00.

Shaykh H. Chishti, Book of Sufi Healing. — Inner Traditions International, Limited, 06/1991. ISBN 0-89281-324-5 Trade Paper. : $16.95.

Hazrat I. Khan, Complete Sayings. — REP ed. — Omega Publications, Incorporated, 09/1991. 299 p. ISBN 0-930872-39-8 Trade Paper. : $14.95.

Nicolaas H. Biegman, Egypt : Moulids, Saints & Sufis. — Routledge, Chapman & Hall, Incorporated, 07/1991. 176 p. : ill. ISBN 0-7103-0415-3 Trade Cloth. : $49.95.

Muhyiddeen Abdul-Qadir Gilani, The Endowment of Divine Grace & the Spread of Divine Mercy, Vol. 1 : Al-Fathu Rabbani. — Pearl Publishing House, 03/1991. 240 p. ISBN 1-879405-01-6 Trade Paper. : $19.50.

Shaikh Muhyiddeen Abdul-Qadir Gilani, The Endowment of Divine Grace & the Spread of Divine Mercy, Vol. 2 : Al-Fathu Rabbani. — Pearl Publishing House, 09/1991. 240 p. ISBN 1-879405-02-4 Trade Paper. : $19.50.

Abd A. Al-Qashani Compiled by. Glossary of Sufi Technical Terms. — Institute for the Study of Human Knowledge, 1991. 278 p. ISBN 0-86304-032-2 Trade Cloth. : $40.00.

A. Reza Arasteh, Growth to Selfhood : The Sufi Contribution. — Viking Penguin, 05/1991. 160 p. ISBN 0-14-019282-4 Trade Paper. : $8.95.

Muzaffer O. Al-Jerrahi, Irshad : Wisdom of a Sufi Master. — Pir Publications, Incorporated, 11/1991. 725 p. ISBN 1-879708-00-0 Trade Cloth. : $29.95.

Soraya S. Behbehani, The Messenger Within : Discovering Love & Wholeness Through Meditation. — Edwin Mellen Press, The, 10/1991. 254 p. : ill. ISBN 0-7734-9882-6 Trade Paper.: $39.95. ISBN 0-685-49871-9 Paper Text. : $19.95

Bruce B. Lawrence, Edited by Nizam Ad-Din Awliya : Morals for the Heart. — Paulist

Press, 12/1991. (Classics of Western Spirituality Ser.) ISBN 0-8091-0451-2 Trade Cloth. : $26.95. ISBN 0-8091-3280-X Trade Paper. : $18.95.

Javad Nurbakhsh, The Nurbakhsh Encyclopedia of Sufi Terminology.— KhaniQahi Nimatullahi Publications, 05/1991. ISBN 0-318-68434-9 Trade Cloth. : .00

Nahid Angha, Principles of Sufism. — International Association Of Sufism, 1991. 114 p. ISBN 0-918437-03-2 Trade Paper. : $8.00.

Seyyed H. Nasr, Sufi Essays. — State University of New York Press, 08/1991. 184 p. ISBN 0-7914-1051-X Trade Cloth. : $49.50. ISBN 0-7914-1052-8 Trade Paper. : $16.95.

Sufi Symbolism Encyclopedia. — Khani Qahi Nimatullahi Publications, 05/1991. ISBN 0-933546-28-9.

Javad Nurbakhsh, Sufi Symbolism, Vol. 5 : Veils & Clothing, Government, Economics & Commerce, Medicine & Healing.—KhaniQahi Nimatullahi Publications, 1991. 194 p. ISBN 0-933546-45-9 Trade Cloth. : $30.00.

Terry Graham, Translated by Sufism V : Gratitude, Patience, Trust in God, Aspiration, Veracity, Zeal, Valor, Altruism, Shame.—KhaniQahi Nimatullahi Publications, 1991. 159 p. ISBN 0-933546-43-2 Trade Cloth. : $11.95.

J. Marvin Spiegelman, Sufism, Islam, & Jungian Psychology. — New Falcon Publications, 02/1991. 200 p. ISBN 1-56184-015-7 Trade Paper. : $12.95.

Hazrat I. Khan, Tales. — REP ed. — Omega Publications, Incorporated, 11/1991. 224 p. ISBN 0-930872-37-1 Trade Paper. : $13.50.

Ibn Al-Husayn Al-Sulami, Way of Sufi Chivalry : Futuwwah. — REP ed. — Inner Traditions International, Limited, 04/1991. 192 p. ISBN 0-89281-317-2 Trade Paper. : $10.95.

Hazrat I. Khan, The Art of Being & Becoming. — REP ed. — Omega Publications, Incorporated, 1990. 296 p. ISBN 0-930872-41-X Trade Paper. : $12.95.

Shaykh F. Haeri, Elements of Sufism. — Element Books, Incorporated, 06/1990. ISBN 1-85230-159-7 Trade Paper. : $9.95.

Titus Burckhardt, An Introduction to Sufism : The Mystical Dimension of Islam. — REP ed. — Borgo Press, 1990. 128 p. ISBN 0-8095-7133-1 Library Binding. : $26.00.

Titus Burckhardt, An Introduction to Sufism : The Mystical Dimensions of Islam. — Thorsons, 06/1990. 126 p. ISBN 1-85274-070-1 Trade Paper. : $9.95.

Fadhlalla, Leaves from Sufi Journal. — Element Books, Incorporated, 1990. ISBN 1-85230-057-4 Trade Paper. : $15.95.

Llewellyn Vaughan-Lee Lover & the Serpent : Dreamwork Within a Sufi Tradition.— Element Books, Incorporated, 06/1990. ISBN 1-85230-147-3 Trade Paper. : $13.95.

M. R. Muhaiyaddeen, A Mystical Journey. — Fellowship Press, 04/1990. 150 p. ISBN 0-914390-28-7 Trade Cloth. : $12.00. ISBN 0-914390-29-5 Trade Paper. : $7.00.

Reshad Feild, Reason Is Powerless in the Expression of Love. — Chalice Guild, 10/1990. ISBN 0-9625412-0-6 Trade Paper.: $9.00.

H. T. Norris, Sufi Mystics of the Niger Desert : Sidi Mahmud & the Hermits of Air. — Oxford University Press, Incorporated, 11/1990. 216 p. : ill. ISBN 0-19-826538-7 Trade Cloth. : $59.00.

Javad Nurbakhsh, Sufi Symbolism, Vol. IV : The Nurbakhsh Encyclopedia of Sufi Terminology the Beloved's Body, Wine, Music, Convivial Gatherings. — KhaniQahi Nimatullahi Publications, 1990. 190 p. ISBN 0-933546-40-8 Trade Cloth.: $30.00.

Idries Shah, Sufi Thought & Action : An Anthology of Important Papers. — Institute for the Study of Human Knowledge, 1990. 272 p. ISBN 0-86304-051-9 Trade Paper. : $17.00.

Nurbakhsh, Sufi Women. — REV ed. — KhaniQahi Nimatullahi Publications, 1990. 264 p. ISBN 0-933546-42-4 Trade Paper.: $11.95.

Spiegelman, Sufism, Islam & Jungian Psychology. — Golden Dawn Publications, 04/1990. 190 p. ISBN 0-9622452-4-0 Trade Paper. : $12.95.

Muhyiddin Shakoor, The Writing on the Water : Chronicles of a Seeker on the Islamic Sufi Path.—Element Books, Incorporated, 1990. 242 p. ISBN 1-85230-026-4 Trade Paper. : $15.95.

Muhammad S. Siddiqi, Bahmani Sufis. — South Asia Books, 1989. ISBN 0-8364-2467-0 Trade Cloth. : $31.00.

Donal B. O'Brien , Edited by Charisma & Brotherhood in African Islam. — Oxford University Press, Incorporated, 01/1989. 232 p. — (Oxford Studies in African Affairs) ISBN 0-19-822723-X Trade Cloth. : $55.00.

Molana-al-Moazam Hazrat, Dawn. — University Press of America, 08/1989. 44 p. — (Shahmaghsoudi (Angha) Heritage Series on Sufism) ISBN 0-8191-7429-7 Paper Text.: $12.00.

Idries Shah, The Dermis Probe. — Institute for the Study of Human Knowledge, 1989. 191 p. ISBN 0-900860-83-9 Trade Cloth.: $25.00. ISBN 0-86304-045-4 Trade Paper. : $12.50.

Javad Nurbakhsh, Dogs from a Sufi Point of View. — KhaniQahi Nimatullahi Publications, 1989. 100 p. : ill. ISBN 0-933546-39-4 Trade Paper. : $11.95.

Sufi I. Khan, Education from Before Birth to Maturity. — Hunter House, Incorporated, 1989. 128 p. ISBN 0-89793-063-0 Trade Paper. : $6.95.

Seyyed Hossein Nasr, Edited by Islamic Spirituality: Manifestations.— Crossroad Publishing Company, 10/1989. 500 p. : ill. — (World Spirituality Ser. ; Vol. 20) ISBN 0-8245-0768-1 Trade Cloth. : $49.50.

Julian Baldick, Mystical Islam : An Introduction to Sufism. — New York University Press, 12/1989. 192 p. ISBN 0-8147-1138-3 Trade Cloth. : $40.00. ISBN 0-8147-1139-1 Trade Paper.: $16.50.

Marietta Stepaniants, Philosophical Aspects of Sufism. — South

Asia Books, 1989. ISBN 81-202-0265-1 Trade Cloth. : $17.00.

Andrew Harvey, Speaking Flame : Re-creations of Rumi. — Meeramma Publications, 12/1989. 120 p. ISBN 0-9622973-1-3 Trade Paper. : $8.95.

Kevin Shepherd, Edited by A Sufi Matriarch : HazratBabajan. — State Mutual Book & Periodical Service, Limited, 1989. 78 p. ISBN 0-9508680-1-9 Trade Cloth. : $60.00.

William C. Chittick, The Sufi Path of Knowledge : Ibn al-Arabi's Metaphysics of Imagination. — State University of New York Press, 07/1989. 478 p. ISBN 0-88706-884-7 Trade Cloth. : $74.50. ISBN 0-88706-885-5 Trade Paper. : $24.95.

Hazrat I. Khan, Awakening of the Human Spirit. — Omega Publications, Incorporated, 09/1988. 224 p. ISBN 0-930872-35-5 Trade Paper. : $12.95.

Idries Shah, Caravan of Dreams. — Institute for the Study of Human Knowledge, 1988. 207 p. ISBN 0-900860-14-6 Trade Cloth.: $25.00. ISBN 0-86304-043-8 Trade Paper. : $12.50.

Hazrat M. Angha, Destination Eternity : Az Janin Ta Janan. — International Association Of Sufism, 1988. 185 p. : ill. — (Sufism Ser.) Original title: Az - Janin Ta-Janan. ISBN 0-918437-02-4 Trade Paper.: $15.50.

Sufi I. Khan, The Development of Spiritual Healing. — Hunter House, Incorporated, 04/1988. 104 p. ISBN 0-89793-060-6 Trade Paper. : $6.95.

Peter L. Wilson , Translated by The Drunken Universe : An Anthology of Persian Sufi Poetry. — Phanes Press, 01/1988. 155 p. ISBN 0-933999-65-8 Trade Paper. : $10.95.

Mohammd Shafii, Freedom from the Self : Sufism, Meditation, & Psychotherapy. — Human Sciences Press, Incorporated, 01/1988. 261 p. ISBN 0-89885-231-5 Trade Cloth. : $32.95. ISBN 0-89885-395-8 Trade Paper. : $17.95.

Hazrat I. Khan, Gayan. — Omega Publications, Incorporated, 02/1988. 88 p. — (Authentic Versions Ser.) ISBN 0-930872-34-7 Trade Paper. : $7.50.

Titus Burckhardt, An Introduction to Sufi Doctrine. — Kazi Publications, Incorporated, 01/1988. 156 p. ISBN 1-56744-217-X Paper Text. : $8.50.

Manifestations of Thought. — University Press of America, 12/1988. 154 p. : ill. — (Shahmaghsoudi (Angha) Heritage Series on Sufism) ISBN 0-8191-7135-2 Library Binding. : $41.50. ISBN 0-8191-7136-0 Paper Text. : $22.50.

Sufi I. Khan, Music. — Hunter House, Incorporated, 04/1988. 104 p. ISBN 0-89793-059-2 Trade Paper. : $6.95.

Hazrat I. Khan, Music of Life. — Omega Publications, Incorporated, 12/1988. 368 p. ISBN 0-930872-38-X Trade Paper. : $14.95.

N. P. Archer, Edited by Sufi Mystery. — Institute for the Study of Human Knowledge, 1988. 218 p. ISBN 0-900860-79-0 Trade Cloth. : $25.00.

Javad Nurbakhsh, Sufi Symbolism, Vol. III : The Nurbakhsh Encyclopedia of Sufi Terminology. — KhaniQahi Nimatullahi Publications, 1988. 263 p. ISBN 0-933546-35-1 Trade Cloth.: $30.00.

William C. Chittick , Translated by Sufism IV : Repentance, Abstinence, Renunciation, Wariness, Humility, Humbleness, Sincerity, Constancy, Courtesy. — KhaniQahi Nimatullahi Publications, 1988. ISBN 0-933546-33-5 Trade Paper. : $11.95.

Coleman Barks, Translated by This Longing - Poetry, Teaching Stories, & Selected Letters of Jelaluddin Rumi. — Threshold Books, 11/1988. 128 p. ISBN 0-939660-29-6 Trade Paper.: $9.00.

Hazrat I. Khan, The Way of Illumination, Vol. 1 : The Sufi Message.—South Asia Books, 1988. ISBN 81-208-0497-X Trade Cloth. : $17.00. ISBN 0-685-37679-6 Trade Paper. : $8.75.

Martin Lings, What Is Sufism?., 11/1988. 136 p. ISBN 0-04-297039-3 Trade Paper. : $9.95 — Routledge, Chapman & Hall, Incorporated. ISBN 0-946621-41-1 Trade Paper.: $8.95—Atrium Publishers Group.

Shahab ud-Din Suhrawardi, Awarif al-Ma'arif. — Kazi Publications, Incorporated, 01/1987. 300 p. ISBN 1-56744-225-0 Cloth Text. : $15.95.

Shaikh A. Ad-Darqawi, Letters of a Sufi Master : The Shaikh Al-'Arabi Ad-Darqawi. — Sophia Perennis Et Universalis, 1987. 38 p. ISBN 0-900588-00-4 Trade Paper. : $9.95.

Muzaffer Ozak, Love Is the Wine : Talks of a Sufi Master in America. — Threshold Books, 09/1987. 108 p. ISBN 0-939660-22-9 Trade Paper. : $9.00.

Shah Maghsoud Sadegh Angha, Ossoul Faghr va Tassavof : Principles of Faghr & Sufism. — M T O Printing & Publication Center, 02/1987. 173 p. ISBN 0-910735-11-5 Trade Cloth. : $55.00. ISBN 0-685-21325-0 Trade Paper. : $29.00.

Mir Valiuddin, Quranic Sufism. — REP ed. — South Asia Books, 1987. ISBN 81-208-0320-5 Trade Cloth. : $14.00.

Eva De Vitray-Meyerovitch, Rumi & Sufism. — REP ed. — Post-Apollo Press, The, 09/1987. ill.(World of Islam Ser.) ISBN 0-942996-08-9 Trade Paper. : $12.95.

Regula B. Qureshi, Sufi Music of India & Pakistan : Sound, Context & Meaning in Qawwali. — Cambridge University Press, 03/1987. 300 p. : ill. — (Cambridge Studies in Ethnomusicology) ISBN 0-521-26767-6 Trade Cloth. : $89.95.

Javad Nurbakhsh, Sufi Symbolism, Vol. II : The Nurbakhsh Encyclopedia of Sufi Terminology. — KhaniQahi Nimatullahi Publications, 1987. 193 p. ISBN 0-933546-31-9 Trade Cloth.: $30.00.

Leleh Bakhtiar, Sufi; Expressions Of The Mystic Quest., 09/01/1987. ISBN 050081015X Trade Paper. : $15.95 Ingram—THAM.

Yunus Emre, The Wandering Fool, Sufi Poems of a Thirteenth-Century Turkish Dervish. — Cadmus Editions, 1987. 100 p. ISBN 0-932274-39-0 Trade Cloth. : $25.00. ISBN 0-932274-38-2 Trade Paper.: $9.00.

Shems Friedlander, When You Hear Hoofbeats, Think of a Zebra :

Talks on Sufism. — HarperCollins Publishers, Incorporated, 02/1987. 128 p. ISBN 0-06-096128-7 Mass Market. : $6.95.

Irina Tweedie, Daughter of Fire : A Diary of a Spiritual Training with a Sufi Master. — Blue Dolphin Publishing, Incorporated, 12/1986. 832 p. ISBN 0-931892-05-8 Trade Cloth. : $29.95. ISBN 0-931892-04-X Trade Paper. : $19.95.

Shaikh Gilani, Futuh al-Ghaib. — Kazi Publications, Incorporated, 01/1986. 213 p. ISBN 1-56744-277-3 Trade Paper. : $6.50.

John Renard , Translated by IBN Abbad of Ronda, Letters on the Sufi Path. — Paulist Press, 03/1986. 256 p. — (Classics of Western Spirituality Ser. ; No. 49) ISBN 0-8091-0365-6 Trade Cloth. : $12.95. ISBN 0-8091-2730-X Trade Paper. : $9.95.

Alexandre Bennigsen, Mystics & Commissars : Sufism in the U. S. S. R.. — University of California Press, 01/1986. ISBN 0-520-05576-4 Trade Cloth. : $45.00.

Shah Maghsoud Sadegh Angha, Padidehaye Fekr : Manifestations of Thought. — M T O Printing & Publication Center, 1986. 75 p. ISBN 0-318-32757-0 Trade Cloth. : $20.00. ISBN 0-910735-13-1 Trade Paper. : $11.00.

Javad Nurbakhsh, Sufi Symbolism, Vol. 1 : The Nurbakhsh Encyclopedia of Sufi Terminology the Natural World, Symbolism of Birds & Other Animals in Sufi Poetry. — KhaniQahi Nimatullahi Publications, 1986. 228 p. ISBN 0-933546-12-2 Trade Cloth. : $30.00.

Samuel L. Lewis, Sufi Vision & Initiation : Meetings with Remarkable Beings. — PeaceWorks International Center for the Dances of Universal Peace, 07/1986. 398 p. : ill. ISBN 0-915424-10-X Trade Paper. : $12.95.

William Stoddart, Sufism : The Mystical Doctrines & Methods of Islam. — Paragon House Publishers, 05/1986. 91 p. — (Patterns of World Spirituality Ser.) ISBN 0-913757-47-0 Trade Paper. : $5.95.

M. R. Bawa Muhaiyaddeen, Come to the Secret Garden : Sufi Tales of Wisdom. — Fellowship Press, 06/1985. 450 p. : ill. ISBN 0-914390-27-9 Trade Cloth. : $20.00.

Alexi Allens, Images of Sai Baba. — Illumination Arts, Incorporated, 11/1985. 104 p. : ill. ISBN 0-318-18477-X Trade Paper. : $11.95.

Arthur Osborne, The Incredible Sai Baba : The Life & Miracles of a Modern-Day Saint. — Apt Books, Incorporated, 07/1985. 102 p. ISBN 0-86125-105-9 Paper Text. : $4.95.

Mir Valiuddin, Love of God : A Sufic Approach. — REP ed. — Borgo Press, 06/1985. 205 p. ISBN 0-89370-577-2 Library Binding. : $26.00.

Muhammad Al-Ghazali, Mysteries of the Human Soul. — Kazi Publications, Incorporated, 01/1985. 64 p. ISBN 1-56744-343-5 Trade Paper. : $6.95.

S. A. Salik, Saint of Jilan. — Kazi Publications, Incorporated, 01/1985. 110 p. ISBN 1-56744-374-5 Trade Paper. : $3.00.

Stuart Litvak, Seeking Wisdom : The Sufi Path. — Samuel Weiser Incorporated, 1985. 128 p. ISBN 0-87728-543-8 Trade Paper. : $6.95.

Javad Nurbakhsh, Sufism-III : Submission, Contentment, Absence, Presence, Intimacy. — KhaniQahi Nimatullahi Publications, 1985. 133 p. ISBN 0-933546-19-X Trade Paper. : $11.95.

Carl W. Ernst, Words of Ecstasy in Sufism. — State University of New York Press, 01/1985. 184 p. ISBN 0-87395-917-5 Trade Cloth. : $59.50. ISBN 0-87395-918-3 Trade Paper. : $19.95.

R. A. Nicholson, The Essence of Sufism. — REP ed. — Holmes Publishing Group, 1984. ISBN 0-916411-49-4 Trade Paper.: $3.95.

W. H. Gairdner, Translated by Four Sufi Classics. — Institute for the Study of Human Knowledge, 1984. 222 p. ISBN 0-900860-69-3 Trade Cloth. : $22.00.

Hafiz of Shiraz, News of Love. — Unicorn Press, 05/1984. 48 p. : ill. — (Keepsake Ser. ; Vol. XI) ISBN 0-87775-155-2 Trade Paper. : $7.95.

Mevlana J. Rumi, Open Secret : Versions of Rumi. — REP ed. — Threshold Books, 09/1984. 96 p. ISBN 0-939660-06-7 Trade Paper. : $9.00.

Margaret Smith, Rabi'a the Mystic & Her Fellow-Saints in Islam. — Cambridge University Press, 12/1984. 256 p. ISBN 0-521-26779-X Trade Cloth. : $39.95. ISBN 0-521-31863-7 Trade Paper. : $14.95.

Nurbakhsh Javad, Spiritual Poverty in Sufism. — KhaniQahi Nimatullahi Publications, 1984. 150 p. ISBN 0-933546-11-4 Trade Paper. : $8.95.

R. A. Nicholson, The Sufi Doctrine of the Perfect Man. — REP ed.— Holmes Publishing Group, 1984. ISBN 0-916411-48-6 Trade Paper. : $3.95.

William C. Chittick, The Sufi Path of Love : The Spiritual Teachings of Rumi.— State University of New York Press, 1984. 433 p. — (SUNY Series in Islam) ISBN 0-87395-723-7 Trade Cloth. : $49.50. ISBN 0-87395-724-5 Trade Paper. : $16.95.

Toshihiko Izutsu, Sufism & Taoism : A Comparative Study of Key Philosophical Concepts. — University of California Press, 01/1984. 493 p. ISBN 0-520-05264-1 Trade Cloth. : $50.00.

Louis Brenner, West African Sufi : The Religious Heritage & Spiritual Quest of Cerno Bokar Saalif Taal. — University of California Press, 01/1984. 215 p. ISBN 0-520-05008-8 Trade Cloth. : $35.00.

M. R. Bawa Muhaiyaddeen, Golden Words of a Sufi Sheikh. — Fellowship Press, 03/1983. 472 p. ISBN 0-914390-24-4 Trade Cloth. : $20.00.

S. A. Rizvi, History of Sufism in India., 1983. ISBN 0-685-13690-6 Cloth Text. : $62.50 — Coronet Books. ISBN 0-318-63156-3 Trade Cloth. : .00 Write/Call Publisher for info. — South Asia Books. ISBN 81-215-0039-7 Trade Cloth. : $44.00 — South Asia Books. ISBN 81-215-0040-0 Trade Cloth.: $44.00 — South Asia Books.

Nurbakhsh Javad, Jesus in the Eyes of the Sufis. — KhaniQahi

Nimatullahi Publications, 1983. ISBN 0-317-07015-0 Trade Paper. : $8.95.

Ernest Scott, The People of the Secret. — Institute for the Study of Human Knowledge, 09/1983. ISBN 0-86304-027-6 Trade Cloth. : $25.00. ISBN 0-86304-038-1 Trade Paper. : $12.50.

Idries Shah, The Sufis. — Institute for the Study of Human Knowledge, 06/1983. ISBN 0-86304-020-9 Trade Cloth. : $24.00.

Idries Shah, The Way of the Sufi., 06/1983. ISBN 0-900860-80-4 Trade Cloth. : $25.00 — Institute for the Study of Human Knowledge. ISBN 0-14-019252-2 Trade Paper.: $11.00 — Viking Penguin.

Chawan Thurlnas, Current Sufi Activity : Work, Literature, Groups & Techniques. — Institute for the Study of Human Knowledge, 06/1982. 40 p. — (Sufi Research Ser.) ISBN 0-86304-004-7 Trade Paper. : $7.00.

Idries Shah, The Elephant in the Dark. — Institute for the Study of Human Knowledge, 06/1982. 76 p. ISBN 0-900860-36-7 Trade Cloth. : $19.00.

Widad El Sakkakini, First among Sufis : The Life & Thought of Rabia al-Adawiyya. — Institute for the Study of Human Knowledge, 06/1982. ISBN 0-900860-45-6 Trade Cloth. : $25.00.

Mah Talat Etemad Moghadam, From the Prophet to the Great Sufi Mir Ghotbeddin Mohammad. — M T O Printing & Publication Center, 09/1982. 231 p. ISBN 0-317-01145-6 Trade Paper.: $12.50.

Pir Vilayat I. Khan, Introducing Spirituality into Counseling & Therapy. — REP ed. — Omega Publications, Incorporated, 10/1982. 176 p. ISBN 0-930872-30-4 Trade Paper. : $9.95.

T. C. Rastogi, Islamic Mysticism Sufism. — Asia Book Corporation of America, 1982. 126 p. ISBN 0-318-37184-7 Trade Cloth. : $23.95.

H. B. M Dervish, Journeys with a Sufi Master. — Institute for the Study of Human Knowledge, 06/1982. ISBN 0-900860-95-

2 Trade Cloth. : $25.00. ISBN 0-86304-041-1 Trade Paper.: $12.50.

Idries Shah, Seeker after Truth. — Institute for the Study of Human Knowledge, 06/1982. ISBN 0-900860-91-X Trade Cloth. : $25.00.

H. Abbas Sufi Principles, Action, Learning Methods, Imitators, Meeting-Places. -— Institute for the Study of Human Knowledge, 06/1982. 64 p. — (Sufi Research Ser.) ISBN 0-86304-001-2 Trade Paper. : $7.00.

Javad Nurbakhsh Sufism II : Fear & Hope, Contraction & Expansion, Gathering & Dispersion, Intoxication, & Sobriety, Annihilation & Subsistence. — KhaniQahi Nimatullahi Publications, 1982. 126 p. ISBN 0-933546-07-6 Trade Paper.: $9.95.

Amina Shah, Tales of Afghanistan. — Institute for the Study of Human Knowledge, 06/1982. ISBN 0-900860-94-4 Trade Cloth. : $21.00.

Javad Nurbakhsh, The Truths of Love. — KhaniQahi Nimatullahi Publications, 1982. ISBN 0-933546-08-4 Trade Paper. : $8.95.

Samuel L. Lewis The Bowl of Saki Commentary. — PeaceWorks International Center for the Dances of Universal Peace, 1981. 180 p. ISBN 0-915424-08-8 Trade Paper. : $18.00.

Ibn Arabi, Journey to the Lord of Power : A Sufi Manual on Retreat.— Inner Traditions International, Limited, 1981. 144 p. : ill. ISBN 0-89281-018-1 Trade Cloth. : $10.95.

Adam Musa, Edited by Letters & Lectures of Idries Shah.— Institute for the Study of Human Knowledge, 06/1981. 40 p. ISBN 0-86304-010-1 Trade Paper. : $7.00.

Seyyed F. Hossain The Sufis of Today. — Institute for the Study of Human Knowledge, 06/1981. (Sufi Research Ser.) ISBN 0-86304-007-1 Trade Paper. : $7.00.

Javad Nurbakhsh Sufism I : Meaning, Knowledge, & Unity. — KhaniQahi Nimatullahi Publications, 06/1981. 111 p. ISBN 0-933546-05-X Trade Paper. : $9.95.

Frithjof Schuon Sufism : Veil & Quintessence. — World Wisdom Books, 1981. 163 p. — (The Library of Traditional Wisdom) ISBN 0-941532-00-3 Trade Paper. : $7.00.

Amina Shah, Assemblies of Al-Hariri. — Institute for the Study of Human Knowledge, 1980. 267 p. ISBN 0-900860-86-3 Trade Cloth. : $25.00.

Arif of Herat, The Book of Ecstasy. — Institute for the Study of Human Knowledge, 1980. ISBN 0-900860-74-X Trade Cloth.: $18.00.

Javad Nurbaksh, Divani Nurbakhsh : Sufi Poetry. — KhaniQahi Nimatullahi Publications, 12/1980. 265 p. ISBN 0-933546-04-1 Trade Cloth. : $30.00.

Sirdar Ikbal Ali Shah, Escape from Central Asia. — Institute for the Study of Human Knowledge, 1980. ISBN 0-900860-78-2 Trade Cloth. : $20.00.

Hazrat I. Khan, The Inner Life : An Introduction to Sufism. — Ind-U. S. Incorporated, 1980. (Orient Paperbacks Ser.) ISBN 0-86578-082-X Trade Paper. : $3.25.

Ramsey Wood, Kalila & Dimna. — Institute for the Study of Human Knowledge, 1980. ISBN 0-394-50693-6 Trade Cloth. : $22.00.

Hafiz Jamal, Edited by Key Concepts in Sufi Understanding.— Institute for the Study of Human Knowledge, 06/1980. 47 p.—(Sufi Research Ser.) ISBN 0-86304-006-3 Trade Paper.: $7.00.

Denise Winn, Edited by Revelation of the Secrets of the Birds & Flowers : Al Muqaddasi. — Institute for the Study of Human Knowledge, 1980. ISBN 0-900860-75-8 Trade Cloth. : $27.00.

Sata'at, Sufism & the Islamic Tradition. — Institute for the Study of Human Knowledge, 1980. 127 p. ISBN 0-900860-81-2 Trade Cloth. : $25.00.

Canon W. H. T. Gairdner,. Theories, Practices & Training Systems of a Sufi School. — Institute for the Study of Human Knowledge, 06/1980. (Sufi Research Ser.) ISBN 0-86304-003-9 Trade Paper.: $7.00.

David Pendlebury, Translated by Yusuf & Zulaika : Jami. — Institute for the Study of Human Knowledge, 1980. ISBN 0-900860-77-4 Trade Cloth. : $22.00.

Hazrat Inayat Khan, The Alchemy of Happiness. — Hunter House, Incorporated, 1979. 262 p. — (Sufi Message of Hazrat Inayat Khan Ser Vol.6) ISBN 90-6077-953-3 Trade Cloth. : .00 Write/Call Publisher for info.

E. Heron-Allen, Translated by A Fool of God : The Mystical Verse of Baba Tahir. — Institute for the Study of Human Knowledge, 1979. ISBN 0-900860-70-7 Trade Cloth. : $21.00.

M. R. Bawa Muhaiyaddeen, Four Steps to Pure Iman. — Fellowship Press, 1979. 70 p. : ill. ISBN 0-914390-17-1 Trade Paper. : $5.00.

Javad Nurbakhsh, In the Paradise of the Sufis. — KhaniQahi Nimatullahi Publications, 1979. 125 p. ISBN 0-933546-01-7 Trade Paper. : $8.95.

Mir Valiuddin, Love of God. — Hunter House, Incorporated, 1979. ISBN 0-900217-02-2 Trade Paper.: $9.95.

Hazrat Inayat Khan, The Mysticism of Sound., 1979. 262 p. — (Sufi Message of Hazrat Inayat Khan Ser.) ISBN 90-6077-569-4 Trade Cloth. : .00 Write/Call Publisher for info. — Hunter House, Incorporated. ISBN 0-7873-1196-0 Trade Cloth. : $4.40 — Mokelumne Hill Press.

David Shea, The Religion of the Sufis. — Institute for the Study of Human Knowledge, 1979. ISBN 0-900860-68-5 Trade Cloth.: $18.00.

Edward Eastwick, Translated by The Rose Garden : Saadi. — Institute for the Study of Human Knowledge, 1979. ISBN 0-900860-65-0 Trade Cloth. : $25.00.

Nader Ardalan, The Sense of Unity : The Sufi Tradition in Persian Architecture. — University of Chicago Press, 12/1979. xx, 152 p. : ill. ISBN 0-226-02560-8 Trade Paper. : $29.95.

Hazrat Inayat Khan, Sufi Teachings. — Hunter House, Incorporated, 1979. 332 p. — (Sufi Message of Hazrat Inayat Khan Ser. ;

Vol. 8) ISBN 90-6077-954-1 Trade Cloth. : .00 Write/Call Publisher for info.

Gertrude Bell, Teachings of Hafiz. — Institute for the Study of Human Knowledge, 1979. ISBN 0-900860-63-4 Trade Cloth.: $18.00.

E. H. Whinfield, Translated by Teachings of Rumi : The Masnavi.— Institute for the Study of Human Knowledge, 1979. ISBN 0-900860-64-2 Trade Cloth. : $30.00.

Hazrat Inayat Khan, The Unity of Religious Ideals. — Hunter House, Incorporated, 1979. 280 p. — (Sufi Message of Hazrat Inayat Khan Ser. ; Vol. 9) ISBN 90-6325-097-5 Trade Cloth. : .00 Write/Call Publisher for info.

Margaret Smith, The Way of the Mystics : The Early Christian Mystics & the Rise of the Sufis. — Oxford University Press, Incorporated, 05/1979. ISBN 0-19-520039-X Trade Cloth. : $16.95. ISBN 0-19-519967-7 Trade Paper. : $6.95.

Idries Shah, The World of the Sufi. — Institute for the Study of Human Knowledge, 1979. ISBN 0-900860-66-9 Trade Cloth.: $23.00.

Shah Maghsoud Sadegh Angha, Al-Salat. — M T O Printing & Publication Center, 03/1978. 116 p. ISBN 0-318-37656-3 Trade Paper. : $5.00.

Idries Shah, The Hundred Tales of Wisdom. — Institute for the Study of Human Knowledge, 1978. ISBN 0-900860-60-X Trade Cloth. : $19.00. ISBN 0-86304-049-7 Trade Paper. : $12.50.

Victor Danner, Ibn 'Ata Illah-Kwaja Abdullah Ansari : The Book of Wisdom-Intimate Conversations. — Paulist Press, 1978. 256 p. — (Classics of Western Spirituality Ser.) ISBN 0-8091-2182-4 Trade Paper. : $8.95.

Javad Nurbakhsh, In the Tavern of Ruin : Seven Essays on Sufism.— KhaniQahi Nimatullahi Publications, 1978. 135 p. ISBN 0-933546-00-9 Trade Paper. : $9.95.

Idries Shah, Learning How to Learn. — Institute for the Study of

Human Knowledge, 1978. 302 p. ISBN 0-900860-59-6 Trade Cloth. : $22.00.

Idries Shah, Special Problems in the Study of Sufi Ideas. — Institute for the Study of Human Knowledge, 1978. 45 p. ISBN 0-900860-21-9 Trade Paper. : $7.00.

Arthur J. Arberry, The Doctrine of the Sufis., 08/1977. ISBN 0-521-21647-8 Trade Cloth. : $32.50 — Cambridge University Press. ISBN 0-521-29218-2 Trade Paper. : $19.95 — Cambridge University Press. ISBN 0-87902-195-0 Trade Cloth. : $12.95 — Orientalia Art, Limited.

James Redhouse, Edited by Legends of the Sufis. — Theosophical Publishing House, 04/1977. ISBN 0-7229-5051-9 Trade Paper. : $9.50.

Idries Shah, Neglected Aspects of Sufi Study. — Institute for the Study of Human Knowledge, 1977. 83 p. ISBN 0-900860-56-1 Trade Cloth. : $16.00.

Idries Shah, Special Illumination : The Sufi Use of Humour. — Institute for the Study of Human Knowledge, 1977. 64 p. ISBN 0-900860-57-X Trade Cloth. : $17.00.

Henry Corbin, Spiritual Body & Celestial Earth : From Mazdean Iran to Shi Ite Iran. — Princeton University Press, 04/1977. (Bollingen Ser. ; No. 91) ISBN 0-691-09937-5 Cloth Text. : $59.50.

Mehdi Nakosteen, Sufism & Human Destiny & Sufi Thought in Persian Literature. — Iran Books, 1977. 236 p. ISBN 0-936347-17-1 Trade Cloth. : $25.00.

Idries Shah, The Book of the Book. — Institute for the Study of Human Knowledge, 1976. 146 p. ISBN 0-900860-12-X Trade Cloth. : $18.00.

Amina Shah, The Tales of the Four Dervishes of Amir Khusru. — Institute for the Study of Human Knowledge, 1976. ISBN 0-900860-44-8 Trade Cloth. : $21.00.

S. A. Rizvi, A History of Sufism in India. — Asia Book Corporation of America, 1975. 467 p. ISBN 0-318-37182-0 Trade Cloth.: $34.95.

Annemarie Schimmel, Mystical Dimensions of Islam. — University of North Carolina Press, 10/1975. xxi, 506 p. : ill. ISBN 0-8078-1271-4 Trade Paper. : $16.95.

E. H. Palmer, Oriental Mysticism .: A Treatise on Sufistic & Unitarian Theosophy of the Persians. — Institute for the Study of Human Knowledge, 01/1974. 84 p. ISBN 0-900860-33-2 Trade Cloth. : $10.00.

Shah Maghsoud Sadegh Angha, Principles of Faghr & Sufism. — M T O Printing & Publication Center, 1974. 173 p. ISBN 0-910735-10-7 Trade Cloth. : $35.00. ISBN 0-317-68047-1 Trade Paper. : $29.00.

O. M. Burke, Among the Dervishes. — Institute for the Study of Human Knowledge, 1973. ISBN 0-900860-17-0 Trade Cloth.: $16.00. ISBN 0-86304-018-7 Trade Paper. : $12.50.

Michael Gilsenan, Saint & Sufi in Modern Egypt : An Essay in the Sociology of Religion. — Oxford University Press, Incorporated, 12/1973. ill.(Monographs in Social Anthropology) ISBN 0-19-823181-4 Trade Cloth. : $49.95.

L. F. Williams, Sufi Studies; East And West., 11/01/1973. ISBN 0525211950 Trade Cloth. : $15.00 Ingram — OCTG.

Idries Shah, The Magic Monastery. — Institute for the Study of Human Knowledge, 1972. 208 p. ISBN 0-900860-89-8 Trade Cloth. : $25.00.

Idries Shah, Reflections., 02/1972. ISBN 0-14-003411-0 Trade Paper. : $2.50 — Viking Penguin. ISBN 0-900860-07-3 Trade Cloth. : $18.00 — Institute for the Study of Human Knowledge.

Idries Shah, Thinkers of the East. — Viking Penguin, 02/1972. 208 p. ISBN 0-14-003410-2 Mass Market. : $5.95. ISBN 0-14-019251-4 Trade Paper. : $9.95.

D. M. Matheson, An Introduction to Sufi Doctrine. — Orientalia Art, Limited, 1971. ISBN 0-87902-175-6 Trade Paper. : $4.75.

Idries Shah, Sufis. — Doubleday & Company, Incorporated, 02/1971. ISBN 0-385-07966-4 Mass Market. : $11.00.

[illegible] ISBN 0-[illegible]-0202-3 Trade Paper $45.00.

Nasrullah S. Fattah [illegible] [illegible] Associated University Presses (Date Not Supplied) ISBN 0-[illegible]-2248-6 Trade Cloth $12.00.

Khalilullah Khalili, The Quintessence Khalilullah Khalili — Institute for the Study of Human Knowledge (Date Not Supplied) ISBN 0-[illegible]-7 Trade Cloth $25.00.

Menahem Milson, A [illegible] Rule for Novices — Kitab Adab Al-Muridin of Abu Al-Najib Al-Suhrawardi [illegible] ed — [illegible] ed. — Books on Demand (Date Not Supplied) 96 p. — (Harvard Middle Eastern Studies, No. 17) ISBN 0-[illegible]-4436-6 Trade Paper $26.[illegible].

Idries [illegible] Ali-Shah, The Sufi Tradition in the W[illegible] [illegible] Publishing Corporation (Date Not Set) [illegible] p. ISBN 1-[illegible] Trade Paper [illegible] Call Publisher for info.

Richard M. Eaton, Sufis of Bijapur, 1300–1700: Social Roles of Sufis in Medieval India — [illegible] — Books on Demand (Date Not Supplied) ISBN 0-[illegible] Trade Paper $105.00.